ALSO BY PAUL MARION

POETRY
Lockdown Letters & Other Poems
Union River: Poems and Sketches
What Is the City?
Strong Place

NONFICTION
Mill Power: The Origin and Impact of Lowell National Historical Park

COAUTHOR
French Class: French Canadian-American Writings on Identity, Culture, and Place
with Susan April, Paul Brouillette, and Marie Louise St. Onge

EDITOR
Atop an Underwood: Early Stories and Other Writings by Jack Kerouac

COEDITOR
Atlantic Currents: Connecting Cork and Lowell
with Tina Neylon and John Wooding
History as It Happens: Citizen Bloggers in Lowell, Mass.
with Richard P. Howe, Jr.
The Generator Room: A Public Art Project
with David Ireland (author) and James Coates
Merrimack: A Poetry Anthology
with Kathleen Aponick and Jane Brox
Essays From the Lowell Conference on Industrial History
with Oliver Ford and Robert Weible

PORTRAITS ALONG THE WAY
1976-2024

PAUL MARION

Loom Press
Amesbury, Massachusetts
2024

Portraits Along the Way: 1976-2024
Copyright © 2024 by Paul Marion
www.paulmarion.com

ISBN 978-0-931507-49-6
All rights reserved.
No part of this book may be reproduced in any manner without written permission from the author and publisher, except in the case of brief quotations in critical articles and reviews.
Printed in the United States of America
First edition

Design: Keith Finch
Author photograph: Tory Wesnofske for UMass Lowell
Font: Helvetica Thin and Adobe Caslon Pro
Printing: Versa Press, Illinois

Front cover images, left to right: Tony Conigliaro, Leymah Gbowee, Louise Glück, and Billy Joel. Thank you to the following for permission to use the images: University of Massachusetts, Lowell (Leymah Gbowee and Billy Joel); Boston Red Sox (Tony Conigliaro); and Academy of American Achievement (Louise Glück).

Loom Press
15 Atlantic View, Amesbury, Massachusetts 01913
www.loompress.com
info@loompress.com

Out of respect for the privacy of individuals, some names have been changed in the writing published here.

For Rosemary and Joseph

CONTENTS

Introduction	i

ONE

Antoinette & Wilfrid	3
Doris & Marcel	15
Marcel Marion	21
Astronauts of Project Mercury	29
Ste. Thérèse de Lisieux	32
John F. Kennedy	38

TWO

Tony Conigliaro	45
Gumba & The Fly	48
Sergei Samsonov	53
Dalton Jones	55
Nathan Eovaldi	57
Paul Marion	61

THREE

Bette Davis	73
Bob Dylan (1)	79
Johnny Depp	82
Joan Baez	84
Dimitri Hadzi	86
Buddy Guy	91
Billy Joel	93
Katherine O'Donnell Murphy & Arshile Gorky	96
Bob Dylan (2)	98

FOUR

The Poets' Lab	103
Alentour Poets	113
Jack Kerouac (1)	133
Gary Snyder	135
Maya Angelou	138
Charles Simic	140
Annie Proulx	143
Benjamin Myers	145
Jack Kerouac (2)	149
Patti Smith	157
Stephen King	162
Jack Kerouac & Bob Dylan	165
Henry David Thoreau	168
Louise Glück	169
Merrimack Valley Authors	174

FIVE

Rosemary & Joseph	185
Frank P. Putnam	187
Jim Casselton	190
Luther C. Ladd & Addison O. Whitney	192
Daniel R. Turner	194
Eddie Franzoni	195
Hamid Ismailov & Juan Ferrer	197
Doug DeNatale	199
Doeun "Duey" Kol	202
Helga Becker	205
Francis "Pinky" Roy	206

SIX

Leymah Gbowee	211
Patrick J. Mogan (1)	214
Patrick J. Mogan (2)	219
Paul E. Tsongas (1)	221
Paul E. Tsongas (2)	225
Harry Callahan	231
Dith Pran & Sophin Chea	232
John Ogonowski	235
Meetinghouse Hill Figures	237
Acknowledgments	248
Index	250
A Note on the Author	251

INTRODUCTION

I've found gold in people's life stories. From a revealing moment to a broad narrative, I've documented an assortment of individuals since I began keeping a notebook. Scottish author Thomas Carlyle proposed that "history is biography," but we need more than his "great men" and colorful heroes to fully appreciate the ongoing human drama.

What can we learn from what people say and do? Are we simply drawn to stories we enjoy hearing and repeating? Sometimes, we see ourselves in others. I'm always looking and listening. I write about people I observe because I don't want to lose the experience. Writing is a preservation technique. I've kept the people in this book around me. We are a community. I want readers to know them.

Reader's Digest magazine for years had a popular monthly feature, "The Most Unforgettable Character I've Met." I didn't choose the subjects in this collection of portraits-in-writing on that basis, but each is unforgettable is his or her own way.

I employ various forms for the portraits: traditional renderings, sprawling treatments, spontaneous sketches, snapshots, monologues, book reviews, in-depth profiles, a journal, an interview, a self-portrayal, and groups in their own frames. The compositions date from the mid-1970s and run through the present. Most of the pieces appeared in books, magazines, and newspapers or as blog posts.

Readers will recognize figures from the fields of music, art, literature, history, sports, and civic life. Beyond the known persons readers will meet remarkable men and women, not household names, whom I've encountered along the way. I hope all their stories will stay with you.

I'm grateful to the friends who read the manuscript of this book and commented helpfully, including Susan April, Paul Brouillette, Roberta Fox, and John Wooding. Also, thank you to the editors and publishers who made room for my writing in their publications. A special thanks to my wife, Rosemary Noon, for her close reading of the text, insightful advice, and love.

Paul Marion, Amesbury, Massachusetts

ONE

… PORTRAITS ALONG THE WAY

Antoinette & Wilfrid

Sunday at the Hi-Low.

There was a white plaster cat on the roof of the house next door. It was a French thing. The cat. Every *mémère* had a *minou*, a real kitty, too.

My father's parents, Antoinette and Wilfrid, known to me as *Mémère* and *Pépère* (sounds like "MEH-may" and "PEH-pay"), bought the house next door after my father, Marcel, and mother, Doris, in 1956 got their compact ranch-style home at the corner of Hildreth Street and Janice Avenue in Dracut, Massachusetts, the only place in the U.S. with that name. In those days, farm-lined New Boston Road curved into the end of Hildreth Street, an area called New Boston Village 350 years ago.

I didn't learn the tribal history and colonial-era names associated with our part of town until much later. More familiar was Crosby Heights, a marketing label from the builders of new houses near us, from Crosby Road across to Janice Ave. The town name comes from an estate in southwest England dating from 1086, Draycot Foliat in Wiltshire County. For centuries, the indigenous Pawtucket and Wamesit peoples called the land *Augumtoocooke*, a place in the woods.

Close to the New Hampshire border, the town lies immediately north of the Merrimack River and Lowell, an historic factory city whose riverfront featured a mile of red-brick textile mills in the nineteenth century. In that era, my ancestors on both sides, along with about a million other Quebeckers, quit the frosted fields and job-scarce villages of eastern Canada to try to earn a living in Lowell and other river-valley mill cities in New England. Dracut remained mostly rural with two small mill complexes along Beaver Brook until the change to a bedroom community, suburbia, after World War II.

My parents were among the millions of families of veterans who bought their first homes using the federal "GI Bill" low-interest home

3

loan benefit. If the mass movement had been filmed, imagine the opening scene:

> All-out war recedes in the rearview mirror of young parents from an urban precinct who cross the city limits into the frontier. The adults up front and backseat kids are war veterans of some kind. Ahead, maple trees air-mail twirling seed pods into the breeze. Pines puff out yellow pollen. Red-breasted robins assemble nests for their fragile blue eggs. On the muddy margin of a pond, green frogs blink in the sun.

Doris and Marcel had lived in a couple of other places in Lowell and Dracut before buying the Hildreth Street house and had been on their own for more than ten years. Mum was not thrilled when her in-laws landed in the back yard. After marrying my father, they had stayed for a short time at his parents' house. Mum was not a person to be fooled with in the wrong way. One night she flashed a steak knife at my horny grandfather when he grabbed her from behind around the waist in the kitchen. He was a "rascal." That's the word she used. He got the message, but not soon enough to know he should have kept his hands off.

An extended family was fine as long as it was at an extended distance. Mum didn't want anyone telling her what to do. As a kid, she wouldn't let her father boss her. She laughed about always having the last word—maybe to an extreme. It's a trait I carry and which I've tried to sand down for the sake of diplomacy. Mum's confrontations with the mother-in-law involved all things domestic, if not foreign. Thinking about the Marion in-laws and the years of altercations small and large, Mum would purse her lips and shake her head.

But where was the historically extended family before Massachusetts? In the 1980s, two of my aunts documented our roots. My aunt Joan (McLaughlin) Roy, a nutritionist who married my mother's brother Bob, traced the LeRoy and Roy side across Normandy on the Atlantic coast of France and then in the province of Quebec in Canada. My Auntie Rollie (Rolande Marion), my dad's sister, married engineer Lionel Patenaude and worked for Lowell's health department. She researched the Marions, who lived in the same places as the LeRoys and Roys. Marriage records from churches in Europe and Canada have the key details.

In 1638, Louis LeRoy or LeRoi, meaning "the King," married Anne LeMaistre in *Église Sainte-Rémy* in Dieppe, about halfway between Le Havre and Calais along the English Channel. Louis' son, Nicholas LeRoy I, in 1658 married Jeanne LeLievre in Honfleur, which is in the department of Calvados on the River Seine, where the LeRoy name is common. The Norsemen/north mer. or Vikings dominated that region after 900. There's no royal sap in our family tree as far as we know. DNA analysis of my brother David's blood revealed Viking, Visigoth, and Roman bits in the family genes, not surprising considering the shifting fortunes of the local inhabitants as conquering bands and entire armies swept through northwest France, rampaging, pillaging, raping, and taking some villagers as mates.

In 1655, Nicholas Marion married Marie Guerier in Bacqueville, close to Les Andelys in upper Normandy. Here, Richard the Lionheart, King of England and Duke of Normandy, in 1196 built Château Gaillard, his castle on high ground above the Seine. A genealogical note from my Auntie Rollie says Marie never made it to Canada. I don't know if she died or stayed behind in France. It isn't clear to me whether Nicholas or his son Georges was the first Marion of my line in North America. Records show Georges marrying Madeleine Dumais Demers in Quebec in 1693. The Marion name is from the "Mary" line of names going back to the time before Jesus of Nazareth in the Aramaic language, Maryam, and Hebrew, Miryam.

The LeRoys appear in Quebec marriage files in 1686; Nicolas LeRoy II marrying Madeleine LeBlond at Ste. Famille. Next, we have Étienne and Marie Casse (m. 1709 with the surname shortened to Roy), Pierre and Hélène DeRouselle (m. 1754), Antoine and Marie-Angelique Letourneau (m. 1787), René and Marie-Joseph Langlois (m. 1816), and Damase and Marie Morin (m. 1857). The immigrants, Philippe and Antoinette Lambert, marry in Massachusetts circa 1890. These are my mother's fraternal grandparents.

In Canada, the Marion lineage after Georges and Madeleine is Étienne and Marie-Jeanne Hunault (m. 1728), Antoine I and Monique Tellier-Lafortune (m. 1762), Pierre and Charlotte Gareau (m. 1801), Antoine II and Marie Dalpe-Parizeau (m. 1831), and Joseph and Claire Charette (m. 1863 in Ste. Elizabeth, Quebec), whom we know as the first Marions in Lowell.

Both the Roys and Marions arrived in Lowell in 1880.

The French Canadians typically married each other until the middle of the twentieth century. Marcel Marion (b. 1919) asked Doris Roy (b. 1921) to be his wife in 1940. Mum's brothers and sisters married outside the French tribe to spouses of Greek, Irish, and German backgrounds in the 1940s and after. My brothers married women with Italian and Irish roots—and the same for me, Irish, 100 percent.

While my father spent part of his childhood in Little Canada, the core of the French district, my mother was raised across the river in Centralville and maintained that she was bred among a higher class of Francos. She joked about not being allowed to cross the Aiken Street bridge to Little Canada as a girl because of the class difference. But she wound up with my father, a Cheever Street product from the "blocks," as tenements were called. I wish I knew why my father crossed that bridge. My recollection is that they met at a dance at St. Louis parish possibly introduced by a friend of one of her friends.

In Centralville, on the river's north bank, where many of the Little Canada residents aspired to take a step up, most people were working class. There were some blocks, for sure, but also cottages, two-story houses, and single-family homes. Mum's family rented, and moved around depending on the money coming in. The third rung on the French socioeconomic ladder was Pawtucketville, counterclockwise to the northwest, whose upwardly mobile business owners and professionals, not exclusively, but enough to count, enjoyed comfortable, well-appointed homes with yards and gardens.

At twenty years old, Wilfrid Marion (b. 1896) married eighteen-year-old Antoinette Héroux (b. 1898), who worked in a hosiery mill in Lowell. Industrious and a genial social navigator, *bon vivant* Wilfrid met her family through grocery work at Robitaille's Market and his future mother-in-law's food cart. Antoinette, an only daughter, had attended a religious school in Quebec.

My father's parents, with the adjacent house in Dracut, slightly nicer than ours, had a garage and an enclosed, heated porch. *Mémère* had a green-and-yellow parakeet in a cage on a stand in the kitchen and usually a fluffy cat padding around. When I was small and my folks had jobs, I'd go to my grandparents' house where I watched reruns of favorite TV shows like *The Real McCoys*, a comedy about an Appalachian farm family relocated in rural California of the time, a show that paved the way for the popular *Beverly Hillbillies*. For my lunch, *Mémère* would make a ham sandwich and pour a cup of milk. We played cards too. Instead of the typical Fish game, we played War. One of us would deal all the cards into two piles, hers and mine, and then we'd flip from the top, one card at a time, the high card best. The winner took the two cards and put them at the bottom of his or her stack. When a pair turned over the piles grew until a third of that kind surfaced. The winner took all the cards from the battle, and the War would go on. Simple rules, no jokers. Nothing wild but chance.

As a kid I didn't understand the details, but *Mémère* made good use of insurance. She collected for this or that damage all the time. When money was scarce there might be a small electrical fire that burned a worn sofa. She slipped and fell in stores. Her thriftiness extended to bank-switching. She moved money around to open a new account if a set of dishes greeted a new customer. I never saw her unhappy. She was clever with money for good reasons, including my *pépère's* checkered business record. One night when her husband didn't appear for supper, she walked to his store and found him with my mother's youngest brother trapped in a frozen food compartment where they had retreated for whiskey to top off the day. There's a photograph of Wilfrid-the-businessman standing proudly in his long, blood-stained butcher's apron, wearing a tie and a straw hat, in the doorway of Marion's Meat Market in Little Canada in 1925. The image has been used in museum exhibits in Lowell.

Wilfrid's Canadian-born mother, Rosalba, worked in a mill as an eight-year-old doffer, moving swiftly between machines to remove full spindles of cotton thread and load on an empty spindle. This was young children's work until state and federal legislators regulated such practices in the 1920s. Married at seventeen years old in 1895 to twenty-one-year-old Doda (or Déodat, meaning "given by God") at *St. Jean Baptiste* church in Lowell, she would have twenty pregnancies. Eight children lived past infancy. She lived to be ninety-seven, burying all but four of her children.

How do we assess the grief carried by the mothers and fathers in her time? Were they ardent believers who did not question God's will? How many tossed their faith in a ditch after the fourth or fifth lost child? What kind of love or duty overrides anguish and sheer fatigue? Was this part of the subordination of women? How much of it was driven by nature, by glands, the seventeen- and nineteen-year-old couples desiring one another? If it is love, then the couples pursue happiness and let God or fate control results. Some scenarios were darker, involving abuse. "Do what I want. Do what you're told"—or an unsaid pressure. However, in the small sample of my ancestors, the women come across as self-assured, hard workers who endure, not passive types. Not all of them, but the men wander, the men stumble as often as they achieve.

The Catholic Church forbade all but the calendar rhythm method of charting ovulation in attempting to manage pregnancies. By the 1850s, male prophylactics were on the market. "Are you kidding? No married man would use a rubber," someone close to me said. The first birth control pill was prescribed in 1960. What were the conversations in Little Canada? In my boxes of family documents, I have no account of the response to the mass casualties, only lists of the dead. Those family voices are gone.

My father's grandmother Héroux, Salomé, had two children. She was a tall, sturdy woman with pulled-back silver hair who had an apron on whenever I saw her. She lived to be ninety-one. Like her mother, Antoinette had two children. There's no record or family speculation as to the reason for these atypical small families.

A British national, Salomé was born in Ottawa, Canada, in 1871. She and her husband, Hormidas, also from Ottawa, emigrated to Lowell, where she ran a small grocery store in Little Canada. Suffering from ill health and "bad tendencies," Hormidas was hospitalized. The authorities told his family that he discharged himself, and with the help of a man on a bicycle headed to the train depot to return to Canada. He got a construction job on a large bridge project and saved $1,800. On his return to Lowell, he lent the bulk of the money to a family member, expecting to obtain a job at the mill where the relative had a senior position. That didn't happen. Some years later, he relapsed and was readmitted for treatment in Worcester, Mass., where he died in 1948. Salomé became a naturalized U.S. citizen in 1946 and lived long, fifty years a member of the St. Anne's Sodality at *St. Jean Baptiste* church. She died of heart disease at D'Youville Manor, the preferred nursing home of the local French.

In two long quiz sessions in the 1980s, the second just months before he died of cancer at ninety-three years old, Wilfrid told my brother Richard and me as much as he could recall about his life. At fourteen years old, eldest of his siblings, he worked for a family with a horse-and-carriage business whose own sons felt they were above such horse-work. He then got a job at Robitaille's Market in Little Canada. Living on the north bank of the river in the Rosemont section of lower Pawtucketville meant he walked to work over the Moody Street Bridge. Aware of this and happy with his employee, Mr. Thaddée Robitaille allowed Wilfrid to board with his own family. On Saturdays and Sundays, Wilfrid's sister Jeanne picked him up with the family's wagon for a meal at home.

I have a photograph of Wilfrid and his crew the year he was married, 1916. Under a clear sky, six young men in long black coats and black fedoras stand in high grass just off Melvin Street in Little Canada, specifically at the "Hi-Low," a favorite small field, more like an empty lot, near the river. Was this a "Sunday in the Park" on an afternoon when somebody had a camera?

Behind them are triple-deckers, three of the dozens jammed together in the ethnic enclave. The lineup looks like a scene from *The Godfather* or a group of undertakers. Everyone has a tie. Several wear gray pants. They look stern, so maybe it was an after-funeral shot?

Wilfrid is far left, his hat tipped up to show his forehead. Next to him are George Bellemare, who delivered bakery goods; Leandre Marion, a relative and later a successful house builder; Hormidas "Bidou" or "Bill" Héroux, a supervisor at the Suffolk Mill and soon-to-be Wilfrid's brother-in-law; Alexandre Durand, a carpenter working with Leandre; and Joe Clermont, a baker with Honeycrust Bread in Centralville, across the river, and later founder of Clermont Market, known locally for its Black Angus beef. There are no mill workers here, although there is a mill supervisor. These guys have their eyes on business and a trade, thirty-five years after the first Marion stepped foot in the city.

Wilfrid's initial business venture was buying the Robitaille grocery, the beginning of a succession of self-proprietorships, bankruptcies, and freelance meat cutting. The Robitaille purchase came unglued when lawyers invalidated the agreement, which gave Wilfrid an opportunity to back out or to sue for damages—but he declined and stayed with it. He hired Joe Clermont from the photo to work for him and a man who had owned a market in St. Jean de Matha in Quebec, one of the rural home plates of the Marion and Héroux clans. One time his store was shut down when he was caught selling horse meat for hamburger. A butcher by trade and grocer by profession, Wilfrid's best run was Marion's Meat Market in Little Canada, which he operated from about 1925 to the late 1930s before it burned.

Waiting for his card-playing friends on New Year's Eve, *Pépère* lit a small kerosene heater. When he and his chums left to go out and drink a good time, papers near the heater caught fire and set the store aflame. Wilfrid had headed home across the river's ice where the rocks make a rack of ribs to hop on from bank to bank. Old Stony, they called it. As soon as he got to the north bank, a neighbor rushed over to tell him about the fire. Angry and distraught, Wilfrid took my father, a teenager, back across the river to assess the damage.

Without insurance, Wilfrid struggled to pay debts to vendors who provided goods for his store. A Lowell meat company placed a lien on Wilfrid's two-story house on Martin Street in the Rosemont, which he eventually lost. The bankruptcy settlement required him to pay all the small businesspeople to whom he owed money, which he did in installments. *Pépère* cried when he described the catastrophe to us.

After losing the store, Wilfrid hired himself out to Greek market owners in Lowell like Mr. Gefteas on Market Street. In his seventies, Wilfrid was still cutting meat for Gefteas, then at Skip's Restaurant in Chelmsford, which was popular among families and truckers coming off nearby Route 495. After closing, he took home leftover steaks and large round commercial pies filled with whole apricots and thick apple slices, which he shared with our family.

Overall, he had managed well enough financially to buy houses on upper Merrimack Street, a former funeral home, and on Sladen Street in Dracut. Wilfrid had clear memories of cars he had bought, and listed them with the purchase price, not the year however: $1,300 for a sedan with Isinglass windows, a celluloid material used in Model T Fords; a Plymouth sedan for $600 followed by another $600 Plymouth; and a fourth car, Plymouth again, for $1,000. For one of his markets, he drove a black delivery truck that had been a police patrol wagon. This vehicle carried him across the iced-over river and over unplowed bumpy streets on his delivery rounds. Even in later years, he had a decent car, and a couple of times offered my father his "old car" when he got a new model.

He and Antoinette enjoyed going out to the many theaters in the city, seeing vaudeville shows and movies. Their two children were born in 1918, Rolande, and 1919, my father. On July Fourth, families pushed baby carriages to the North Common for picnic outings and festivities topped off by fireworks. Mischievous youngsters captured rats from the canals and released them on the streets, blowing some of them up with firecrackers. In summer, kids swam in the river near the Old Stony rock-ribs, diving into favorite pools between the rocks called "*le ti kibby*" and "*le grand kibby*." For the adults, the Strand and Rialto theaters had live shows, plays, and even a tightrope walker one time. The Christmas Eve and New Year's Eve celebrations, *le Réveillon*, ranked high for the French, with family and friends gathering to eat holiday foods. Wilfrid said, "Our parties were full of laughing, singing, and loud talking. Christmas gifts were for people who had a lot of money." They took road trips to Quebec to visit relatives, one time bringing my father and young son Richard along to the Three Rivers region.

Wilfrid or "*Ti Noir*" (Blackie) was known to have "*une blonde*" on the side at times. He laughed, telling us about the night one of his cousins bumped into him and a woman who was not my grandmother at a carnival on the fairgrounds. He said, "How are you, Irene? This is Gertrude, one of my best customers." Well into his eighties, he joked about his younger self seeing vaudeville shows at the Keith Theatre on Bridge Street downtown after which he'd visit the "girls upstairs" in the boarding house across the street.

Near the end of his life, during a Christmas visit to his nursing home, my brothers and I showed *Pépère* the Meat Market photograph. Joyous, he began naming people standing next to him in the picture, mentioning a Chinese man who ran a laundry near the market—though he couldn't recall the man's name. He did pick out *Pépère* Chalifoux in a straw hat. We didn't have a tape recorder, but I made notes later.

The last time visiting him at the nursing home in Lowell, in the corridor I passed a woman with one hand amputated and a hook on the other. A half-naked man waited for an attendant to help him bathe. My grandfather remembered without a pattern and wore a bracelet that read: Forgetful. He spent thirty minutes in his room looking for a dollar bill. He said the residents watch TV all day.

Some years after my grandfather died, I spoke to an older man, Alphonse Hudon, brother of a longtime friend of mine, standing on a canal bridge in what had been Little Canada. I wrote a poem about our conversation.

Here it is in sentences instead of short lines of poetry:

> Mr. Hudon wears a blue parka and a dress hat and leans on his cane, surveying the freshly tarred walkway and grove of short pines along the Northern Canal, close to where my father had lived for a time.
>
> "Looks good, doesn't?" I ask.
>
> "I liked it better the way it was," he says, which opens up a line of talk because I know he misses the French village that had colored this shoulder of land at the wide bend in the river.
>
> "My father was raised on Cheever Street," I say.
>
> "I knew your father and his father, Wilfrid, who had the meat market at the corner of Austin and Moody streets."

"My father had his car serviced at Marquis' Garage before the wrecking cranes pulled up to wipe out the buildings."

He corrects me on the address of Marquis' place.

"There was a house across the street with a tree poking through the front porch roof," I say.

"Oh, yes, that was Mr. Marquis house. And he had a monkey there."

A black-and-white sign on the canal bridge reads: "Jean-Paul Frechette, The Blond Tiger," with his two dates underneath. It's a remnant like the Little Canada memorial, a bronze plaque mounted on a granite stone salvaged from a tenement foundation that was among the last to be demolished. The monument was placed by the Franco community and the priests of *St. Jean Baptiste* parish, whose French congregation died one by one or seeped into the surrounding suburbs to such an extent that the church was conveyed to the city's Latino community and renamed *Nuestra Señora del Carmen*. After several years of struggling financially to keep the cathedral-like building in safe condition, the Latino worshippers had to move on.

The monument shows a fleur-de-lis in each corner and beginning and end dates of the neighborhood, 1875-1964, like a gravestone, and street names around the frame: Aiken, Cabot, Cheever, Coolidge, Hall, Melvin, Montcalm, Pawtucket, Perkins, Suffolk, Tucker, Ward. The amen is Quebec's motto: *Je Me Souviens!*—Lest We Forget!

The district's history and geography are packed into that supersaturated marker tucked between evergreen shrubs on Aiken Street in the middle of what was once an enclave so dense only Hell's Kitchen in New York City beat it for people per city block. Sticking an arm out a window, a person could touch the next tenement.

For blocks, a resident or visitor heard one tongue. People ate, slept, drank, worked, loved, reproduced, and dreamt in a native language arranged like code. Rag man, ice box, coal chute, baseball. Pork pie, Rochette's beans, mill rat, whiskey. High Mass, *soirée, L'Étoile, soupe rouge*.

What was here is what Mr. Hudon liked better, a familiar world that seemed to work for people who got up in the morning with something to do. Even I recall, although I was just a kid when the politicians and bankers clear-cut the neighborhood.

The way he looks down the long canal makes me want to say something hopeful to him. I admire the new trees, the sweeping path, whose design takes us to the manmade channel and black water that still moves the power wheels.

The rough, stubby foundation stone is a local version of the monolith in the film *2001: A Space Odyssey*, the one that made the monkey go ape, the one the moon-men couldn't figure out, the floating answer-bar. This hunk of rock on Earth states its case for the record like the metal message boards shipped out with satellites, telling somebody out there who we are.

2022

Doris & Marcel

Stuck with the blanks.

My brothers and I examined the small items our parents had saved. We had folded and packed Mum's clothes. The junk-drawer junk, linen, and bric-a-brac had been sorted. She had dealt with Dad's things eight years before. We were down to the fine grains. My father's war souvenirs were in the dresser: colorful campaign ribbons, Good Conduct Medal, metal "dog tags" that told us his blood type was "A." He'd kept a few issues of *Stars and Stripes*, the military newspaper, one with the headline: HITLER DEAD.

She kept envelopes filled with holy cards of saints. A "retreat lady" who went on weekend spiritual getaways, Mum believed what the Church taught and yet talked like the most practical Catholic you would meet. Dad had the crucifix he had worn at the junior seminary for priests-in-training in northern New Hampshire, the same place he washed out of for reasons that remain mysterious to his sons.

In a 1930s notebook, Dad listed his reading, from Zane Grey westerns to the classics of French literature (in French). Not long after he died in 1982, I drove across country to California, a trip he had pictured taking. On the road he had driven as far west as northern Illinois on the highway when he and Mum visited number two son David and his wife, Dianne, and grandson Eric in the 1970s. Going west, I stopped in Zanesville, Ohio, and thought of him reading those cowboy novels. There's a pencil portrait of Dad in his twenties made by a travel companion. Later, a friend of mine said he resembled actor Ray Walston from *My Favorite Martian* on TV.

Our family was lower middle class on the economic-and-social dial. Some analysts would label us working class. At times our financial condition was precarious. We thought of ourselves as middle-class regarding money and mores, carried there by my determined parents, a rising standard of living in our part of the country, and government support when needed: veterans' housing benefits, organized-labor laws, unemployment insurance, public education, college tuition assistance, a federal jobs program, subsidized housing for elders, Social Security, and Medicare.

My father and mother worked full- and part-time out of the house, respectively. We owned a car, never a new one until my parents in 1972 sold the snug suburban house they had bought in Dracut in 1956. When he got his new bronze Ford Gran Torino with part of the house proceeds, Dad said, "I can die now." He had reached the mountaintop.

From the time I was two years old until my mid-twenties (my brothers were out of the house by the time I started college), we lived in the middle landscape, not the dense streetscape of the city next to us, Lowell, and unlike rural parts of the town. A community of 8,666 people in 1950, which had gained 5,000 people in the past 100 years, Dracut expanded to more than 21,000 in the next 30 years. We enjoyed easy access to Lowell with its then-92,000 people, where my ancestors had settled in 1880, and bigger Boston, an hour away, as well as woods, fields, ponds, dairies, and farm stands of the close countryside.

It was the middle of the twentieth century. I didn't think of us as middlebrow, although we may have looked and acted that way. My parents had high-school educations, my father at the junior seminary where courses matched those of today's community colleges, and my mother in Lowell public schools and commercial classes. They read avidly and followed current events in the broadcast and print news and watched "educational TV" along with popular network shows. My two older brothers earned college degrees in teaching (art) and political science (culminating in a PhD). I earned two degrees, in political science and community social psychology, and studied in a master's level program in creative writing in California.

We proceeded in the broad middle lane of the American experience when I was growing up, not speeding ahead to pass others on the outside edge and largely avoiding the breakdown lane. We felt lucky: proper clothes, doctors and dentists, a turkey at Thanksgiving, money for the collection basket in church, birthday gifts, a TV and record player, parochial school tuitions, and trips to the White Mountains of New Hampshire, Hampton Beach on the Atlantic Ocean thirty miles away, and the 1964 World's Fair in New York City, where we stayed with an unofficial aunt who worked in the post office in Queens.

My mother had boyfriends or at least pursuers in her late teens, including "Nick the Greek" who had a pilot's license. She was a beautiful young woman with long brown hair, short in height and attractive in a bathing suit, with a bright smile and one cracked tooth from a toboggan accident. Mum looked like Vivien Leigh in *Gone with the Wind*. Photographs from the 1940s show her and Dad like Hollywood stars. One pair of their portraits graced a downtown studio for months. My father, five feet, eight in height, resembled the skinny, young Frank Sinatra. When he and my mother were newlyweds, their friends called him "Frankie."

Later in her life, my mother told me, "Count yourself lucky if you have your health, a nice place to live, enough money to get by, and a good sex life." When a cousin of mine was shattered by a broken romance, she said, "Look, if he was with her, he'd be in heaven, and this, where we are right now, this is not heaven."

Working at the kitchen stove when I was very young, my mother spilled a pan of boiling water on her midsection and a little on me in a bassinet close by. We were treated at St. Joseph's Hospital, where I'd been born. My father climbed a set of tenement stairs in the Little Canada neighborhood to see a man known to have healing power, a medicine man, seventh son of a seventh son. Whatever the mystical man did, my mother recovered and testified to this

My mother loved lobster, chocolates, maple walnut ice cream, the Boston Pops, and talking to her sisters and brothers on the phone. She sold coats and dresses in a downtown department store for twenty-five years. As much as the family needed her earnings, the job at times was a source of friction. My father complained that she "left her paycheck at the store" because of the cost of clothes she needed to look good at work. She'd snap back: "You can't hold your liquor." And they'd go back-and-forth for a few rounds.

When I was small, my father, brothers, and I drove her to South

Station in Boston, where she boarded a silver rail car bound for a retail-training program at Charles of the Ritz in Manhattan. We thought it was her big career break, possibly becoming a "buyer" of merchandise for her company. She returned a day early with the flu. I found the training manual while cleaning out her bureau after she died in 1989. To this day, long after the clothing store closed, her customers tell me about her courtesy, enthusiasm, and fine taste in recommending just the right thing to wear.

Dad was a big sports fan and good at baseball in the back yard and at family picnics with the relatives. Dad's excellent hand-eye coordination made him a better-than-average golfer, one year winning the Most Valuable Player trophy of the Men's Club of St. Therese parish. With a cold beer, or two, he watched as many Red Sox games on TV as possible and occasionally got tickets for us to see games in Boston.

Mum saved one piece of V-Mail sent by Dad from "Somewhere in Germany" on March 10, 1945. The army examiner's censor stamp is initialed on the miniaturized version of my father's letter shipped home with countless other missives shrunken to palm-size by the authorities for ease of handling:

> Sweetheart
>
> Darling, I'm now somewhere in Germany, and I'm fine and well dear. Don't you worry sweet because I'm somewhere in Germany. Honey, believe me I'll take very good care of myself dear. I've been assigned to the Third Army. I'm still with some of the boys I know, but I've lost contact with Vic, he must be assigned to the Third Army too. Now you can send me a box dear, candy bars, fudge, tissues, a box of good Fanny Farmer's Candy. Don't send any cigarettes or blades, or gum, I've got plenty of that.
>
> Honey, I love you with all my heart and the baby too. I miss the both of you an awful lot too. This war will end soon, and I'll be coming back home again for good, honey. Darling don't worry about me. I might not be able to write every day from now on, but whenever I'm able to I will dear, you can depend on that sweet. Give my address to everybody and give them

my regards. All my love to you and Richard and loads of kisses to honey. Good night and pleasant dreams honey. I love you terribly hard dear.

>
> Love and kisses
> Yours lovingly
> Marcel

He returned in July 1945, bringing home a few things including a small bone-handled jackknife that he got from a French farmer in a swap for a can of peaches that showed up in his meal ration. Whenever he left our house, he put the little knife, no longer than his thumb, in his front right pants pocket along with a spray of quarters, pennies, and dimes. The knife blade was worn and sharpened down to a sliver that was perfect for cleaning his fingernails or cutting a piece of string.

We distributed Mum's jewelry to her daughters-in-law, sisters, relatives, and special friends except for a few pieces we could not let go. We found Mother's Day cards we had crayoned and decks of cards from a Lake Tahoe casino where she and Dad had vacationed. Her charm bracelet with a cable car marks the California years, the 1960s, when Dad had been a sought-after tradesman, a wool grader, working for the wool co-ops of the Great Central Valley eight months a year. In his diary from 1967, he writes over and over how much he misses his "Honey."

Richard said the personal effects seemed "thin," this collection of keepsakes. David surprised me, saying, keep what's left together, don't divide by three. Mum and Dad had clipped every news story about the three of us. They had been in the paper, too: one dark photo shows my father and co-workers taking a strike vote in the 1940s. He was a shop steward until the company broke the union by keeping the mill shut down. He rarely mentioned this. Another yellowed clipping reports that my family "chose Indian Head in the White Mountains and Hampton Beach in New Hampshire as their vacation spots."

What does it all come to? The German money and hammered gold earrings. The letter opener from Monticello. A golf tee and a store employee badge for "Doris." The blue diaper pin and Kennedy half-dollars. Ticket stubs from Fenway Park. The small bone-handled knife from

France. Shoehorns and scissors. Eyeglasses, expired house keys, and matchbooks from fancy restaurants. The snapshots and birthday cards. The missing interview tapes and transcripts. We didn't write down the answers.

1989

Marcel Marion

Laid off.

One of my pre-school memories is a composite of scenes with my father during the day when he was not working at the mill, when he was "laid off." That was the term I heard. Laid off. Told by the boss to stay home because the company did not have enough business activity to keep him employed. When this happened, he qualified for unemployment insurance. He would be "collecting," as people said. Collecting unemployment checks. He was also said to be "loafing," but that was not precise and even cruel. Loafing makes me think of Walt Whitman: "I loafe and invite my soul,/I lean and loafe at my ease observing a spear of summer grass." For my father there was little of this kind of sauntering. It was not his choice to be out of work in the 1950s, sometimes for months at a stretch.

I was too young to know that the national economy was right in our kitchen. According to federal economic reports, the textile industry took one of the worse hits in the recession of 1957-58, which knocked five million people out of all kinds of work. The Northeast had high job losses. The post-World War II economic surge had topped off. Business growth lagged, and personal spending contracted. Also, an Asian flu pandemic slowed exports in manufacturing, and interest rates rose as the Federal Reserve banking system countered inflation. Nationwide, the unemployment rate reached 7.5 percent by mid-1958. After the highest joblessness since the 1930s, the rate dropped to below 5 percent by 1960. Lowell from 1950 to 1957 ranked as an area of "persistent high unemployment" with an average rate of 7.9 percent. Another term I heard when I was a bit older was "a depressed area."

I was assigned to Dad on the days when my mother worked in the women's clothing store in downtown Lowell. One vivid scenario: My father drives my mother to work downtown with me in the back seat of the car. After dropping her off at the corner of Merrimack and John streets, Dad parks the car at a meter near the store. The two of us walk down Paige Street on the back side of the five-and-ten cent stores to a bar called Marty's, known for having one of the longest bar tops in the state, stretching the length of the building from Paige Street over to Merrimack, from back door to front. We sit in a booth upholstered with slippery red material, not cloth. My father orders a glass of draft beer for himself and an orangeade for me. Always a glass of orangeade from the soda fountain. I'm four years old. We have one drink and then go. Never two drinks. Sometimes we make a pit stop at the men's restroom that was under the sidewalk on the back side of the five-and-tens. The men's and women's facilities here were the only public restrooms in the city. Many years later the stairs were sealed over. One day an urban archeologist will discover the toilets under Paige Street.

At home in Dracut, the "laid off" days passed. Time must have dragged for my father. He kept busy around the house, working in the yard or down cellar or helping his parents next door. There's always something to maintain or clean when you own a house. He built a solid workbench in the cellar using scrap wood and his few tools. When he was younger, he had done a little carpentry with his Marion cousins who ran a construction company. The Marion name is associated with building in the area. Louis Marion's company built one of the yellow-brick buildings in the historic quadrangle of the old Lowell Textile School, one of the predecessors of today's Lowell campus of the University of Massachusetts. An old friend of mine says the Marions were cathedral builders. Sometimes when my father was driving the family around, he would point out a house that he had helped build. (My mother never got a driver's license because she was too nervous to drive a car. She took lessons but could never get the hang of it. For years, she called taxis to pick her up in Dracut to go to work in downtown Lowell.)

John Mullen worked with my father at Gilet Carbonizing, at first in Lowell and then in North Chelmsford. Carbonizing removes seeds, burrs, lanolin, and other organic matter from raw wool before it is sent on for the next step in production. He supervised scouring machines on the lower level of the mill, a job I did for two days in the summer of 1972. Here's my take on what it felt like in Satan's glowing red, infected bowels:

> No adjective for the heat. My olive-green T-shirt blackens before work starts on the scouring train in the cellar of this mill. I'm the keeper of the vats, three linked in a fifty-foot machine, my train between two more.
> A chute drops raw wool into harsh detergent soup, bubbling the shit out of it, then a big claw rakes acrid slop from vat one to the next until the whole mess hits the dryers. Like an underground sentry, I march up and down a yard-wide walk, using a hoe to unclog grates beneath each vat where steaming liquid strains into a waste-way. There are regular red alerts—when a section plugs, muck flows over, and scalding soapy stew boils up, I run down to scoop out crap.
> The stink of cooked sheep dung, bleach, oil, and sweat makes me plan to burn my jeans at home.
> With no fans, no relief, and the sight of my twenty-year-man teacher, I know there's no tomorrow.

I'm in awe of the will it must have required for a man like Mullen to report every day to that underworld. The commitment baffles me, but his is another example of the sacrifices made by people who were determined to make a life and earn a living in America.

John said it straight: "When I first went there in 1939, let me tell you, you wouldn't want a dog to work in the place. And I was a dog at the time, lucky to get a job. I did all the shit jobs in the world that were lousy there. When you're a new guy, you get, well, you know what you get."

John talked about the boss, George Noval.

> He probably was the only one that could really speak English and knew every process in the mill. The people in the Pawtucketville neighborhood of Lowell can be thankful to him because if there was an opening, somebody from Pawtucketville got the job. The place was ninety percent French other than the early people that were there, who were Portuguese and Polish.

My father had lined up the summer job for me, which meant asking for a favor unlike he had ever done at the mill. I'm sure I caused a problem, even embarrassment, when I told him the stench of the scouring machines made me nauseous to the point of vomiting and that I could not make it past the morning on the second day. He didn't chew me out, however, and sucked up the news that he had to give to the big boss. I told him I'd apply for a job at a fast-food place.

Lucky for me, my mother got me in at the women's clothing store where she was a senior salesclerk. The manager hired me part-time to run the manual elevator. I could hardly have painted a more different job setting. I needed to help pay for college tuition and to put gas in the creaky 1966 Ford Galaxie 500 that had been handed down to me when my father got my grandfather's black Mercury sedan after he bought a new pine-green, two-door Comet. The Galaxie looked like it had leprosy, the silver-blue paint flaking off from hood to trunk.

In October, I gained a windfall benefit. My parents sold their small ranch house in Dracut because Dad wanted to get out of house-care worries. We moved to a two-bedroom, garden-style apartment on the west side of town, Whitecliff Manor—how upscale British sounding. With a small profit from the house sale, my parents bought themselves their first new car, a bronze 1972 Ford Gran Torino, automatic transmission with a stick shift, and got a new, chocolate-brown Ford Pinto hatchback for me—for commuting to Merrimack College in North Andover, where Red Sox star outfielder Carl Yastrzemski had earned a bachelor's degree in off-season classes. I ran the Pinto for ten years, until the engine burst into flames one afternoon outside my mechanic's shop while I was inside explaining the car's latest problem. I know the Pinto is a cultural punchline in 1970s humor, but I squeezed every ounce of value out of that car, which took me all over New England. My folks had paid less than $2,000 for my "ride" ten years before.

John Mullen spoke with Mehmed Ali of the Lowell Historical Society for two hours in June 2002, recollecting the mill work and labor organizing of his day. I was invited to sit in. He was eighty-five-years old, articulate, white-haired, and had a face like the actor Kirk Douglas. He remembered one strike whose aim was to get a ten-cent raise for the textile workers. He laughed: "Even if you ask for nothing, the owners can't afford it." Industry executives considered Gilet to be a top plant in woolens and worsteds. He counted four strikes in the 1940s when my father was hired at the Lowell mill, which stood at the Lower Locks complex of the Pawtucket Canal, the site of today's UMass Lowell Inn & Conference Center (a former Hilton hotel in the 1980s). Gilet's later moved to a mill complex in North Chelmsford near a railroad line.

John ticked off names of men who worked with my father: Joe Halloran, Bucky Landry, Bill Jezek, George Brouillard, and Marcel Vervaert, "Big Marcel," who taught my father, "Little Marcel," how to sort wool, a trade that served him for forty years. One time an anthrax scare shook up the employees. "An old French guy on the third floor who opened the bales of sheep fleeces got sick enough to see a doctor," said John. A doctor saved his infected eye. He never returned to work. In the business, anthrax is known as "the wool sorter's disease," and it was a constant concern. John said:

> Wool sorters were the elite in the mill in the early days. You can be proud of your father. They can take a handful of wool and make three or four different sorts, grades of wool [like Prime and Choice for beef grades]. It was amazing to see those fellows in action. People from Rhode Island and Lawrence, Mass., came to work at the Gilet factory because of the high pay we were able to get for the wool sorters. That skill was hard to find anyway. I never had any trouble negotiating a wage for the wool sorters.

John smiled as he recalled a colorful character from his time.

> There was a fellow named Harry Healey who believed that wool sorters were the top of the heap. He came to work all dressed up. At the shop he'd put on a white frock. And guess what he had in his briefcase? His lunch. But he would take a shower after work every day and put his suit back on to go home. You should see that white frock after eight hours of

sorting wool. Oh, oh! Well, you know, raw wool is full of burrs, dirt, and shit.

He admitted he was an irritant to the boss, but John said:

> We improved operations 1,000 percent—1,000. In the early 1950s, I got the hell out of there, and then went to work for the United Fund in 1955. I should have stayed with the union, because in the textile thing I was president. We had a Woolen and Worsted Division of the United Textile Workers of America from the AFofL-CIO. We had several plants, Southwell and others, so with my big mouth they elected me president of the council.
>
> Your father was one of the union stewards. I'm sure he was because I was smart enough to make sure that even with the elite that I got the guys that I wanted. And I know Marcel was always up front. He was always up front.

The 1953-55 Labor Agreement between the Gilet company of Lowell and the United Textile Workers of America, A.F. of L., Local No. 734 is a fifty-two-page document detailing the terms and conditions for union security, hours of employment (forty hours a week, eight hours a day), seniority, basic force level, wages and cost of living adjustment, holiday pay and vacation, military service, management and discharge, union notices, safety and health, grievances and arbitration, health benefits, miscellaneous items and the term of the contract. The wool sorters would be paid $1.86 per hour, second only to over-lookers who would earn $1.97. Scourers like John's first slot came in at $1.39. The agreement was signed by the company president Albert J. Gilet. Kenneth G. Clark signed for the national union, and for Local 734 six names are listed: John J. Mullen, William J. Landry, Gerard Morrissette, George Brouillard, Marcel Marion, and William Jezek.

And even with all John Mullen describes the owners and managers in the 1950s ridded themselves of the union. By the time I was old enough to understand, the collective protection of organized labor was gone from my father's workplace. Conditions deteriorated, he was furloughed more often, and the once well-compensated wool sorting no longer drew top dollar. John Mullen chalks up the decline to increasing competition, shifting markets, and technological changes.

In the months out of the mill, Dad explored other options such as a job in electronics. He kept a notebook with mimeograph drawings of tubes and circuits. This may have been a TV repair class. I can't tell. The diagrams show audio output, amplifier operation, grid voltage, electron-emitting cathode, photo-sensitive material. The notes are about transformer couplings, plate resistor, capacitor, and transconductance. Stored with the notebook was an exam book for a police services job. This may have been something he looked into after the war.

The workbench was Dad's area in the cellar. It was eight feet long and the height of a kitchen counter. Built like a box against the back wall of the house foundation, the bench was open in the front and had a tabletop surface about a yard deep. When I was small, I had to stand on a stool to reach the back of the top counter. Underneath there were used paint cans, boards of various sizes, large and small saws, pieces of metal, and other items that were too useful to throw out. On top he kept his mix-and-match tools: no two screwdrivers were from the same family. A couple of dozen jars and small boxes held nails, screws, hooks, brass hinges.

One winter he organized the nails and screws in old jelly and peanut butter jars whose covers were nailed into a board that was in turn nailed to beams above the workbench so that Dad could reach up and unscrew the jar containing the needed nail or hook. I've seen this arrangement in cellars of old houses in the area. Baby food jars are a good size for small screws and washers. At the back of the countertop more remnant parts and supplies were stacked, waiting for the next home improvement.

In the months out of work, my father had a lot of time to think and read. He enjoyed the writings of the longshoreman-philosopher Eric Hoffer and Edward Bellamy's social critique *Looking Backward: From 2000 to 1887*. In his own way he was spiritual, without the dogma and clerical trappings. He said the Pope should sell all the gold ornaments in the Vatican and use the money to feed hungry people. His anticlerical views made me take a pass on the chance to be an altar server, which baffled nuns who taught me. I preferred not to do that. On top of Sunday Mass with my family, the school required weekly Crusader Masses, First Friday Mass, Easter Week and Christmas Masses, and Holy Day of Obligation Masses, which gave me plenty of capital in the God Bank.

A few years before my father died of cancer in 1982, I published a meditation on him in my first pamphlet of writing:

> Dad's middle name was super-French, *Réal,* in the category of *Hormidas, Salomé,* and *Déodat* from the older generations. I pictured him trudging down muddy German roads in 1945, one eye on Bavaria, his combat boots worn thin. Did he see himself, twenty years ahead, sorting raw wool in the San Joaquin Valley of California, touring the sheep spreads, and talking French to the Basque farmers?
>
> State dinners in Washington with ambassadors and movie stars made him sick to his daily-bread stomach. It's a good thing he enjoyed the Red Sox. "Jefferson was a genius," he'd say. "Something went wrong. Mazuma did it. Money corrupts absolutely."
>
> Taking off his glasses, he'd sigh. "I dunno what's gonna happen." There were no political junkets for him, no study trips to Sweden and Japan. He had to be happy with native corn and tomatoes in August. Who knows that Corporal Marcel Marion studied Greek and Latin and geometry in the junior seminary in the White Mountains of New Hampshire?
>
> Once, watching a TV symphony, he said to my mother, "Now there's a guy who did something in his life. He composed music. What did I do?"
>
> "You had a family, three sons, that's something."
>
> My father used to say he had seen our country's best days. He worked, read, wanted to travel, enjoyed his grandsons, liked to bet a buck, drank a beer. My father had questions.

2019

Astronauts of Project Mercury

In a nutshell, the universe is 13.7 billion years old, plus or minus one percent; a recent previous estimate had a margin of error three times as much. By weight it is four percent atoms, 23 percent dark matter—presumably undiscovered elementary particles left over from the Big Bang—and 73 percent dark energy. And it is geometrically 'flat,' meaning that parallel lines will not meet over cosmic scales. The result, the astronomers said, is a seamless and consistent history of the universe, from its first few seconds, when it was a sizzling soup of particles and energy, to the modern day and a sky beribboned with chains of pearly galaxies inhabited by at least one race of puzzled and ambitious bipeds.

—Dennis Overbye, writing about a map of the universe compiled by a satellite called the Wilkinson Microwave Anisotropy Probe, The New York Times, *February 12, 2003*

I carried a blue metal Space-themed lunch box to my first-grade classroom in a wooden schoolhouse. On my lunch box were two Earth pilots wearing clear round helmets walking toward a rocket vehicle. Around the sides were illustrations of silver spaceships on an arid plain ringed by jagged hills over which shone a massive orange moon. It was a cartoon version of outer space, a vision from science fiction stories at a time when our idea of interplanetary travel was shaped by flying-saucer movies like *The Day the Earth Stood Still*, from 1951, which introduced the mysterious Klaatu, a kind and stern spaceman, and his robot, Gort. (The indelible line: "Gort, Klaatu barada nikto," whose meaning remains a science fiction mystery even though many guesses have been made.)

My teachers taught the basic subjects and good conduct. When the day was rainy or too cold for my classmates and me to go into the play yard for recess, we listened to phonograph records on a hand-cranked music-playing machine called a Victrola. We took turns requesting music. I usually picked "My Old Kentucky Home" by Stephen Foster. I don't know why other than I liked the melody. We didn't have Elvis, Little Richard, or even Jimmie Rodgers in the stack of recordings, and anyway I didn't know rock 'n' roll in the fall of 1959.

I probably heard the Russians had fired a metal orb named Sputnik into Earth orbit in 1957 and sparked what came to be known as the Space Race. An older friend of mine who was then in the Navy in Rhode Island saw tiny Sputnik low overhead in the gray dawn. Waiting with fellow sailors to march to breakfast, he heard buzzing, a whoosh as it passed. "That damn Russian spacecraft was flying over us."

I would not have known that the National Aeronautics and Space Administration (NASA) of the United States had been formed in 1959 and that one of the first men recruited was Lt. Col. Alan B. Shepard, Jr., of Derry, New Hampshire, where Robert Frost had his first farm, and not far from my hometown, but I certainly knew about Shepard in May 1961, when he shot into the clouds inside the *Freedom 7* capsule atop a Redstone rocket and landed in a ticker-tape parade in New York City draped in praise from our new young president, John F. Kennedy of Massachusetts. Shepard stayed with NASA long enough to hit golf balls on the moon.

I kept that space-themed lunch box for years, later using it to store small plastic pill bottles filled with dimes and nickels from a coin collection. For me, in those days, space as a concept meant the future. It was the next chapter of the American story. My father had fought in World War II, which was the previous big chapter. I was too young to grasp the happenings of the 1950s, from the bloody Korean War to bloody racial strife. Unlike my father, who said the country slept for eight years under President Eisenhower, I liked Ike, war hero and grandfather, and stood with a glass of milk with the other "small fry" in pre-school days for my daily Toast to the President when "Big Brother" Bob Emery turned to the official portrait on the set of his Boston TV show.

My mind's eye opened for good around 1960. One of the first things I saw was space exploration. Through the early years of grammar school, each time an astronaut blasted into space or splashed down in the ocean, my class was allowed to watch the event on a television mounted on a tall, wheeled cart in front of the room. The nation tracked those launches and recoveries. Kids may not have been able to pronounce the name of the Russian cosmonaut Yuri Gagarin, the first human to orbit the Earth, but we knew America and the Soviet Union were competing in "Can you top this?" The names of America's Project Mercury astronauts were as familiar to us as Rudolph's reindeer group—Scott Carpenter, Gordon Cooper, John Glenn, Virgil "Gus" Grissom, Wally Schirra, Alan Shepard, and Donald "Deke" Slayton.

Soon we had the space story in packs of trading cards with bubble-gum on the variety store counter next to baseball stars like Sandy Koufax and Willie Mays. In 1957, my brothers collected the first space cards with comic-book illustrations of a dog in a capsule, meteor showers, and men in protective gear frying eggs on the surface of Mercury. That set stepped its way to a moon landing and return, complete with imaginary flight-control centers and lunar greenhouses to feed a colony. The pictures on my cards came from color news photographs. I was in the future.

2014

PAUL MARION

Ste. Thérèse de Lisieux

"A shower of roses."

My family belonged to a French Catholic parish in Dracut, Massachusetts: *Ste. Thérèse*. Known as the Little Flower of Jesus, *Thérèse* of Lisieux in France is pictured on holy cards as a beautiful young Carmelite nun with a dark veil and high white collar around her delicate throat. She is usually portrayed holding a crucifix and a bouquet of roses. Her life model was the child Jesus of Nazareth. She is remembered as simple, humble, patient, kind, and pure—a perfect even if impossible example of a loving and genial youth in the eyes of French Catholic parents. She wrote holy poetry. *Thérèse* was twenty-four when she died of tuberculosis in 1897.

In her autobiography, completed just before she died, she writes: "I have never given to the good God anything but love. He will return that love. After my death I will let fall a ceaseless shower of roses upon earth." She is considered extraordinary among Catholic saints because of the vast following she won after being canonized in 1925. She was young, she was an ideal, she delivered miracles, and she was French, which made her a rock star among the Franco-American faithful.

Soon after *Ste. Thérèse* parish was founded due to an overflow of French families from *St. Louis de France* parish in the Centralville neighborhood of Lowell, the next-door city, there were grand prayer sessions with Catholics coming in buses for the healing services at a grotto built to honor the saint before the church was constructed. In the artificial grotto between the church and the parish school, a plaster cast of the saint lay in a glass-covered case set among flowering bushes and a stone shrine. When I started Catholic school in 1960, the side altars in the church were hung with crutches and braces of those believed to have been cured through her intercession. It was the era of polio, the infectious disease poliomyelitis, which can cause full or partial paralysis. My classmates and I drank small cups of the oral vaccine at school each year.

Soeur Thérèse de L'Enfant Jesus taught me in the first grade. How old was she? Maybe 22? The Sisters of the Assumption held us to a godly standard. In addition to the basic subjects, English-Math-History-Geography-Science, we studied French grammar and practiced speaking French. At least once, we were assigned a nun who spoke only French. That made Geography a higher hill to climb. Fortunately, the maps and textbook were in English. On Thursdays, for a few years, half the classes were taught in French. In the play yard, a student could earn a *jeton*, meaning you got a little credit ticket redeemable for something of value if you said a sentence in French to the nun on patrol during recess. The something of value might be a holy card or a glow-in-the-dark statue of St. Joseph carrying a hammer. There would be a small flock of model students hovering around the nun outside during the thirty-minute lunch break. With all that training, plus four years of French classes in high school and two semesters of grammar refreshing in college (I did not do well because I had been doing mostly reading and conversation in high school classes)—with all that in the language bank I still lost my fluency in French for lack of use.

If I was dropped down into Montreal or Paris for three months, I think the skill would work its way forward from a network of deep brain caves. I can read well enough to get a sense of what's going on. Writing is a struggle, although I had fun in the 2000s writing poems back and forth with a Canadian writer with whom I was engaged in a poetry challenge tied to the hockey playoffs with the Boston Bruins battling Montreal's *Canadiens*. If Montreal won, I had to write a poem in French, and François Pelletier was required to compose in English if the Bruins prevailed. Crazy as it sounds, we wound up on nationwide public radio in Canada being interviewed about our poetry "face-off." We did this for two playoff series and collected the poems in a chapbook published by bookstore-owner Richard Gingras in Montreal (*Librairie Le Chercheur de Trésors*)—popular enough to warrant a second printing. Both of us deviated from the original rules and wrote in French and English with all the associated fractures and foolishness.

By the end of my eighth grade in the school, the crumbling grotto had been removed, opening up the barrier between the girls' yard and boys' yard, which was major progress in our eyes. Keeping the sexes apart at playtime had been consistent with the teaching of moral purity it would seem, even before the adolescent download of hormones that set us on our way to teen-age. Of course, all the blockades and warning signals still had not prevented a Bernadette from taking a rawhide bracelet from a Eugene on the school bus going home.

We were young Catholics when the altar in church had been turned around, allowing the priest to look at the congregation during the Mass, and second, the language of the service changed to English from Latin, which had been the liturgical language all our lives. In most cases the traditional altar remained in place while a simple long table draped in the appropriate cloth had been installed for a forward-facing holy celebration.

The dramatic outward changes had emerged from the Second Vatican Council (1962-65), a worldwide event. Convened by Pope John XXIII, the proceedings registered like a Constitutional Convention in the secular nation. The goals and objectives were high-minded and complex, much of which was lost on us, but we took the visible result as modernization. And now only an invisible line separated the boys' and girls' yards. The old-world grip loosened on past rules and procedures. When the bishop withdrew the longstanding ban on eating meat on Fridays, a modified fasting, we knew the modern world had arrived. That weekly penance, abstaining from something as simple as a pork chop, had been a way to remind Catholics that strength of spiritual character matters. We believed Jesus had suffered and died on earth to ensure we could have everlasting life in Catholic heaven. "Suffer it up," one of my aunts would say.

The big losers were the fresh-fish markets and fish-fry places like Nichols' on Lakeview Avenue in Lowell where my mother had worked part-time for a short while. On Fridays, the line of customers stretched out to the sidewalk. Happy, hungry, obedient Catholics emerged with their oil-stained brown paper bags of fried haddock and hand-cut French fries. Overnight, hamburgers were allowed on Fridays.

Ham sandwiches instead of tuna fish salad. No more tomato-rice soup with saltines in the school cafeteria on Fridays.

The reforms, the changes, made it easier for me to choose public high school rather than continued Catholic education like my brother David had done at St. Joseph's in Lowell. He walked a mile to a bus stop on Lakeview Avenue and then took a bus (two buses) into Lowell his first year, and later car-pooled with Skippy Paquette who lived up the hill off Janice Ave. Our older brother Richard had broken the pattern and gone to Dracut High after going to school for eight years with the nuns. David had made his own decision. My parents had no problem with me choosing public school.

While I may not have been able to articulate in eighth grade the lasting effects of Catholic instruction and Jesus' example, I can say now that the models of simple kindness towards others and long practice of interior reflection have stayed with me all this time. For reflection, we sat quietly at our desks and examined our souls before walking the short distance to the church where we would confess sins, sometimes made up to have something to say, and be absolved of wrongdoing by the priest. Parochial school spoke to the metaphysical in life. We contended with sin, eternity, mysteries, and miraculous healing. That's big for ten-year-olds.

Ralph Waldo Emerson writes that the young in New England of the early nineteenth century "were born with knives in their brain, a tendency to introversion, self-dissection, anatomizing of motives." Reform movements would follow as engaged individuals contested established structures and ways of being and acting. They were alert for the transcendent. In our own way, using the Catholic map, my classmates were shown a direct route to the supreme, the ultimate, the invisible unknown source of the universe. The nuns encouraged us to speak to God, to pray, even if much of our expression was mimicry. The repeated practice developed in us a spiritual muscle memory with the potential to flex in an authentic moment and draw a clarifying insight from the mind.

Many years ago, while driving north on Pawtucket Boulevard along the Merrimack River, I had a moment that I can't fully explain. All of a sudden, passing the Heritage Ice Cream Stand, my brain gave me an image of a seemingly endless sequence of open doors, one swinging open onto another in an advancing line, that is, going away from me in the direction toward which I drove. Although I was looking at the road ahead, my mind's eye was seeing something else above tree height. I could have been looking at a movie scene. If this was a satori moment out of Buddhist practice, it was embarrassingly ordinary. Doors opening? More important than what I was seeing, however, was the feeling of "getting it."

Words are not adequate in describing the sensation of understanding. "Okay, I see what this all means" was unstated in my head. I felt an overall sense of coherence as if a secret explanation had been revealed to me. I'm not sure I can interpret the message, if that's what it was, but I've come to think of it as "Everything is connected" and "Way leads on to way" (as Robert Frost writes in a poem). There was something ecological and holistic about the vision if it can be given such a high-status label.

Midway through high school I told my parents that I would not go to Sunday church services anymore. They objected, and so I walked to the early Mass by myself for about three months, complaining all the way, after which the struggle subsided. I didn't want the ritual anymore. The authorities may have made a mistake with me by forcing me to go along with the system for so many years. I didn't have a choice, really. For a reason or reasons unknown to me my father had dropped out (or been kicked out) of the junior seminary in New Hampshire at about the same age that I quit the church ceremonies and rejected the dogma. He remained a populist Catholic who saw the wisdom in Christ's teachings as presented in the New Testament of the Bible: "Do unto others as you would have them do unto you." At the same time, he was anticlerical and skeptical of the claimed sacramental powers of priests. "Those guys have no magic," he said. "They like having a big new car and a housekeeper in the rectory. The church should sell all its gold and use the money to help poor people."

In 1980, I worked on a poem about a different Therese, also a Carmelite sister, Spanish mystic St. Teresa of Ávila (1515-1582) whom I had become fascinated with after reading about her life. I made eight pages of handwritten notes as I researched and used these to write a poem that I sent to *The Paris Review*, one of the many literary journals I submitted work to in those years. I aimed high—maybe being over-confident. Sister Teresa grew up in a Christian family with Jewish lineage, people with resources but not wealthy, in mountainous Spain, Castile.

As a child she was headstrong and once ran away with her brother, hoping to be martyred for her faith. In a convent at sixteen, the other sisters thought her to be happy. Ailments plagued her from teenage years to age forty-five. Teresa associated her bodily trials with Christ's sufferings. Teresa's ecstatic seizures set her apart as a figure in rapture. She believed her extreme physical episodes were spiritually sparked. My poem ends: "a mad Fire gets the bones as if marrow were to luminesce/ with the light of a thousand suns./The body brims in cool peace, aching to stay lit, aching to release, alive,/hot blood in a jar of ice." Productive beyond compare, she established more than thirty convents and monasteries while teaching and writing a sprawling autobiography—maybe the first Western woman to write this way.

My Teresa poem came back from *The Paris Review* with a form rejection slip on which poetry editor Jonathan Galassi wrote: "I found 'St. Teresa' impressive and would like to see more work from you." He made a few suggestions on the poem typescript and added, "Is this finished?" I made the changes and sent back the poem with a few others—but he didn't take anything. It was a big step for me, though, to get the attention of an elite editor. I was twenty-six years old. I never published that St. Teresa of Ávila poem, forever paused by the editor's decision to pass on it.

2019

PAUL MARION

John F. Kennedy

"Ask what you can do."

Sister Irene opens the door to my classroom and tells Sister Marie standing in front of the class, "President Kennedy has been shot." (How does she know? Was she listening to a radio in the school office? Did a parishioner call the convent next door?) In a minute, a different nun pushes a wheeled metal cart with a TV on the top rack into our classroom and turns it on. The time is about 1:45 p.m. Cardboard turkeys and pilgrims in tall black hats decorate the windows facing the line of maple trees on Goodhue Avenue. The kids sit quietly. We look at each other and then at the TV. A framed color photograph of the President hangs in the front left corner of the class near the American flag and the provincial flag of Quebec, Canada, with a *fleur-de-lis* in the center. A color picture of Pope Paul VI in the right corner balances the President's photo. By the time yellow buses pull up alongside the school we know the President is dead. November 22, 1963.

At home, the TV stayed on during waking hours from Friday evening through Monday afternoon. Networks covered every step of the ritual after the shooting and death. The word assassination was a word from the history books, from President Abraham Lincoln's murder in 1865. It wasn't a word we knew or had any reason to use, but now the word was everywhere. In Massachusetts, in Catholic families, the killing was a death in the family. We referred to him as JFK, like FDR, President Franklin D. Roosevelt—the acronym could have come from Boston tabloid headline writers who would have written "Hub Man Tabbed Pontiff" if Boston's Cardinal, Archbishop Richard Cushing, had been selected to be pope. In his large family, then and later, the second oldest Kennedy brother was "The President." Massachusetts households, especially Irish Americans, displayed his portrait in the kitchen as if he was a living saint. Some of the older Irish called him "Jack."

We followed each stage. From Texas, the arrival in darkness of the casket in Washington, D.C., with a new President, Lyndon B. Johnson, already sworn in and in charge. Mrs. Jacqueline Kennedy. "Jackie," in the bloody pink jacket and skirt smeared with her husband's brain matter, stepped down from the plane's boarding stairs. The lying-in-state on Saturday. Thousands passed by. 250,000 in a line three miles long. Elegant white horses pulled a caisson or wagon bearing the flag-draped coffin to the Capitol, shining white like the Washington Monument, Lincoln Memorial, and house where Presidents live.

On Sunday a little after noon, on live TV, the grotesque scene in the basement of Dallas police headquarters. Mobbed-up nightclub owner and cop-shop rink rat Jack Ruby pushes through the crowd of onlookers and jabs his pistol toward Lee Harvey Oswald's abdomen, firing the gun. Police gripping Oswald recoil in shock. Officers swarm Ruby. Confusion doubles, triples. Ruby has cut out Oswald's tongue. The public will not hear his story beyond his shout of "I'm just a patsy." when the authorities briefly displayed him to the media like a captured dog. "We have the assassin." Wrestled into custody, Ruby is a history-crasher.

What is going on with the three-name motif? John Fitzgerald Kennedy. Lee Harvey Oswald. Lyndon Baines Johnson. John Wilkes Booth. Martin Luther King, Jr., James Earl Ray. Bobby Kennedy broke the pattern, but he could be Robert Francis Kennedy sometimes. And Sirhan Sirhan, Bobby Kennedy's killer, had his own strange slot, the same name twice. It's as if we needed three names to contain the weight of the presence of these figures. The rhythm tells us the information is substantial.

In Washington, funeral preparations came together with military precision. Mrs. Kennedy asked the White House staff to model the arrangements on the funeral of President Abraham Lincoln. World leaders flew in to pay respects. President Charles de Gaulle wore his French army dress uniform holding in his right hand the traditional cap that looks like an upside-down saucepan. Queen Frederica of Greece in her mourning-black coat. In his commander's jacket, chest lined with medals, bearded Emperor Haile Selassie of Ethiopia. Ranks and ranks of other dignitaries.

Behind the caisson, the riderless horse, Black Jack, with high boots backwards in the stirrups, led by a young soldier. After the funeral Mass at St. Matthew's Cathedral, John junior in light-blue coat with matching short pants saluted like the soldiers had when his dad's body was on its way to Arlington Cemetery. His sister Caroline, also in blue, stood on her mother's right. Hearts broke.

John F. Kennedy was forty-six years old when he was shot dead. Two years older than my father. The World War II generation. I had borrowed *John F. Kennedy and P.T.-109* by Richard Tregaskis from the Dracut library, the story of a young Navy lieutenant in the Pacific islands whose patrol boat was split by a Japanese ship. He and his crew thrashed in the gas-soaked sea. They swam to a nearby island, Kennedy stroking with the belt of a life jacket in his teeth as he pulled an injured crewmate behind him. Actor Cliff Robertson did a credible job as the future president in the movie version. Debunkers questioned the melodramatic storyline in the book, charging that Kennedy had recklessly put his boat in harm's way. As with almost anything Kennedy, before and after his death, the truth is a polyhedron.

The day of JFK's inauguration in January 1961, a snowstorm swept through New England. My mother kept me home from school, and we watched on TV in the living room of our small ranch-style house with the picture window facing west, the slanted snow fuzzing the scene like "snow" on a black-and-white TV screen on the fritz. The former Supreme Commander of Allied Forces in Europe, now former President Dwight D. Eisenhower, sat with top hat on the platform. New Englander Robert Frost in a long winter coat recited his poem for the occasion.* Almost seven years old, I heard the President's call to action in real time. Reporters picked up the quotable lines that distilled the attitude of the new administration.

Hatless in the freezing temperature, President Kennedy poked the air and declared, "Ask not what your country can do for you. Ask what you can do for your country."

That was it. The challenge. The assignment. The homework. The call to action that sank into me deeply over the next five years. I believed it. I wanted to respond.

I began to think that I might be able to become president. I even picked the year: 2000, when I would be forty-six. That was the plan. True story. At the time it was not highly unusual for a kid to say he wanted to be president. The adage was that anyone in America could grow up to be president. Why not?

> *On October 26, 1963, nearly three years after the inauguration and less than a month before he was shot dead, President Kennedy attended a groundbreaking for the Robert Frost Library at Amherst College in Massachusetts. In his speech, according to the John F. Kennedy Presidential Library and Museum, "he describes the role of an artist in society, noting Frost's contributions to American arts, culture, and ideology. The President discusses the nature of strength and power, famously stating, 'When power leads men towards arrogance, poetry reminds him of his limitations. When power narrows the areas of man's concern, poetry reminds him of the richness and diversity of existence. When power corrupts, poetry cleanses.'"

2019

Tony Conigliaro

Topps 1964 All-Star Rookie.

If a nineteen-year-old from St. Mary's High in Lynn, Mass., could make the Red Sox, then a kid in Dracut could dream. I was ten when Tony Conigliaro homered on his first swing at Fenway Park in 1964. It was as if one of the Beatles had put on a Boston uniform. He was tall and dark-haired with Hollywood looks.

I had discovered baseball five years before. My father taught me how to catch and hit in our back yard. My older brother David took up where my dad left off. He let me tag along for games at Gendreau's Field next to our house, where one time I took a pitch to the forehead because I didn't know enough to duck. In those days we'd wrap a baseball in black electrical tape to keep the string from unraveling after the cover had let go under the beating of a thousand clouts.

My brother had Ted Williams and the early Carl Yastrzemski. My half-generation had Tony C and Triple Crown Yaz. When my pals and I played Home Run Derby in the back yard, someone would always say, "I'm Tony C." He won the American League home run title in 1965, the youngest champ ever. "Conig" even cut a rock 'n' roll record. Soon he was hanging out with New York Jets quarterback Joe Namath, Broadway Joe, and dating sexy blonde nightclub singers.

That was about the same time that I received the sacrament of Confirmation at St. Therese's Church. To prepare for this rite of passage, a young Catholic selects a confirmation name, preferably that of a saint who can be a life model and spiritual guide. Parents and godparents announce your Christian name at Baptism. Confirmation signals full membership in the church. You pick your own name the second time around. I chose "Anthony," and the nuns thought I meant the saint.

A few years back, I paid $8.00 for an old Conig card at a baseball memorabilia show. The card is a Topps brand, 1965. Along the way I lost the one I'd pulled out of a pack at the Hovey Square Variety. My old Red Sox had gone the way of Beatles cards of the same period, all those holy pictures tossed out in a fit of adolescence. There comes a moment when it's shameful to have heroes. The card show guy said Tony C sold well across the country. It's my favorite Conigliaro card—he's in three-quarter profile in his crisp white home uniform and looks as if he's staring a hole in a batter from his post in right field. There's a small gold trophy in the right corner for being named a Topps 1964 All-Star Rookie.

In the summer of 1966, I bought a Conigliaro-autographed model bat at Stuart's department store in Lowell. My father drove me to the store on a Saturday morning, then rushed me home to play ball in the abandoned farmer's field my friends and I had turned into a baseball field at the top of the Janice Avenue hill past my house. The regulars were there, joined that morning by a greasy punk from Crosby Road. He was fifteen going on twenty-five: duck's-ass hairstyle, pack of Winston cigarettes rolled up in the sleeve of his white T-shirt, and pegged black chinos. He always wore pointy fence-climber dress shoes, which made him slip all over the grass. He never brought a glove either. That day my team took the field first. I was at shortstop. The hood came up to the plate, a butt stuck in his mouth. He had my shiny bat with the white handle and brown barrel.

When he hit the ball, I heard a loud crack and felt sick. I knew he had hit the ball on the bat's label, which everyone else knew not to do. We were so conscious of that, especially with a new bat.

"Turn the label away from the pitcher. Don't hit the ball on the grain." How many times did we hear that? I should have made him buy me a new bat. He said it was a mistake. I fumed. When I got home, I nailed and taped the bat, but it was dead.

In 1967, I was living with my family in California during Boston's Impossible Dream summer, on the way to the World Series for the first time in decades. That August, pitcher Jack Hamilton of the California Angels hit Tony C with a fastball that fractured his left cheekbone in a game at Fenway Park. The *Sports Illustrated* photo of him in the hospital is gruesome, the closed left eye purplish black and swollen. He didn't play for a year-and-a-half. By 1970, he hit 36 homers and drove in 116 runs. The Sox traded him that winter.

In high school, I wore number 25 for four years on Junior Varsity and Varsity, but it didn't make me a power hitter. As a college student, I saw one of his second-comeback home runs at Fenway, a patented Green Monster job. Years later, he collapsed in his brother's car on the way to an interview with a Boston TV station. He was being considered for the color-man position on the Red Sox broadcasting team. By the time he reached the emergency room he had brain damage. After years of round-the-clock care, Tony Conigliaro died on February 24, 1990. He was a thrilling hitter with a big swing. I didn't expect anything from him except a homer every time he stepped into the batter's box. I tracked down that old baseball card because the cracked bat is long gone.

1990

PAUL MARION

Gumba & The Fly

"Havlicek stole the ball!"

At fifteen, I hung around with Andy Dubois. It may have been four months max, but in those days a third of a year was a long time. He was from one of the many French families in my area. We pronounced the name "Doo-BWA," unlike the non-French who said "DOO-boys."

Our parish, *Ste. Thérèse*, was a spillover from *St. Louis de France* in the Centralville section of Lowell, contiguous with our part of Dracut. Even today, Dracut has a high percentage of residents with French-Canadian roots. Andy's father ran a plumbing business, which he started when he returned from fighting the Japanese army on Pacific islands in World War II. He served in the Seabees, the U.S. Navy's Construction Battalion (CB became Seabee), building supply depots and runways for fighter planes. Most of the fathers I knew were combat veterans. One of my friends who didn't want to be left out when the subject came up would tell us that his father was in the Boy Scouts during World War II because he was too young for the army. We were good with that.

I smoked cigarettes with Andy every day for two weeks until I got sick of it. Somehow, we got a full pack and hid it in a stone wall lining a farmer's hay field that was a five-minute walk from my house. We had skin magazines stashed between the rocks too. We'd meet there to smoke a few cigarettes, talking about what's in the minds of teenaged guys. Next day, the same thing.

My father smoked unfiltered Camel cigarettes when I was a kid. Years later, he stopped one day, just quit. I can still see the package with blue lettering, brown camel, and golden palm trees and pyramid on the front. There was a weak joke related to the package. One of my uncles would ask me where I would hide if it started raining in the desert, under the camel or palm tree or inside the pyramid? If I answered, "The tree," he would say, "All you have to do is turn the package around and go to the city on the back." I don't recall taking a package from my father, so we must have gotten the cigarettes another way.

Andy introduced me to Mitch Gumbington. We called him "Gumba." He was in his early twenties. Gumba had a basketball hoop with a fresh white net at the end of the driveway at his house about halfway up the Crosby Road hill. And this began the Gumba basketball fad. We played there constantly one spring. With a group of friends, I'd show up after supper and play until streetlights clicked on or even later. Two outdoor spotlights above the kitchen window in the back of the house were trained on the driveway and backboard.

Gumba was six feet tall and thin with buzzed black hair. His five-o'clock shadow beard was so dark on his white cheeks and jaw that it made him look like a cartoon character. He did a weird thing constantly. He'd snort, loud and long, as if he was clearing out a hawker from his nostrils, a big gooey clam, then stretch out the neck of his T-shirt and pretend to spit down onto his chest—and rub it in satisfyingly. He grossed us out each time until we caught on to the fake. Gumba had played high school ball, so he made the games interesting. He was all elbows on rebounds. The hook shot from eight feet was deadly.

We had another character in our group around the same time. He was a couple of years older than me, but we hit it off as pals and I surfed on his wave, so to say, for a while. I had a stand-up comedian at my side, quick-witted and up-to-the-minute with the news. He anticipated today's 500 channels on cable. He'd roll through the latest in sports, politics, movies, music, and history in two minutes. For a while we called him "Fly" for his love of cool Walt Frazier of the New York Knicks basketball team. Here he is:

> As if in a lounge chair, Fly leaned back on his 650 Triumph chopper that growled up my driveway. He got the flag gas tank and Captain America helmet from *Easy Rider*. He saved money for the bike from his job as a bagger at the Demoulas supermarket across town.

Fly changed sports persona each season: on hockey ice, the Golden Jet and slapshot king, Bobby Hull; spinning to a basketball hoop, Walt Frazier; holding high a baseball bat, Yaz of the Red Sox; and scrambling quarterback Fran Tarkenton of the New York Giants when it was time to launch autumn bombs to speedy Homer Jones.

His red plastic comb remained hidden in a back pocket, "a foreign object," until he raked it across the skull of anyone who would play front-lawn Big Time Wrestling, starring Professor Tanaka, Bruno, and Chief Jay.

An inventor, he tagged nicknames rapid-fire on a defenseless population. William F. Buckley and Bee Gees mimic, he specialized in the "high above courtside" rasp of Boston Celtics' radio voice Johnny Most, who gargled razor blades, Fly said.

He turned that Johnny Most imitation into season tickets one manic Boston Garden halftime when he nearly blew a lung in a soundalike duel, screaming, "Havlicek stole the ball! Havlicek stole the ball!" The crowd went nuts. He won tickets for the coming year, a weekend ski trip in New Hampshire, and a $500 gift certificate from Sears. I went to a lot of basketball games the next year, sometimes running to get the last train to Lowell out of Boston's North Station downstairs from the Garden.

We met in elementary school. He was a new kid. On the bus one day he carried a clear plastic box sectioned off to hold turquoise rocks, pink quartz, mica, pyrite, the gems of his father's collection for show-and-tell.

Fly's name was Rudy Lavalley. His parents were fans of the singer and old-time radio entertainer Hubert Prior "Rudy" Vallée, who had French roots like theirs. Fly (Rudy) worshipped the Boston Bruins of the Bobby Orr years. Whenever he had enough spending money, he would ride the train to Boston Garden and buy the cheapest ticket to sit in the nosebleed section, hovering over the ice surface. I was with him at high altitude on March 2, 1969, the night when Boston centerman Phil Esposito scored two goals in a shutout against Pittsburgh and became the first National Hockey League player to score 100 points in a season.

On skates Fly was Olympian Peggy Fleming with a nasty wrist shot. His specialty was a pirouette hip-check to an opponent's shoulder, not hip, yelling, "Clear the track, here comes Shack!," meaning Eddie Shack, a Bruins hacker. He'd knock an unsuspecting stickhandler into the frozen weeds, sweep the stolen puck ahead, deke the defense(less)man, and flip a little backhander over the spread-legged goalie. (As smooth as he was on ice, Fly's vertical leap in basketball was a marvel for a five-eight Frenchman.) He called himself "A Streetcar Named Frank," after the lumbering forward Frank Mahovlich of the Detroit Red Wings.

On weekends or during winter school vacation, it was common to see kids walking to a pond after a snowfall with a hockey stick in one hand and a snow shovel in the other. This was before our hockey gang progressed from neighborhood ponds to the new indoor rinks opening because of Bruins-mania. We'd chip in five or ten dollars each, pile into somebody's car for the drive to the Billerica Forum or Nashua Gardens upriver and rent time on the ice at midnight for pickup games when town league players were in bed at home.

Gumba moved after a couple of years, and Andy took me with him one night to visit our old basketball pal at an apartment in a Victorian home next to a senior housing high-rise across the river in Lowell. By this time, both Andy and I had a driver's license. Gumba's place had the first black lights I'd seen. In the darkened second-floor apartment, white objects shined like glow-in-the-dark plastic saints that the nuns gave as rewards at the end of the year in grade school. Gumba lived alone, having split from his wife, Judy, the young wife from the basketball game nights. His hair was combed forward in black bangs, and a thick gold chain circled his neck. A huge waterbed dominated the bedroom, which smelled of incense and pot. On the bureau beside a stack of magazines was a large plastic container of Vaseline. He didn't offer us a joint but gave us beer.

"You should see the women I'm meeting at the Triple Mark in Tyngsborough. I've had four or five of them back here, not all at the same time. There's only so much a man can handle." He gave us details. "Remember, boys, it's the penmanship and not the pen that makes a woman smile."

He complained about the black light exposing the spotted black silk sheets on the waterbed. "The one thing you can't get out is jism. The stains are brutal."

On the stereo, Iron Butterfly droned "In-A-Gadda-Da-Vida," the thumping bass turned way up. In a lumpy bean-bag seat, Gumba bobbed his head with eyes closed. The song takes up one whole side of a record. Seventeen minutes. We got out of there at ten minutes. I don't think he noticed because he didn't say a word.

2019

Sergei Samsonov

Say it ain't so, Sammy.

We would have needed a bench full of Sammies to overcome the 20,000 zealots in *le Centre Bell*. Our compact rugged Russian kid blazed end-to-end all night. The only brown bear with a nose for the net was the Moscow Magician, Sir Sergei Viktorovich Samsonov, former Red Army national star. He tried to stickhandle his way to *La Coupe Stanley* through a swarm of red-and-blue bees who must have had honey or maple syrup on their blades last night, the way the puck stuck and kept finding Canadian branches in the Boston woods.

"Where have you gone Joe Thorntonaggio?" Paul Simon would have sung in this series if singing to Larry Robinson instead of Mrs. Robinson. *Montréal* goalie José Théodore imitated a reverse matador whose quick glove and splits stopped most of the Boston bulls, *Olé, Olé*.

When Steve Bégin got his face smashed into the boards and rushed back, sewn up behind plexiglass, to keep pounding Bruins in the corners, we knew the *Québec* Crusade was true. Boston could not rob the Hockey Treasury before the wide eyes of a crowd standing on guard for Lord Stanley.

Those small towels twirled by screaming French fans were never for crying on the drive home to Rosemont, no, the towels were for wiping spilled beer from thousands of bartops, dance floors, and dashboards after the Ice Mass ended and the faithful left in peace.

The struggle now returns to Boston, where the Gallery Gods and Beantown fanatics must channel the ancient essence of flying Bobby "Hoar" and his mate "Exmozito," as my *Pépère* Marion called brilliant Bobby and the centerman Phil Esposito, about whom it was said: "Jesus saves, and Espo scores on the rebound." Believers of this generation will scrape gold from the Massachusetts State House dome to fortify home uniforms of Patrice Bergeron and crew.

2004

Dalton Jones

"A lot of big hits."

Last week, I received a surprise call at my UMass Lowell office. I was in a meeting off campus, so was not there to pick up the phone. Later in the day, I got an email message explaining what had happened and telling me to check the voicemail.

I joined the Facebook universe in January 2011. That spring, when baseball season came around, for fun I changed my profile picture on Facebook (for nonusers, that's the one that identifies you on all your postings). I put up an image of a Topps baseball card from 1965. It was Dalton Jones, the infielder with the beautiful left-handed swing who played for the Red Sox in the mid-1960s. He wasn't a superstar, but he was a great contributor to the team. As my friend and baseball wiseman Jack Neary says, "He got a lot of big hits in 1967," when the Sox made it to the World Series.

I played baseball for Dracut High School for four years. I wasn't a regular starter. I played shortstop, second base, outfield, wherever I could help. I was a much better hitter in neighborhood games and in pickup softball later in my life, but I held my own in high school—one time broke up a no-hitter with two outs in the last inning against Billerica.

In 1965 when I was eleven years old, Dalton Jones was already my favorite Red Sox player. Dalton was such a good prospect coming out of high school that the Red Sox asked another great left-handed hitter to recruit him: Ted Williams. He batted .389 in the 1967 World Series, playing third base in games one through four. He was 7 for 18 with a .421 on-base percentage in the Series. Boston lost to St. Louis, as old-time fans recall. I remember a newspaper cartoon the day after the series showing a sad kid in a Red Sox cap who had scrawled these words on a wall: "Julián Javier is a Jerk"—Javier was the Cardinals' second baseman.

When my Facebook and real-life friend Bill Lipchitz saw Dalton Jones on my Facebook page, he wrote to me and said you probably don't know this, but Meredith Fife Day went to high school with Dalton Jones in Louisiana around 1960. Bill said she still talks to him and visits when she goes back to her hometown. Meredith has been the artist-in-residence at the Whistler House Museum of Art in Lowell for several years. One of her paintings hangs in my family's living room.

Bill is a friend of Meredith's, so he told her about Dalton and me. Meredith wrote to me and said it was great to hear this, and that she would tell her baseball-playing friend that he had a big fan in Lowell. She said Dalton was expected to attend the Fenway Park centennial celebration in April 2012. As it turned out, he was not able to get to Boston this spring.

Imagine my surprise and happiness when I listened to the voicemail message. "Hi Paul. This is Dalton Jones. I'm sitting here with a good friend, Meredith, and we're talking about you. Sorry I didn't get through to you. She's going to bring back a couple of things for you. Goodbye."

2012

Nathan Eovaldi

Diamond heroes and villains.

This email message from October 2018 was sent to my friend John Suiter in Chicago at 6:30 a.m., about three hours after the mythic contest between the Boston Red Sox and Los Angeles Dodgers ended with an 18th-inning victory in game three of the World Series. I quit watching TV after the top of the 15th inning when the Red Sox blew a good chance to break the 2-2 tie with at least one run. That was at 2:30 a.m. The game of over seven hours, longest in World Series history, began at 8:00 p.m. Eastern Standard Time. I've loved baseball for sixty years, brought along by my father and brother David from the time I was four or five. I've followed the Red Sox all this time, watching them miss being champions until the now-legendary 2004 defeat of the dreaded New York Yankees and ensuing World Series win against the St. Louis Cardinals. The game last night and into this morning spurred me to tell John what I was feeling. He had sent me an email message from Chicago after waking up and seeing the game was still on. He wanted to know if I was up in New England and watching the action. Here's what I wrote to him—I added the title just now.

John,

It was baseball like opera, like a Russian novel, baseball binge-watched in real time. I turned off the game after the top of the 15th when the main man Mookie (is he nicknamed for Mookie Wilson of the Mets or for Mookie in Spike Lee's movie?) took a whiff pitch with two outs and Jackie-Bradley-Junior on second. Backwards K. Our proven-MVP Mookie broke a record with 0-7 in a World Series game, matched by shortstop Xander B., 0-8. The top three slots for the Red Sox were, like, 0-23. Terrible. But they had a chance to win.

I couldn't watch more. It was 2:30 a.m. The game did not end for another hour. I couldn't watch with all the horror movies of past Red Sox seasons in my head. Even with them up 2-0 in the World Series, I felt total dread. The sporting life is never safe for a Red Sox fan.

Nate Eovaldi. What a superman. He pitched a whole game, 97 pitches until he got stung by Max Muncy. Max. The new Kirk Gibson of LA-LA Land. 18th inning. Bottom. What more could Nathan do for us? Fly to Nathan's in New York and get that man a red-hot, a Coney Island, a foursome with onions, relish, and mustard as yellow as Tweety Bird in the Sylvester cartoons.

Eduardo Núñez. A *Boston Globe* writer said he was in the wrong sport last night. The BoSox third baseman should have been in soccer shorts for all the tumbling, diving, and lurching he did from the 12th inning on. Is he dead yet? I was thinking after each of three falling-diving up-ends. A Facebook friend posted a clip from a Monty Python film with the knight missing two arms and a leg saying, "I'm invincible."

The game was Boston's but for a skid in the near-outfield grass by second baseman Ian Kinsler, who is what on the side? A bagpipes salesman? A kilt manufacturer? No, it turns out he's in business with rock star Jack White in Texas, making baseball bats called Warstic. But Kinsler, who got beat out for his college shortstop spot at Arizona State by Dustin "Pedey" Pedroia (who would go to the Sox), causing Ian to transfer to Missouri—Kinsler slips and makes a wild throw to first that never-before-playing-first-base Christian Vázquez (catcher) cannot haul in, not his fault—the throw goes wide to the photographers' corral. Run scores. Run scores. Tie game instead of a win for Boston. Nate must have died inside. Fellow pitcher Rick Porcello told the *Globe* he cried for Nate when it was over because Eovaldi left nothing on the field. An epic relief job. Magic Manager Alex Cora pushed him to the brink. 97 pitches. Leaving the scary Drew Pomeranz, lefty, sitting alone in the bullpen for what seemed like eternity, afraid to bring in Drew who could blow up in an L.A. Minute. It was Drew "Don't-Go-There" Pomeranz unless Nate had taken a line drive to the forehead. Even then maybe Cora would have made Brock Holt pitch. Brock-star has played everywhere else this year but catcher.

PORTRAITS ALONG THE WAY

Oh, the pain. Insufferable *Globe* scribe Dan Shaughnessy with his insufferable tics (the Sons of Cora, like the Sons of Farrell and the Sons of every other Boston manager, plus his pop music name-drops) is already writing the obituary for the 2018 Sox. They were up two games, and now they're dog meat.

For 14-plus innings I watched one of the most magnetic baseball games I've seen on TV, even if only 4 runs had scored at that point. They had me. The prospect of going up 3-0 vs. L.A. was not to be believed but suddenly possible before Mookie got whiffed and then the Sons of Dave Roberts hung in by their fingernails until Max Muncy, released by Oakland in 2017, blew a hole in the imaginary surreal HOOD dairy company blimp of Fenway Park fame floating beyond the outfield wall in Chavez Ravine, a stadium whose loaded origin can be learned in Ry Cooder's concept album of the same name that tells us about the working-class Mexican-American neighborhood that got bulldozed and wound up in hands of Brooklyn baseball money-men who brought their product to the West Coast. But that's another story for another day.

Here, this morning, it's all hail Nate Eovaldi, the fallen almost-hero of the Carmine Hose who grew up in Alvin, Texas, also hometown of hardball god Nolan Ryan. Can you say "synchronicity?" Nate Eovaldi who came back from Tommy John surgery and pitched like Babe Ruth last night, the way the Babe in red socks pitched 14 innings in 1916 against the Brooklyn Robins on the borrowed Boston Braves field in Beantown. Nathan Eovaldi who performed under the Olympian gaze of Sandy Koufax sitting close to the field in a Dodger comp seat and looking like ten million bucks, a survivor of the Rat Pack era who has kept his dignity and handsome locks. We remember Sandy Koufax. We will remember Nathan Eovaldi even though he got the "L" in game three of the World Series of 2018.

So, it's on to the field tonight after a seven-hour game. Ernie Banks used to say, "Let's play two," and they did last night.

I'm writing from the high hill in Amesbury, Mass., whose Main Street mural poet, John Greenleaf, gave the name to Whittier, California, where the Quakers put down roots and up grew a toxic plant called *Richius Nixonium*, but that's another story. The Whittier Quakers of today were surely wearing Dodger-blue caps and rooting for Max Muncy at midnight. Root, root, root for the home team.

Au revoir, my dark hours correspondent.

Your fellow fanatic

2018

Paul Marion

Hometown baseball.

In the 1950s and 1960s, small bottling companies "popped" up around the state. I grew up with Dracut Home Beverages, produced in the Collinsville section of town. The plant was little more than a retrofitted garage on a side street in a residential area off Lakeview Avenue. I still have one of the branded bottles, now valued as a collectible in the region. We always called soft drinks "a tonic" because of the local source of tonics like Moxie that came out of the once-lucrative patent medicine business in Lowell.

For several years in the mid-1960s, my cousins Tommy and Danny Brady, about the same age as me, a year younger and a year older, had a small business selling cold drinks to players and spectators at softball games of the Lowell Industrial League at Hovey Field across the street from their house. Half the park was in Dracut with a baseball diamond at each end. My cousins packed ice between the bottles of vivid tonic and pulled the wooden soda crates in a little red wagon to the park. On Saturdays, their father drove them to the bottling plant to buy eight cases of twenty-four.

Companies of that time included Raytheon Missile Systems, Joan Fabrics, Pandel-Bradford, Prince Spaghetti, and Avco Space Systems (a NASA contractor developing designs for Mars exploration). When we were twelve, the players appeared to be immense in size and as old as our fathers even though most of them would have been in their twenties or early thirties. I had a similar impression as a freshman baseball player in high school with eighteen-year-old seniors the size of forty-year-old men stomping around the locker room—a few of them bearded but not tattooed. Their home run clouts matched those of hammerin' Harmon

Killebrew of the Minnesota Twins. We knew the better players by names and numbers.

Between innings, softball guys paid a quarter for a seven-ounce bottle—maybe lime, strawberry, or ginger ale in crayon colors, among the many flavors. My cousins had the edge on the ice cream man in his ring-a-ding truck who swung by only once during the game.

"Hey, you kids, I sell the Cokes in this park!"

"Too bad, Mr. Softee. We've got it from here."

We were getting to be business-minded in more ways than tonic sales. In 1968, my cousins and I discovered that we could buy a carton of Topps baseball cards for the wholesale price at the Notini Tobacco Company distribution warehouse in the old Little Canada section of Lowell. What a revelation. Cut out the middleman. In those days the price at the corner variety store was five cents a pack. Each time Topps released a new series for sale, we'd get a carton with twenty-four packs of five cards each at a discount. What wealth we had when we spread our fresh cards on the kitchen table. The thin, hard, flat rectangles of pink bubble gum got tossed in the garbage.

Around this time, Tommy and I were happy to be included in regular weekend pickup games organized by my brother David and his friends, some high school buddies, some new college pals, who played six or seven on a side (the hitting team provided the catcher) if there were enough guys or alternatively played scrub with two men up at a time and others in the field. The regular field was the worn-down but usable Hovey Field reserved for softball on weeknights. There was one day when Hovey was unavailable, so everyone saddled up in their cars and drove a half-mile up the street to a park on Pleasant Street in Dracut where there were two diamonds with outfields back-to-back. Past the outfield looking east rises the distinctive wooden bell tower of the Old Yellow Meeting House built in the late 1700s. We found a large squad of neighborhood kids, closer in age to Tommy and me than to the older guys in our gang.

After a quick negotiation, the locals accepted the challenge, and we had a full-on game set up with nine players on each side, maybe ten on the "home team," each side providing an umpire calling strikes and balls from behind the pitcher during its turn at bat. What spooled out was epic, a full nine-inning game with fantastic fielding and clutch hitting, shortstops diving left and right to stab hard grounders, outfielders making impossible catches on long drives over their heads.

We could have played eighteen innings. We were semi-unconscious in our giddy good fortune. Time stopped for this field-of-dreams game. One kid ran across the street to his house to get jugs of water after the fourth inning. The absolute spontaneity, serendipity, harmonic convergence of factors lights me up even now. An "away" team shows up at your neighborhood field and challenges your crew to a game. This scene is from a book, a movie, a made-up memory like walking to school in a blizzard in the old days. We rhapsodize about the magic and mojo of hardball. The game on this day was pure for three hours. Two bunches of birds landed in the same open space and flashed their feathers. Everything anybody had in raw ability or learned-skill from thousands of bat-swings, rounds of playing catch, and friendly pickup contests found expression in the heightened moment. We played for the joy of it. In high school I became friends with several of the kids we played against in the game of the decade. Bobby and Mouse Dionne, Bones Beaudry, Donnie Beaudry, Gene Topjian, Dennis Doucette who lived across the street, and Gary Sullivan, who later joined the priesthood, and a couple more.

Monahan Park, then Pleasant Street Park before it was dedicated to Michael Monahan who had been killed in Vietnam, was already part of town baseball lore, remembered in a poem by Bob Schaefer, who had been at second base during a Little League game in the early 1960s when emerging sports-god Larry Adams (later a college football star and after that my high school gym teacher) belted a titanic home run that soared past the outfield, over the chain-link fence along the sidewalk, and across Pleasant Street into the front yard of the Fox family home. Nobody had a tape measure, but spectators knew they had seen something for the first time. In Dracut this was in the Ted Williams orbit.

I have no idea who won the ballgame in Dracut Center. The contest is etched in my mind like no other in many years of what some would call unorganized baseball but for me was a long-running series of entrepreneurial ballgames, as democratic a thing as you will find. Everyone got chosen for a team. We followed official baseball regulations and applied local ground rules, depending on location, whether farmer's field or taken-over Little League diamond. For example, second base might be a flat stone too large to dig up. Disputes were negotiated by team captains if there was no agreed-upon umpire at the start. Having an umpire was once in a hundred games—maybe somebody's dad showed up and offered to call safe-and-out on the bases. The next day your team would be a new mix of friends competing against yesterday's teammates. We learned a lot about getting along.

We used our own just practices like "bucking up" for first time at bat. We decided "first ups" in one of two ways. In the bat toss, one kid tosses a bat to another who catches it with one hand half-way up the barrel. Then the kid who tossed the bat closes his fist above the catcher's hand—and so forth until there is no room for another hand. The top hand wins. Unless, of course, a crafty kid calls "tops" and wins by slapping his palm on the knob of the bat. For "odds and evens," two kids, each with a closed fist, say "Once, twice, three," shaking their closed fists three times. On the fourth shake, "Shoot," each puts out one or more fingers. Before any counting or showing fingers, one or the other of the kids, by mutual agreement, would have called either "odds" or "evens," meaning the total number fingers shown determines who wins.

Everyone played. Take "Rollies at the Bat." Except for the batter and a catcher, all the players take the field. There's no pitcher. The batter hits the ball out of his or her own hand: toss it up and take a cut. The hitter then lays down the bat lengthwise at his or her feet. Whoever catches or stops the ball then throws the ball in from the field, trying to hit the bat on a bounce or a roll (the source of "rollies"). Rare is the throw that plunks the bat on the fly. If your ball knocks the bat, you become the next hitter. And a hitter stays up until a ball meets the bat.

One day when I was sixteen, the assembled neighborhood stars in the farm field at the top of Janice Avenue made me king for the day or something like that. We had six players. One kid pitched to me for an hour. I swung the bat until my arms ached. One after another, I drove line drives and deep flies to four kids in the outfield who were having a fielding bonanza, chasing down balls in the gap, backing up on high pops, and grabbing liners over their shoulders. I was hitting so many balls that I started placing drives so that all fielders were getting their chances. This is something that does not happen. One person hitting for such a long time. It never happened to me again. Anyone who has played baseball knows the existential jolt a hitter feels from wrist to gut when the sweet spot of the bat connects with a thrown hardball. Boom, boom, boom. When he was playing hardcore fast-pitch softball in his twenties, my friend Mark used to say that hitting a home run was better than sex for him. He was into it. Like the nine-on-nine pickup game that materialized out of park air in Dracut Center in the summer of 1968, my day in the trampled-down farm field with woods bordering three quarters of the outfield remains a peak day in my years of unorganized ball.

My organized baseball time lasted four years. The old neighborhood at Hildreth Street and Janice Avenue with its full supply of kids gave me all the happy baseball that I wanted until I turned fourteen years old and wondered what it would be like to play in the town Babe Ruth League. With a fifteen-year-old age limit, the spring of 1969 would be my last chance to compete against the best players my age.

I signed up for the player draft in January and waited. My brother David had played a season or two of Little League and tells the story of wanting badly to play on a real team. We have a photograph of him in his itchy woolen uniform standing in our front yard with his fist jammed into the pocket of his fielder's glove and looking serious, dark cap tilted a little on his head. He felt guilty because my father had to buy him a new glove to play. I'm sure whatever glove he had been using around the yard was a ragged leather thing: rawhide lace through the fingers tied together where it had broken from wear and the palm with a hole in it taped over with black electrical tape. He got a new glove. I watched him in a game at Intervale Field in the Kenwood section of town to the east and not far from the Merrimack River. He cracked a bat hitting a double down the left field line, a ground-rule double that bounced into the woods. After the game, the coach gave him the bat to take home. It was like a war souvenir, a saint's holy relic, an actual new Louisville Slugger that had been carried to the field in the coach's army duffle bag, a trophy whose handle David wrapped as tightly as possible to allow for further play at home. We made a bat rack out of a board and ten-penny nails for our three family bats including the cracked one. The bat handles were wedged between two nails that were not pounded in all the way. The knob overlapped the nails to keep the bat from sliding out. It was as fine as a gun rack in Kentucky.

Waiting for the Babe Ruth League team announcement, I tried out for the high-school freshman baseball team. We had enough good players to field freshman, junior varsity, and varsity squads. The coach posted the roster with typed names on the gymnasium door. Without having played an inning of town baseball, I somehow made the team as an infielder. A couple of weeks later, the Babe Ruth teams were set. Several freshmen played on Babe Ruth teams. If a schedule conflict arose, the high-school team had priority.

Returning Babe Ruth players stayed on their teams from the previous year. New player names, either first-year kids stepping up from Little League or entirely new names like mine, were put in a pool for league coaches to draw from. Coach Norm Miller selected me for the Yankees, which was a new team added to the expanding league. Dracut had so many kids my age that the school committee instituted double-session attendance for my ninth grade. Not only was my 330-member class split between the high school and junior high buildings, but we also were on staggered schedules. For half the year, half of us started school an hour early and ended after lunch while the other half began at 9 a.m. and stayed until 3:30 p.m. The bus schedule was crazy as were after-school activities. I wound up in the junior high building. The teenage overflow spilled into town baseball. Hello, Yankees.

Norm Miller was Donald Trump before Trump was a thing. Coach Miller had golden-hay hair swept across the top of his head not to cover baldness like Trump's but to manage the full mane atop his wide skull. He was in real estate, of course, and drove a late-model Pontiac. He looked like Trump did at his peak. He swaggered like that Trump, but he wasn't shady as far as we knew. He was an enthusiast who clapped his hands a lot on the sidelines. He often dressed in golf gear from white cap to stylish slacks and sporty shoes. I never saw him in sneakers.

I heard that he chose me sight unseen because of a rumor that I was a "ringer" who had played in California the year before. (In those years, my dad worked eight months a year in the wool business in central California. The family tried living there, but my mother couldn't stand being away from her life back East.) The coach didn't know I had been in town my whole life, almost, except for the six months out west. But I got picked and proved myself when the new team met to practice. I wanted to pitch. Coach Miller let me try throwing from a regulation mound. He loved it when I dropped down and threw sidearm fastballs without tipping my delivery until the last second.

Years of practice in my back yard paid off. Bobby across the street from my house had a catcher's mitt and had always been ready to take throws. I fired my pitches to Yankee catcher Gary Wilson from the Korner Kitchen Krewe in the Collinsville part of town, with whom I played in high school when he stepped up. I mixed in a few curves, but I threw heat mostly, high-low, inside-outside. In my father's time, these were called riser, sinker, in-shoot, out-shoot. We had a top-notch shortstop candidate, so I gladly played third base in the games when I didn't pitch.

We did not disappoint our coach even though the Cardinals finished first. They were loaded, including the best high school freshman player, D.J., who had made the junior varsity team. Artie St. Marie from my own neighborhood hummed fastballs for the Cards. All's fair. At mid-season the league sponsored an All-Star Game. Because the Yankees had the second-best record, Coach Miller was in charge of our side. He gave me a new ball to start the game. With my dark blue baseball cap pulled down low to shield my eyes from the sun, my mother said I looked like Denny McLain of the Detroit Tigers who had won thirty-one games the previous year. Halfway through the season, my pitching and hitting had gone remarkably well.

On a night when we started with a game that had been suspended due to darkness a couple of days before, I singled in the winning run with a man on third base in our last "ups." After a fifteen-minute break, the umpire said "Play ball" to begin the second game. We played all seven innings of this one, and I threw a one-hitter. The next day, I got my only headline of the season: "Marion Dracut Babe Ruth Star."

I had a patchy high-school baseball career. Overall, I was simply thrilled to make the freshman team and to stay on the roster the next three years. I didn't play in many games the first year, but I showed the coaches that I could hit fast pitching. If I had opted for an outfield position instead of insisting on shortstop or third base, or even said I could pitch, I probably would have played in more games over four years.

Sophomore year, a couple of my classmates moved up to the varsity team. The coaches kept me in play as starting shortstop for the junior varsity squad. I hit well enough in the first half of the season to be promoted to the varsity for a few games to give them an extra bat. One game stood out. Billerica, another of the Greater Lowell suburbs, had a pitching juggernaut even several years before Tom Glavine starred for the Billerica Indians on his way to the Atlanta Braves and Baseball Hall of Fame. In this Billerica home game, we were being no-hit by Fred Wiroll and Ed Minishak, the Merrimack Valley Conference's dominant hurlers, our region's Sandy Koufax and Don Drysdale.

"Get a helmet and a bat, Paul, you're going to pinch hit," said my coach Tom Tobin, motioning to home plate.

Coach Tobin, medium height with dark hair, slightly resembling President Kennedy, taught history at the junior high in town. He encouraged the players and never yelled at anyone. He knew his baseball and taught me to crouch lower when fielding ground balls, where I made my share of errors. He didn't want me to go the route of Don Buddin, a Red Sox infielder of the late 1950s whose nickname was "E-6" (error-shortstop on the scorecard).

Neither team had scored until the bottom of the sixth inning. The situation had Billerica ahead 2-0 with two outs in the top of the seventh, our last chance at bat. I stepped to the plate, took a ball low and inside and swung through the next pitch, a waist-high fastball. Minishak in his green-and-white uniform must have been thinking that I was a sacrificial lamb, some JV benchwarmer thrown up there in a desperation move. I knew I had to hit the next pitch or else I'd be hacking to stay alive. Everybody on the bench stood up.

"Just get a piece of it! Good eye, now! Swing hard! You hit that ball, Paul Marion!" When they say your two names, you know it's serious.

I dug in my back foot. The heater tailed to the outside. I half-stepped with my left leg and took a short stroke, quick and level. Crack! The skipping ground ball found a hole between the first baseman and second baseman. Clean single. I got on. Broke up the no-hitter.

An ounce of pride was saved for the Middies. (The source of the school's sports name is a long story involving a hurricane and the U. S. Naval Academy.) The next batter grounded out. Beating us in the final game of the season gave Billerica the Conference championship. Our record was three wins and thirteen losses.

My other varsity highlight, two in total, comes from a senior-year extra-innings game in which I played the outfield and got three hits, a double and two singles, against Andover High School, which always fielded a strong team. In the top of the tenth inning, our shortstop got an infield hit, stole second and third, and came home on an error with what proved to be the winning run, 5-4. We didn't win often, our record that year being five wins and seven losses with three games to go.

The next game I was pumped up, expecting to be penciled into the starting lineup. Coach Tobin pulled me aside.

"Paul, I'm putting Taylor in right field today so I can swap him out for our starter, Ricky, without having to take Ricky out of the lineup if we need a pitching change. I want to keep a lefty in the batting order."

This sounded reasonable even if bad news for me. I nodded and headed to the bench. So much for getting three hits in Andover. For my cooperation, I received a gold trophy at senior awards day which reads: "A Really Great Team Player." I've got it here on my desk as I'm writing. (Skip ahead to the fall when I started at Merrimack College in North Andover. Coach Tobin called me at home to say he'd given my name to the *Lowell Sun* sports editor who was looking for correspondents for high school football games. I took the assignment, my first writing job and byline.)

The lowlight of high-school baseball is that my father never got to see me play. He didn't see Babe Ruth games either because at that time he worked spring and summer in the California wool industry. In the years when he was back in Dracut, he had a late-day work schedule. Once in my senior year he came to a home game at the field behind the high school gym. We talked a little before the game. I rode the bench one more time. My big contribution was coaching third base. Lots of chatter for the batters, relaying signals to men on base, and waving a few runners in to score.

My love of baseball has as much to do with my father's passion for the game as anything else. On a Sunday in May 1964, the year before the Minnesota Twins had a 102-win season and gained the American League pennant, my father took me to Fenway Park to see them in a doubleheader against the Sox. I may have liked the Twins more than the Red Sox that summer. Tony Oliva, Zoilo Versalles, Jim Kaat, Don Mincher, and Bobby Allison. With the 1964 baseball cards, I began to follow the players.

Dad drove to Boston without complaint, in fact, I think he was glad to have somebody to go with. He parked the car, and we walked to the ballpark, always a stunning sight inside, the greenest lawn-green, white chalk lines, tan infield. I had been there once or twice before. Dad bought standing-room tickets because the grandstand was full, and he didn't want to sit in the bleachers. We found a good spot on the concourse behind the last row of seats, not directly behind the catcher but looking slightly up the first base line. We stayed for the two games. He knew I wanted to see every minute. He stood for six hours of baseball. We got hot dogs and drinks, a tonic for me and beer for him, twice. In the eighth inning of the second game some fans had left, which opened up a couple of seats for us. The teams split the games, 2-6, 6-5. That's what I remembered when I looked over at him in the bleachers from my spot in the third-base coaching box.

In its way, baseball prepared me for the high degree of failure in the writing trade. Hitting safely one out of three times makes a top-notch major-league hitter. For batters, the game assumes regular failure. Collecting rejection slips from magazine editors and book publishers can make a writer humble and thicken his or her skin—which is what makes writing success such a thing to savor.

2023

THREE

Bette Davis

"She did it the hard way."

Bette Davis is in the Lowell telephone book. Her picture and biography are there along with those of James McNeill Whistler and Jack Kerouac in a section on Famous Folk. These three are the city's artistic trinity, no matter that Whistler and Davis were kids when they left town. The painter's birthplace is preserved as an art museum; the writer is remembered in a granite sculpture plaza; and, shortly after Bette Davis' death last October, the Lowell City Council asked the City Manager to establish a memorial to her.

Anyone from Lowell probably knows Bette Davis was born in the city. Her mother, Ruth Favor Davis, described her daughter's first entrance: "Bette Davis, christened Ruth Elizabeth Davis, was born on April 5, 1908... She was quiet and easy to care for the first years of her life, perhaps compensation for years to come. She had one outstanding quality, an indomitable will."

The baby arrived while her parents were living in her mother's family home at 22 Chester Street in the Highlands neighborhood. Harlow Morrell Davis and Ruth Favor had been married in the house soon after Harlow's graduation from Bates College in 1907. Bette Davis has deep New England roots: ancestors on both sides of the family arrived in the region in the 1600s. Her great-grandmother, Augusta Freeman Favor, worked at a loom beside the "mill girl poet" Lucy Larcom in one of Lowell's textile mills. Bette's grandfather, William A. Favor, was a civil engineer who worked as a park planner in the city.

Much is made of future star's background as a way of explaining her tough, independent character. Bette credits her mother for her success as an artist. In her biography, *The Lonely Life*, she writes: "... without you this famed and after 'de-famed' creature known as Bette Davis would never have materialized."

In an unpublished memoir, Ruth's brother Paul remembers that Ruth excelled in English and chemistry and was Senior Commanding Officer of the Girls' Battalion at Lowell High School. She was also the literary editor of the monthly school magazine. More a "tomboy" than a "glamour girl," she had her own theatrical aspirations, which may explain her determination to give Bette a chance to pursue a career in drama. After graduating from Lowell High School, Ruth attended the Lowell Normal School, one of the predecessors of today's University of Lowell [Now UMass Lowell], a school that trained teachers.

Bette's parents met as summer friends in Ocean Park, Maine, where the two families had vacationed for years. The Davis-Favor union wasn't a good marriage. From Lowell, the family moved to Winchester, Mass., where a second daughter, Barbara, was born. Her father, a patent attorney, divorced her mother when Bette was seven. For the next ten years, Ruth supported her young family, moving constantly and working at various jobs, including as a portrait photographer. The trail finally led to New York City where seventeen-year-old Bette enrolled in drama school.

Within four years, Bette Davis was performing in Broadway theaters. Hollywood producer Samuel Goldwyn offered her a screen test and then a contract with Universal Pictures in 1930. With $50 in their pockets, Bette and her mother boarded a train to Los Angeles.

The motion picture industry was in the midst of great change following the successful release of *The Jazz Singer* in 1927; movies had added voices—the business now needed performers who could act and deliver lines effectively. Bette's rise is a chart of the modern film industry. After her debut in *Bad Sister* in 1931, she made twenty films in four years, leading to her breakthrough as Mildred, the cruel English waitress, in *Of Human Bondage*. The role made her a contender for the Best Actress award in 1934, which she would win the next year for her role in *Dangerous*.

The gold statuette known as "Oscar" gets its name from the middle name of Bette's first husband, Harmon O. Nelson. The rear end of the figure reminded her of "Ham," as she called him, but she was not about to apply that name to an acting award. She won a second Academy Award in 1938 for her portrayal of the feisty Southern belle Julie Marsden in *Jezebel*.

Through more than eighty films and four husbands, Bette Davis reigned in Hollywood. She had power, took risks, and played strong women characters. She wasn't afraid to be seen ugly. She was a working actress, some say a character actress, who became a "leading lady." The film titles read like a list from a classic film library: *The Petrified Forest* (1936), *Dark Victory* (1939), *The Little Foxes* (1941), *The Corn Is Green* (1945), *All About Eve* (1950), *What Ever Happened to Baby Jane?* (1962), and *Hush . . . Hush, Sweet Charlotte* (1964).

A child when she left, Bette's connection to Lowell is not tenuous. She visited the city at least three times after becoming an American cultural icon. One visit is part of the university's history. The year 1956 marked the fiftieth anniversary of the Lowell Tech Players, the dramatic organization of Lowell Technological Institute (LTI), the other predecessor school of today's UMass Lowell. Hoping to make the anniversary memorable, Professor Ernest James, an unofficial advisor to the Players, suggested to club officers Fred Obear '56 and Philip Lamprey '56 that they invite a Hollywood star like Bette Davis to the event.

According to Lamprey, now a professor in the school's chemistry department, Obear wrote the letter "half-heartedly, not thinking it would work." He invited the star to attend the performance of *Mister Roberts* at which she would be presented an award for her "significant work and interest in the little-theater movement and college dramatic groups."

"She wrote back and said 'Great,' she would be there," said Lamprey.

Bette Davis and husband Gary Merrill drove to Lowell from their home on the Maine coast on a Friday afternoon in May. That evening, they dined at the Vesper Country Club in Tyngsboro, upriver from the campus, with LTI President Martin Lydon and a member of the school's board of trustees. A limousine from James F. O'Donnell & Sons Funeral Home arrived at Vesper with a police escort before dinner was over, at which point Bette excused herself, saying "I'm here for the students."

According to Lamprey, "Gary Merrill was thrilled because they came tearing down Pawtucket Boulevard at high speed in a new sports car."

Merrill said, "It was the first time I've ever had the cops on my side going that speed!"

Cumnock Hall, the administration building with columns at the entrance, was filled for the show. LTI's campus newspaper, *The Text*, had reported the upcoming visit weeks before. The Hollywood star accepted a silver bowl from Obear, who is now Chancellor of the University of Tennessee at Chattanooga.

Obear described Davis and Merrill as a "sporty couple who could not have been nicer to us," and recalled that she spoke to him after the play about the possibility of attending acting school. "Of course, we were all chemists and engineers and doing it for fun. I wonder how we dared to take it all on. We just did it."

"I remember her sitting up in the president's office with a cigarette just like in one of her movie roles. She didn't disappoint us. She was exactly what we expected," Lamprey said.

To Professor James, Bette Davis was "a luminous presence."

Lamprey said Davis's visit was driven more by her interest in young people involved in theater than by a desire to return to her native city. Her next appearance in Lowell was more of a homecoming. On October 14th, 1959, Bette Davis and Gary Merrill appeared in *The World of Carl Sandburg* by Norman Corwin at Lowell Memorial Auditorium. The front page of the next day's *Lowell Sun* carried a large photo of Davis and Merrill with Mayor Samuel S. Pollard and his wife, Helen (Callahan), at City Hall, where Lowell resident Ruth Meehan recalls seeing Davis in a mink coat on the front steps. The mayor proclaimed it to be "Bette Davis Day," citing her contributions to the arts and "causes which personify the American way of life."

Sun correspondent Alfred W. Burke declared the production "a brilliant stage vehicle" that would be a top attraction for audiences. In her *Lowell Sun* column, "Pertinax" reported that "Bette, trim in a grey suit, was highly keyed up with excitement. 'Did it go well? Oh, I'm so happy! Because it was here, especially!' her mother wrote in a telegram from California. 'Welcome to your birthplace.'"

A third stop in Lowell was a quick trip on a Sunday morning in 1971.

Davis was in Boston for a fundraising event for the Special Collections division of the Mugar Memorial Library at Boston University, which has more than 100,000 items of Bette Davis memorabilia. Dr. Howard Gottleib, curator of the world's largest twentieth-century archive, said he and "Miss Davis" drove by places where she had lived as a girl, including in Lowell and Newton, Mass.

The Davis collection includes a curious item that arrived five years ago, an old Victorian-style time clock sent by Davis. According to Gottleib, she said: "It was the clock I had to punch when I worked in that 'expletive' factory and hated it. I swore that someday when I'm famous I will get that for my own."

Some sixty years later, she tracked it down. But something doesn't fit here. Gottleib said she claimed it was from a factory in Lowell, however, there is no documentation with the clock. While the media reported the anecdote without question, it is useful to refer to one of Davis's favorite nuggets of wisdom that Gottleib repeats: "Never let the facts get in the way of a good story."

Andy Warhol predicted fifteen minutes of fame for each of us in the era of mass-consumed image-based information. Bette Davis has survived the cultural shredder of the audience. Her films, professional and personal battles, even the disposition of her will made hot copy for screen magazines and supermarket tabloids. One Hollywood insider said that she became a monster in order to survive in a beastly business. She survived because of the quality of her artistic work. Performances in *All About Eve* and *Of Human Bondage* will thrill audiences as long as they are seen. True, some of her work is considered high camp. The one-liners live: "I'd love to kiss you, but I just washed my hair" and "What a dump!" and "Fasten your seatbelt, it's going to be a bumpy ride." Her "Bette Davis Eyes" are as much a Hollywood sign as the large letters in the hills overlooking the dream factories.

She was the first woman elected president of the Academy of Motion Picture Arts and Sciences and the first woman to receive the Life Achievement Award of the American Film Institute. In 1987, she was selected for the Kennedy Center Honors in Washington, D.C. Like Julie

Marsden in *Jezebel*, she was determined to wear the red dress to the ball. She wrote her epitaph: "Bette Davis—She Did It the Hard Way."

1990

Bob Dylan (1)

Bold for the Lord.

Bob Dylan opened a New England tour on May 4th with the first of two concerts at the city auditorium in Worcester, in central Massachusetts, a good spot to draw out-of-state fans from the region. He presented himself as a wise man traveling from the west unto the east with a sure-footed spiritual stance rooted in his newfound Christian beliefs. Rock journalists who chart Dylan's progression much as art critics discuss Picasso in terms of his Blue Period and so forth may rank this dramatic change in the musician-poet alongside his disruption of the folk music scene at the 1965 Newport Folk Festival when he turned to an electric guitar. Dylan produced an evangelical church service presided over by a convert and a gospel group which brought a holy message minus pipe organ and purple robes.

From the outset it was a strange event. In 1975, he pulled up in Lowell with the Rolling Thunder Revue, a mix of old folkies and compatriots, making a film on the road, *Renaldo and Clara*. In 1978, I caught up with him in Augusta, Maine, where he had a stage loaded with musicians and backup singers who helped him power through new material and upbeat versions of early songs. This year, Dylan showed up declaring he would play only Bible-ish songs from his most recent album, *Slow Train Coming*, and songs in the same vein from a forthcoming record.

Christian rock music is big where Dylan lives in Southern California. The Orange County Evangelical Christian radio station, KYMS, caters to a generation raised on pop, rock, and soul music who are now drawing religious sustenance through that medium. Last summer I heard that Dylan was "born again" through the network of evangelical musicians when I visited a woman who was a friend of Karen Lafferty's, a popular young Christian singer. With Dylan, Donna Summer, and Arlo Guthrie being more forthright about their spiritual journeys, I would not be surprised to see the audience grow.

The average age of the conservatively dressed ushers was fifty years old. Maybe they were regular auditorium employees. They looked like the ancient and honorable who collect donations and hand out bulletins at the local church. The audience was a blend of loyal Dylan fans (some with their kids), compulsive concertgoers, senior citizens, leather-clad bikers, high school students, and a large contingent of born-again Christians who may have arrived in buses. They were thrilled with Christian Bob. One woman said to me, "Dylan has always been outspoken, and now he's bold for the Lord." She then asked, "Are you a Christian?" making me think that my Catholic upbringing somehow didn't qualify for her brand of belief. Behind me, a man told his friends: "Look, you just have to adapt to him. The music is still super."

I was surprised to find tickets available at the door and more surprised to see many empty seats. How is it that Dylan, ranking with The Beatles and the Rolling Stones, could not fill a 3000-seat hall? The show began a half-hour late or for Dylan-specific fans an hour late because the first thirty minutes featured five gospel singers who delivered richly sung although little appreciated pieces. At times their solos were interrupted by rude shouts of "Dylan, Dylan, Dylan!"

Finally, the man himself appeared, kicking off with "Gotta Serve Somebody." He sang-shouted, "It may be the devil or it may be the Lord, but you gotta serve somebody." He stuck to a limited program, cuts from his latest album and new Christian numbers. His unique phrasing and voice quality challenge the ear even when one knows the words, but with new material and a poor sound system he was nearly impossible to understand. The over-amplified sound just about ruined the vocals. Of the new songs, I caught the choruses on some and figured the titles might be "Ain't Gonna Go to Hell for Anybody" and "What Can I Do for You?"

All evening people paraded down the center aisle where they stopped squarely in front of the stage, just a few feet away from Dylan. Before being ushered aside, person after person peered deeply into his form, as if checking to be sure he was there like a kid pulling a Santa Claus beard.

Dylan played electric and acoustic guitar. On "What Can I Do for You?" he took his famous harmonica from his famous pocket to the cheers of the crowd and wailed a virtuoso piece that held the place up and drove applause through the roof. He's always been a front-end loader pushing private and public emotions onto Main Street, shifting elaborate gears as he plows ahead for justice and romance. The guitar-plucking lynx at the wheel, his mouth-harp flashing in red stage light, white boots as shiny as the microphone chrome, sang with such conviction that I expected him to begin calling the faithful down to the front to dedicate themselves to Christ. The Jesus focus magnifies his poetic power, and the new truth-smacking songs sting the soul like the best of his early work.

Between songs, Dylan delivered mini sermons, punctuating his assertions with guitar chords. At one point he said, "There are a lot of people running for president this year saying they're gonna save the country. Well, they can't save anything unless they've saved themselves. I'm not gonna say, 'God bless you,' I'm gonna say, 'God save you!'"

He said, "We're living in dangerous times," and many in the crowd hooted their approval and raised index fingers high in the sign for "One Way."

I slipped out during the stomping and hollering for an encore. In the stairwell a man handed me a holy card from a Bible church, and then another guy running back into the main hall yelled to me, "Whatever you do, don't give up on Jesus!"

In the spring of 1980, Bob Dylan toured the country to promote his second born-again Christian album, *Saved*, which was released in June. The year before he had given the record industry and music culture a shake by releasing *Slow Train Coming*, which sold at the Platinum level in America. The hit song on the album, "Gotta Serve Somebody," won him a Grammy for Best Rock Vocal Performance, Male.

1980

PAUL MARION

Johnny Depp

"Hollywood is a small town."

You were a serious young guy wearing a gray-green plaid shirt over a tan T-shirt, brown pants with cuffs rolled, combat boots, and an Atlanta Falcons cap turned backwards. You set your black attaché case at your feet and sat down at the dining room table. You had a cigarette behind one ear. Your voice was deep, and your lingo was street.

I watched Edward Scissorhands hold by an edge a photo of Jack Kerouac shoveling snow on Sanders Avenue in 1967, another of Jack petting a black cat. You studied typed letters to his friends Neal Cassady and Sebastian Sampas, flipped through the uncut, illuminated *Book of Dreams* typescript with its title page collaged with blocky words and lingerie models clipped from newspapers. You came to Lowell to buy Jack's raincoat—a plain, dark wrap with a balled-up tissue in the left pocket.

The week before you had been in New York to shoot final scenes for a film with Faye Dunaway and Marlon Brando. You were engaged to Winona Ryder. I liked your polite, easy manner. After you arrived mid-afternoon, we examined documents and talked K for hours.

"I can't believe I'm in Lowell. This is like touching the robes of Christ," you said.

We toasted the author with cognac while an acetate Jack scatted and read passages from *Vanity of Duluoz*. Upstairs you looked through boxes filled with socks, cancelled checks from 1958 to 1968, a Horace Mann prep school yearbook, rolled Japanese calendars from a Tokyo publisher, a worn address book, Zig-Zag papers, ancient hard candy.

After dark, we drove in the executor's vintage Mercedes to a bistro downtown, a makeover of one of Kerouac's hideouts. On the wall hang framed snapshots of a scruffy Jack with a whiskey, circa the Summer of Love. You talked about growing up in Kentucky and Florida. You said you didn't consider yourself a proven box office star, and said your latest work is an art film.

"The paparazzi are horrible. People steal my mail. Hollywood is a small town."

You signed a menu for the owner. At ten o'clock we dropped you off at your idling limo and promised to write.

1991

Joan Baez

Always of her time.

In the end it was like church. A generational church. A church of humanity. Of joy. Of suffering. Of soulful community. She had brought us together one more time, and there was a poignancy to it because a lot of us are "getting up there" and have seen a lot of water flow under our bridges. A big part of the familiar sound of that water we've heard rushing toward us and running under the bridges came back to us last night in the auditorium at Lowell High School. She was in the city for the Lowell Summer Music Series.

Poet Walt Whitman writes that he contains multitudes. Joan Baez has gathered up a multitude of experiences and people that layer her performances as an artist. In a city where history is front and center, Joan Baez shared her remarkable history. She played folk standards as purely as she did when just a long-haired girl with a guitar in coffeehouses. She gave us selections of Americana, spirituals, and pop among choices from her catalogue of compositions—both hits and deep cuts.

Always of her time, whether she was singing for civil rights or pushing for human rights in Latin America, she name-checked the Supreme Court and this week's decisions on the Voting Rights Act and gay marriage—one minus, one plus—and sang her commentary.

She has a forever bond with Bob Dylan that gets richer and deeper as each of them ages. Her renderings of "It's All Over Now, Baby Blue" and "The Lonesome Death of Hattie Carroll" were exquisite, heartbreaking, really, for all the profound emotional freight the music and lyrics carry. We got it straight from the source last night. She played "Hattie Carroll" with "Bob" when the song was new in the very Maryland county in which the brutal act had occurred. "We had to get out of there fast after the show," she said. On "Baby Blue," she mimicked Dylan's outlaw croon on a few key lines, drawing a laugh from the crowd. The night began and ended with standing ovations.

Her repertoire includes brilliant interpretations of work by the extended family of composers, those long gone and others more recent. The encore featured a gorgeous version of "The Boxer" by Paul Simon. Did anyone tell her that Lowell is a fighters' town? Throughout the evening her guitar-playing was a joy to absorb. Other than Carole King on piano, how many other women of her generation are delivering a ninety-minute show of singing and instrumentation? Joni Mitchell sang a few songs on stage last week at an event in Canada. She's younger, and I don't think on the road these days.

Joan Baez first played in Lowell in November 1975 as a member of the Rolling Thunder Revue, barnstorming the northeast on the Bob Dylan bus. I remember their crystalline singing of "Blowin' in the Wind" in a cozy college gym. After the intermission, the lights came up with the two of them on stools, strumming behind a see-through curtain that slowly rose. The crowd bloomed. Late in the show last night Joan Baez thrilled us with a beautiful and sly version of "Diamonds and Rust," her monument to their legendary relationship.

She closed the show with a group sing of John Lennon's wishful anthem "Imagine," a thousand of us in unison on the modern hymn, singing for what might have been or what still could be. The thoughts point in a good direction, a clearing in the woods to which we can head. We knew all the words.

2013

PAUL MARION

Dimitri Hadzi

When I have shed my skin and bone,
Perhaps I'll be a polished stone.
      —Seamus Heaney ©1988

(Entry in the Hadzi studio guest book by his Harvard University colleague)

Dimitri Hadzi's exhibition of sculptures and prints at the Brush Gallery in the Market Mills complex in Lowell coincides with the installation of his new sculpture in the city. For the first time, the community is hosting an art show in connection with the unveiling of a new piece in the Lowell Public Art Collection. The Hadzi exhibition involves the Hellenic Culture Society, Paul and Niki Tsongas and their families, and "the Brush."

    Hadzi is a good match for a place where the Hellenic tradition is a proud one. Ancestors drawn by the prospect of work in the burgeoning textile-manufacturing center established an ethnic community whose progeny have made significant cultural and civic contributions. Hadzi is rooted in this tradition. His intellect, energy, and curiosity have served him well. He is considered to be one of the most important sculptors of his time.

    Combining the exhibition with the unveiling of Hadzi's monumental piece at the junction of the Pawtucket and Eastern canals gives the public a chance to see the relationship between the new sculpture and the smaller bronzes and works on paper in the gallery.

    "I'm basically a traditional sculptor," says Hadzi. Works in the show reflect the artist's diverse interests, ranging from the early sculpture *Centaur and Lapith*, a figurative piece with the two mythic antagonists entwined, to rich black-and-white monotypes fresh from the press.

Hadzi's fascination with weapons and tools—helmets, shields, swords, and hammers—is evident in several of the works. The title of *Elmo III* refers to the Italian word for helmet. In the late 1950s, Hadzi entered a design competition for a memorial at Auschwitz, the Nazi-run extermination camp in Poland where at least one million people, mostly Jewish prisoners, died as slave laborers or were killed in gas chambers between 1940 and 1945. In the process Hadzi delved into the history of war and revisited his own experiences in World War II.

"The Auschwitz Sculpture Competition in 1958 was very important. Looking at photographs of the death camps, I realized the numbing effect of all the bodies. After a while it was just a gray mass I felt that a simple, abstract form suggesting terror and struggle could make a more dramatic statement."

He exhibited his "Projects for a Concentration Camp Monument" at the Auschwitz-Birkenau museum in Poland in 1958. About his preference for abstraction, Hadzi says

> My student work was figurative and representational. Little by little the work became more abstract. Of course, I was very influenced by Henry Moore, and was also intrigued by Cubism. I come from a science background and have always been interested in formal structure.
>
> A lot of people don't think I'm a complete abstractionist. My shapes are based on natural forms. Some things in nature are pretty abstract—snow crystals, geological formations. What is more abstract than a beehive, a hexagonal shape?

The cast bronze elements of *Hephaestus III* allude to weapons and ceremonial objects, products of the forge. In Greek mythology, Hephaestus is the god of the forge and the workman of the gods. *Tevere* is a fine example of the way Hadzi's bronze works, though seemingly abstract, relate to nature. He calls this sculpture "a subconscious piece" that developed from drawings. Only afterwards did he see a river-like form. Hadzi's expressive bronzes have an organic quality. The heft and texture of the modeled forms suggest flesh and bone. Though harder than most stones, the cast bronze seems more alive than cold.

Art critic Gerald Nordland writes that Hadzi is "one of the outstanding figures of his generation." Although he spent twenty-five years in the middle of his life in Europe and is clearly cosmopolitan, Hadzi exudes a quintessential Americanness, especially as the character has evolved in this century: independent, vital, and—ethnic. A bootstrapper conditioned to hard work and few expectations, he seems to be a man who has made an artist's life for himself with the same force applied in shaping the materials of his prodigious public sculptures.

The son of a Greek immigrant from Kastoria, Hadzi grew up speaking Greek and was nourished by the local community. Living in Greece and traveling there often, the artist has cultivated a relationship with the country. He mines mythology to make sense of the world. Born in 1921 in New York City, he and his family scraped through the Depression, relying on their wits and some generosity to survive. With his first painting kit he copied the icons in the local Greek Orthodox church. Always quick-minded, Hadzi was accepted at the Brooklyn Technical High School, where he majored in chemistry. In 1940, he took a job in a research laboratory.

Hadzi says, "The discipline and thinking I learned from working in a research lab has made a huge impact on my life. I can work on three or four projects at one time and keep control of them, and still be constantly alert for any kind of accident that might happen and which I can take advantage of."

Following service in the Air Force in World War II and graduation from The Cooper Union in New York City, Hadzi was awarded a Fulbright Fellowship to study in Greece. In Athens he met Henry Moore and began a long friendship with the great sculptor. Hadzi then moved to Rome, using his veteran's benefits to support his new family while he studied casting and foundry work.

Shipping work from Rome to dealers and museums throughout Europe and across the Atlantic to America, Hadzi began to make his mark. In 1956, he was chosen to represent the United States in the prestigious Venice *Biennale*. A few years later Hadzi was again asked to represent the United States in Venice, this time with another artist, Louise Nevelson.

Hadzi remained in Italy as his reputation grew and his artistic powers developed. Although he was based in Europe, he was becoming more active in the United States, installing works on the West Coast; in Minneapolis, Minn.; and at Lincoln Center in New York City. In Boston, he installed *Thermopylae* at the John F. Kennedy Federal Building on City Hall Plaza, a project designed by architects Walter Gropius and Samuel Glaser.

In 1975, Harvard University offered Hadzi a residency. That same year he completed one of his most important commissions, the bronze doors of St. Paul's Within the Walls Episcopal Church in Rome. Hadzi maintained his position as artist-in-residence at Harvard until his retirement last year. The professor emeritus lives with his wife, Cynthia, in Cambridge, and keeps a studio in East Cambridge.

Hadzi's schedule is as busy as ever. Among his current projects are a sculpture commission for the Hugo L. Black United States Courthouse in Birmingham, Alabama, and shows on the east and west coasts. Last year, his works were exhibited in Tokyo, and next year he will have an exhibition in Athens, his first one-man show in that city.

Hadzi's recent monumental sculptures in the Boston area may be more familiar to the public than his signature. Among those works are the massive wall fountain at Copley Place; the tall multicolored granite sculpture in the center of Harvard Square in Cambridge; and *Primavera* on the campus of Pine Manor College in Chestnut Hill.

Asked about the responsibility of the public artist, he offers:

> I can't always explain my work. I keep discovering things myself because a good part of what I'm doing is intuitive. I think the sculptor should carefully consider, without compromise, what he or she is creating for a public space. It shouldn't upset people too much. It's something they have to live with. You have to try to be sympathetic to the public. They are trying to understand something. Of course, the other side of the coin is that people should make more of an effort to learn about contemporary art. After all, chamber music and poetry were very difficult for me.

I have had to put a lot of time into it. Still, I do understand that contemporary art can be hard. Perhaps it is because there are so many baffling directions in sculpture right now.

In 1987, former U.S. Senator Paul Tsongas and his wife, Niki, commissioned Hadzi to create a work in honor of their parents. The sculptor and Tsongas had previously discussed the growing art collection in Lowell. About a year later, the Tsongas family asked him to begin thinking about a design for the project they envisioned. Hadzi's sculpture is the first work in the Lowell Public Art Collection that is entirely privately funded.

Speaking about the lengthy design process, Hadzi says, "The two commissions that I have found most difficult were the doors of St. Paul's Church in Rome and this one. Unlike other commissions, I needed to get close to the people who commissioned me." In the end, Hadzi arrived at a solution that he describes as "simple and embracing." He says, "The forms possibly suggest a family group or trees. There's a sense of something strong, yet warm." The bronze sculpture is a group of three elements, the tallest of which rises about ten feet. Hadzi used a translucent black patina to add crispness to the forms. The title, *Agápetimé*, means "love and honor."

1990

Buddy Guy

"Don't let the blues die."

Wearing a gray flat cap and black-and-white shirt printed with ovals, Buddy Guy drove his musical Mack truck right through the center of a packed Boarding House Park this past Saturday night and left everybody staggering from the blues wallop that he put on us.

We go to the downtown Lowell pavilion on these nights like lowly moths drawn to lamps, hoping to be lifted up, to be transported, to be moved in a visceral way—sometimes soothingly and sometimes getting all fired up. Because that's what the live amplified music does. It gets inside our bones, runs up and down our capillaries, and vibrates our nerves. Buddy Guy and his guitar (Buddy Guy-tar?) make one organism.

He's seventy-seven years young. *Rolling Stone* magazine put him on the list of the 100 best guitar players ever. He's in the Rock & Roll Hall of Fame in Cleveland, Ohio. He holds the National Medal for Arts and was honored by the Kennedy Center for the Performing Arts. His history stretches from Muddy Waters and B. B. King to Eric Clapton and Jimmy Page. Music is music because it isn't words, so it's difficult to try to frame in language what happens when he puts his mind and hands to work on the instrument. I was listening and being swarmed by the sound, and at the same time thinking about how to describe what I was experiencing. He turns the guitar into an electric voice of its own, especially when he's in overdrive on the strings. The guitar becomes a creature in his hands as he slings his fist and picks the notes and plucks the strings. It's more than a machine, which of course it is, but it seems to come alive at his touch—and the sounds they make together go right to a person's core. Our reflex is to start moving. Head bobbing. Foot tapping. Hand slapping thigh. Whole body going to the beat. He played loud, and he played soft. He shouted. He crooned. He wailed. He smoothed. He had a force that belied eight decades on earth.

Early in the show he walked into the audience and played among the people, calling a town meeting on the grass. Toward the end he went back to the edge of the stage and handed out guitar picks, maybe fifty. He signed a guitar that one man offered up in homage to the king. He told stories and encouraged people to read his book. He played "Hoochie Coochie Man," "Skin Deep," "Fever," and Cream's "Strange Brew." He lamented that people can't hear blues music on the radio. He told us what Muddy Waters told him at the end: "Don't let the blues die."

There was something else going on all night. Buddy Guy kept praising the young guitar virtuoso Quinn Sullivan, who had opened the show with forty-five minutes of blistering blues, channeling all the guitar gods of the known world. Quinn is fourteen years old. Repeat, fourteen years old. He has been artistically adopted by Guy. Do you remember that *TIME* magazine cover story about Bruce Springsteen that said Bruce was "Rock's New Sensation?" He had already been declared "the future of rock 'n' roll" by critic Jon Landau. Buddy Guy sees high-school freshman Quinn Sullivan of New Bedford, Mass., as "the future of the blues." This is master territory. Genius land. The kid is amazing. And Buddy Guy kept telling people to support him, buy his album, help him make it big. Buddy brought Quinn back up at the end to join the fabulous band and play some tunes including an extended riff on "Sunshine of Your Love." The pavilion was shaking. The wisteria on the green pipes grew and twisted another six inches during the show, its fibers so stimulated by the sonic Miracle-Gro.

And then Buddy Guy did the coolest thing I've seen at Boarding House Park. After doling out more guitar picks to the crowd, and while the band was thumping away and wringing the guts out of their guitars and drums and keyboards, Mr. Buddy Guy slipped offstage—with the audience on its feet and applauding madly for the encore. Through the breaks in the stage backdrop a careful observer could see red taillights moving towards the foot of John Street at the corner of the park. He was gone. Like that. Always leave them wanting more. So sayeth the show biz lords. There and gone.

2013

Billy Joel

There was no "book" to follow.

I'm just back from a "performance" by Billy Joel in Durgin Concert Hall on UMass Lowell's South Campus. He didn't throw a dart to pick his next destination on an informal tour of American campuses. Veteran music reviewer Dave Perry, now a university staff writer, wrote a winning letter in the contest to bring Billy to town. The competition drew hundreds of appeals. It's nice to have a ringer on the team.

For two hours the music megastar engaged in a lively conversation with the audience, 900 strong, using a green laser pointer to call on this or that eager person in a sea of hands. The stage talk format is Joel's preferred situation for college visits these days. He says he found his route into the music business by trial and error, with a lot of mistakes, so this is his way of giving back to those who are thinking of music as a way to make a living or to make a life. After some early success he decided to do what he could "to help people do this job" in a business full of "treacherous and larcenous" characters.

For credentials, he's got scars from a ragged ascent up the career ladder, a lifetime on stages, and six Grammy Awards, plus Rock and Roll Hall of Fame membership. At sixty-two years old, the scruffy white goatee is good for his wise man air. Or he could just be the guy at the end of the bar.

There was no "book" to follow back in 1964 when he joined his first band in the days of Beatlemania. He says he "fell hard" for the music life and didn't look back, playing obsessively during his teenage years, so much so that he didn't finish high school. He doesn't point to himself as a model of anything, he says, but he has plenty to offer from the school of learning-by-doing.

Dressed in a gray sports jacket over a black T-shirt and wearing a black Moto Guzzi ball cap (he geeks for Italian motorcycles), Joel was at ease, joking with the audience and making himself the butt of most of the fooling, including the unlikely pairing of an "incredibly not good-looking guy" who used to be five feet seven inches and supermodels like Elle MacPherson (six feet), and the Brinkley woman, Christie, who agreed to marry the "Innocent Man."

Joel goofed on some of his classic songs like "Piano Man" and "We Didn't Start the Fire." But in between the banter and storytelling, he did his best to give up some of the trade secrets of his business and tell the truth about what it took for him to become a rock star. He said luck and timing were key ingredients, on top of the dogged performing night after night that sharpened his artistic genius and allowed him to master the craft.

As he responded to questions he hopped from the standing mike to one of the two pianos, illustrating at times the point he was just making. When a guy in the balcony asked if he started with music or words, Joel said, "Ninety-nine percent of the time it was music, which was and is what I like best." But he had an example of starting with words, the lyrics to "We Didn't Start the Fire," a recitation of key names and phrases that summarize his life and times up to that point in 1989. He must have played all or part of about a dozen songs, including "Piano Man" and Elton John's "Candle in the Wind."

The highlight of the night was near the end when a music major hollered out "Leningrad," a song I had not heard or had forgotten if I had heard it. Joel had earlier replied to a woman who asked about his greatest achievement, saying he was proud of his visit to the USSR in 1987 when Mikhail Gorbachev was the nation's leader. He said the Russians went crazy when they heard his songs on the giant sound system that had been shipped over from the United States.

When Joel heard "Leningrad," he paused and said, "I haven't played that live." Maybe he said he hadn't played it live for a while. The student yelled, "Let me play it." Joel, who had been a good sport all night with all kinds of requests, invited the guy on stage to take the smaller piano while he sat at the grand piano.

Joel asked the student if he knew the intro. "Of course," came the answer, and they were off. The audience hung on every note and word of the song about an American who grew up during the Cold War versus the Soviets finally meeting face-to-face a Russian of the same age. It was exhilarating to watch the two piano players, note perfect. When the song ended the audience erupted.

Joel said, "He played it better than I did," and called him over to the microphone and announced the student's name—I missed it in the uproar. Not about to waste his opportunity, the tall, thin young guy handed Joel a CD in a case, no doubt his own recordings. Nobody will forget that duet.

Joel closed out the program with Christmas songs, starting with a rich version of "Have Yourself a Merry Little Christmas," and then inviting the music majors to harmonize on a sing-along as he played and sang "Angels We Have Heard on High."

We were privileged to be in the seats for a Hall of Fame artist telling and showing how he makes art and what it's been like living an artist's life. What he has created bounced back to him. Joel-Lowell rhymes.

2011

PAUL MARION

Katherine O'Donnell Murphy & Arshile Gorky

Between two worlds.

Katherine O'Donnell Murphy, saver and giver—her "small oil painting" bought from Arshile Gorky in Spring 1924, fresh from the Boston Public Garden where he liked to sketch, and that day painted in oil Boston's Park Street Church—bought the work from him when he returned to his studio at the New School of Design where Katherine was also a student.

She would later lend it to the Whitney Museum in New York and Washington Gallery (1962). With fountain pen she wrote in the exhibition catalogue, "It has been in my home since then, a reminder of my own carefree days"—small lavender-toned scene purchased from the artist, dressed that day in a worn tweed jacket at the school "where Arshile Gorky and I were students," she tells us in blue ink in the same hand as in another note quoting critic Hilton Kramer on Gorky in 1969: "He was between two worlds, the European and American"—half-sheet tucked in the catalogue conveyed to the Lowell Art Association, along with the oil she bought from the tall man with curly black hair, a gift in the U.S. Bicentennial year, 1976, artwork by an Armenian immigrant who, in 1946, had seen eight of his paintings and two of his drawings picked for a major-league show titled "Fourteen Americans"—

this artist, having buried cousins slain in the Armenian Genocide, left his village in 1920 for New York City, then Boston and Watertown, Mass.—he studied at Rhode Island School of Design, Providence Tech, and Boston's New School of Design, where Katherine O'Donnell of Lowell got the painting one spring day, took it from his wide field-worker's hands, same hands he used to hang himself—after a barn fire ate thirty of his paintings, after cancer, after the car crash in which he broke his neck, after the rack of love—

but on that spring day he was satisfied with the day's picture, a painting later borrowed for a 1980 Guggenheim Museum retrospective that traveled—Dallas, Los Angeles County, before returning to Lowell—a small oil, *Park Street Church, Boston*, the "little impressionist cityscape," so unlike the long free lines and morphology of his signal compositions, this early scene bought from Gorky by a fellow student, who hung it in her house and followed his trajectory.

2017

Bob Dylan (2)

"The hour is getting late."

I'm glad I went down to the river last night. The preacher was in town, and the congregation was called to assemble. He made his fourth tour through the city of smokestacks and steeples, the small city with the world on its streets. The people arrived with eager, happy looks on their faces, a blend of loyalists who grew up with the artist and younger adventurers. We had a beautiful scene at the riverfront Paul E. Tsongas Center. Music lovers streamed toward the arena and the regular Tuesday night Riverwalk runners wove between clusters of people on the pathways. I met a woman who had been with Dylan on the 1975-76 Rolling Thunder Revue tour from the Plymouth, Mass., concert through Lowell and New York City's Madison Square Garden and on to the Zimmerman homestead in Hibbing, Minn. Mysteriously, she said, "I was one of the unknowns."

A couple of the fans had been to Jack Kerouac's grave earlier in the day, making the pilgrimage to the grave the same way Dylan himself paid respects to one of the writers who influenced him as a young man. We had a reporter from San Francisco who writes a daily column on Dylan for an online publication. I met a teacher who told me he is the person he is today because of Dylan's music and ideas. I haven't seen so many gray ponytails in one place in a long time, probably since the last Dylan concert. I thought of the Gray Panthers activists from the 1970s.

Dave Lewis, who teaches business at UMass Lowell, parked his green 1965 VW bus parked outside the Tsongas with doors open as a living artifact of the root-times of Dylan. Dave, Mary Lou Hubbell of the campus communications office, and I handed out 700 copies of a commemorative pamphlet about Dylan, UMass Lowell, and the city to appreciative concertgoers—an instantly collectible essay by writer Dave Perry with pictures.

In the parking lot, I talked to a guy who had been to the two previous shows, and he extolled the performance: "You're going to enjoy this tonight, but he will only play about three songs from the old days." The event had something of a feel of a high-school reunion, a gathering of the faithful for another dose of the sound and the voice that have already gone down in history. In the same way we drop the names of Edgar Allan Poe and Charles Dickens as legendary visitors, this man will be spoken of for a hundred years in the cultural chronicles of Lowell.

Bob Dylan was in good spirits. I've seen him perform eight times, and he offered a fine show, better in my view than in his last appearance at the Tsongas. He leaned into the songs and honored the words, shaping the phrases to fit his older throat. He opened strongly with "Things Have Changed," and on the sixth number thrilled the audience with the first notes of "Tangled Up in Blue." The floor was semi-packed, and the seating bowl filled about a third of the way around, not a capacity crowd or even close, but the people who attend now are connoisseurs and newcomers. The recreational rubberneckers have been drained out of the "endless tour." I understand the reason for the smaller crowds. This edition of Dylan is an acquired taste, and I take some of it like medicine. But it's a unified field of creative work. You are there because you need to be there. The preacher comes to town. The congregation assembles. "So let us not talk falsely now, the hour is getting late."

2013

FOUR

The Poets' Lab

From late 1976 through 1979, I was involved with writers, mostly from the Andover, Mass., area, who called themselves the Poets' Lab and later the Merrimack Valley Poets. Other than one creative writing workshop at the University of Lowell (now UMass Lowell) in 1975, I had no experience in a writers' group. I didn't know published writers or aspiring poets. There wasn't a poetry scene in Lowell. People in the city "doing" history generated the publishing energy—fueled by enthusiasm about the U.S. Bicentennial celebration and the prospect of a national park commemorating Lowell's role in the Industrial Revolution. The Lowell Historical Society released a new history of Lowell. Activist women at the university launched The New Lowell Offering, *a magazine named for the well-regarded* Lowell Offering *written by women factory workers in the 1840s.*

I had published poems in the university's student newspaper and in the city's alternative newspaper, The Communicator, *and had been to one poetry reading at Keene State College in New Hampshire, featuring a Native American woman. Michael Casey, from Lowell and also from my university (he was a physics major, 1968 graduate), won the Yale Younger Poets award (1972) for his book,* Obscenities, *about his time in the military and in the Vietnam War. I didn't know him but had his book. My models were writers I knew from books or those I had heard on radio or seen on TV. The timing of this opportunity was good for me. I was twenty-two years old with a bachelor's degree in political science and had published a pamphlet of my poems, working with a local printer. I thought that was the thing to do, get my work out there. I had read a lot about early twentieth-century poets and the little literary magazines and independent small presses where their work often appeared first. I liked the entrepreneurial attitude of self-publishing. Joining a new writing group seemed a smart next step.*

What began as an informal workshop whose members met every other Wednesday evening at the public library evolved into a collective whose writers gave readings up and down the river valley from Haverhill, Lawrence, and North Andover to Dracut and Lowell. One of the spin-off projects was a broadside series called LOOM *that is the root of my small publishing company, Loom Press, which got going in 1978.*

The Poets' Lab writers represented the full spectrum of development, ambition, and accomplishment. Esther Weisslitz, who often signed her poems E. F. Weisslitz, had published in The New Yorker *in the 1960s and was on a first-name basis with then-poetry editor Howard Moss, while other members like Charlie Brunault had only ever written for themselves. (Esther was so generous that she sent a batch of my poems to Moss with a note urging him to consider them for* The New Yorker. *I never forgot that kind gesture.)*

Dozens of writers filtered through the workshop meetings, the attendance sometimes exceeding the capacity of our second-floor conference room. Ken Skulski of Andover had issued the call for writers in the fall of 1976, using the regional public library network as an organizing tool. News of the workshop spread after the first few gatherings, drawing writers from close by and an hour's drive away. Ten writers formed the core and stayed together for the duration. Some of the friendships endure to this day.

The Poets' Lab Journal (Selected Entries)

October 13, 1976
Tonight, I attended the first meeting of the Poets' Lab at the Andover, Mass., public library, with fourteen other writers representing a variety of ages and backgrounds. Several are good poets. One bubbly African American man, Rudy, is attuned to the sounds in poems. The moderator, Ken, is into audio poetry and reads dramatically. He's forceful, the leader there. He said he corresponds with poet James Dickey. Stephen, tall and bearded, about fifteen years older than me, makes concrete poetry but also writes in traditional forms. One middle-aged man is highly opinionated and demonstrative. He's in love with poetry. There were several women, one with a British accent knitted during the meeting. Her poems are short but not compelling.

We had three or four college-aged men, one who works at a prison. They are energetic, sensitive, anxious. Four young women shared their poems. Their themes were not surprising. An older woman who had studied at Yale has aspired to publish for thirty years. Rudy is from Cambridge. The rest are from Andover and Greater Lawrence. I was the only one from my end of the river valley around Lowell. Many people seemed to be shy. The comfort level rose as we went on. Everyone read something. I said my poem "Meditation on Winter Trees" from memory.

October 28, 1976

The poetry group gathered again in Andover last night. I met Helen Allen, a poet in Lowell and director of the local YWCA. She liked my work and bought a copy of my new chapbook, *Horsefeathers & Aquarius*, offering to take copies for the Y gift shop. When she read her poems, I felt a deep connection to her work. She's a passionate feminist. I got to know Tom better, an intense writer and archivist at Andover Town Hall, a former reference librarian. Cindy read two neat short poems. A lively discussion about poets and poetry arose with people talking about workshop groups, favorite poems, William Carlos Williams, the Beats, Gary Snyder, Yevtushenko, and more. I enjoy being with folks who know something about poetry, like cooks talking food. Rudy has a fine sense of humor. He understands the subtleties in people's writing. Listening, he nods and says, "Yes," "Yeah," "Mmnn," and smiles a lot.

December 23, 1976

Last night I read "December Canticle" at the Poets' Lab, and Steve Perrin said it was the most positive thing he'd heard in a while. I introduced it as a kind of song, a hymn or chant, and after reading it said it is an affirmation that rides close to the Buddhist expression "Tat Tvam Asi," meaning "Thou Art That."

 A Portuguese priest-poet joined us. He has published books of sonnets in Portuguese. A professor of Romance Languages at Harvard University uses the books in his course. I missed his name. He's been told he's one of the most well-known Portuguese poets to come to the U.S. His recent book is called *Sonnets from America*. He read one in Portuguese, and then Ken said the English version in his marvelous way of speaking: "I hear your voice in the swallows on the wire."

Steve Perrin read several hard-hitting pieces written by children in a learning disabilities school where he teaches two writing classes. "I am a pistol that shoots off its mouth" began one poem. Another was by a girl who wrote that "a man in a white suit" gave her brain damage at birth, and that she wished her sisters would have brain damage too.

We had a man who teaches in Manchester, N.H., who read a narrative poem, "Hank and Alice" or something like that. In the poem a man chews razor blades to earn money to support his wife through the Great Depression and then gets hit by shrapnel in World War II, leaving the wife to run their restaurant alone and care for her broken husband. The poem was read in a matter-of-fact manner, reminding me of the painting *Nighthawks* by Edward Hopper. We had fewer people than usual because Christmas is almost here.

January 6, 1977
A good meeting last night that spilled over into a beer-pumping joint, Shag's, in Andover center, and then overflowed to photographer Lynn's house. Good talk and much fact-finding. Tom Mofford's been a teacher in Spain, the West Indies, and Japan as well as in this country. He was born in the last year of the Herbert Hoover administration. His wife, Julie, is a writer also. Ken is dedicated to writing "sound poetry" and has been around. He "knows people" and is informed about "the avant-garde scene," wherever that is. He sits in the seat of abdication as he chairs meetings. A lot of personal talk tonight. Here I sit in judgement of the asteroids in this galaxy.

January 20, 1977
Exciting meeting in Andover last night. There's talk of doing a public reading. People experimented this week. The group is evolving and showing more depth of talent each time that we gather.

February 3, 1977
We will read for the public at the Andover library on a Sunday in April. We may go on the road and do one group reading each month. Last night, Annie Fleming from Chelmsford joined us. She read a

poem called "Jamie with the Swaggers," with this line: "That Jamie he had sounds inside him." Wayne the night guard read two pieces that reminded me of my work, going deep into place and ethnic identity. Mary Lou showed her pen-and-ink drawings of the group members, interpretations of our personalities as animals. I was a raccoon. Some of the others: Tom/ram, Steve/lion, Ken/timber wolf, Florence/cockatoo, Mary Lou/dodo bird, Charlie/monkey, Cindy/deer, and others. Steve read some one-line poems like "Black holes suck." He also read a fifteen-page tiny, one-sentence per page, book called *Time Is*. We did a group poem, titling it "No Constraints." Ken enjoyed the hell out of the impromptu composition. Each of us added a line to the preceding one. Cindy later read some warmly erotic poems. Florence read a poem about the group, and in another compared a cloud to a long duck. Afterwards, we rushed over to Shag's across the street to carry on with talk, music, and general give-and-take and beer.

February 17, 1977

Ken and Rudy last night presented a taped piece called "Rampages"—the first part of a trilogy based on Baudelaire's statement that there are only three professions: the priest, the soldier, and the poet. This section was on the soldier, a bold weird work. Rudy improvised on guitar. Thirteen minutes long. Sounded like "A Season in Hell" madman philosopher ranting in stark images: "Luminous objects pregnant with heat." Tom also gave us a long composition called "Odyssey Since We Last Met," a collage poem of what bombarded him and filtered into him in the last two weeks. He goes on rampages, too. Rudy later read a poem about a February day teasing with Spring: "Birds withdraw their boundary of flight at the smell of our shadow." Wayne read a fine emotional poem about immigrant ancestors and their life on Laurel Hill, as well as the suburban life of the present generation. We also did a second group poem, "No Constraints II."

March 2, 1977

Doing the Beat poetry bit: Anne/Snyder, Tom/Ferlinghetti, Steve/Rexroth, Ken/Kerouac, me/Corso. Steve says to me, "You are so audial, you sound like a blind man reading."

March 17, 1977

St. Patrick's Day. An unpredictable meeting. Three new poets showed up, one, Esther, published in *The New Yorker* and *The Nation* in the 1960s; another, Paula, a near-psychiatrist, read richly worded persona poems about a carnival and Dancing Bear; and the third writer, a wacky talky woman calling herself the Erma Bombeck of poetry, jabbered at the podium and read a few things. Many of us went to Lynn's after the meeting, where we drew lots for the April reading: I will go 18th. Tom had clippings and papers to show me. He is enthusiastic. A wild session.

May 1, 1977

My letter to Tom Mofford:

> Saturday was a fine day. I told Annie Fleming, "I feel like an outlaw, a cultural bandit, when I go into Cambridge like this."
>
> We stopped to watch an inning of a pickup softball game on the common. Lilacs on residential streets. Tall walls of blue steel & glass. Italian steeple, brown triple-decker tenement, Anglican church, white Episcopalians, full decks of apartments street by street. At the Blue Parrot eatery, thick chicken salad sandwiches, rippled chips, and iced tea.
>
> In Cambridge, we got us some live Robert Lowell. An afternoon full house in Sanders Theatre at Harvard University. Lowell reading golden oldies and recent work. The one about the mother skunk in Maine who "jabs her wedge-head in a cup/of sour cream, drops her ostrich tail,/and will not scare." And the jail memory: "I was a fire-breathing Catholic C.O.,/and made my manic statement, telling off the state and president . . ." And later, from *The Dolphin*: "I roam from bookstore to bookstore browsing books . . ."
>
> His over-the-podium furtive stare and understated mid-poem remarks. With his pushed-back white mane, he seemed aged and far away on stage. He's some kind of world-class "local poet" in this setting, which is almost like a family room but extra-large. In the audience, wasn't it good to spot celebrities like one of our own, esteemed Andover poet Stephen G.

Perrin, and that other important author from the neighborhood, John Updike, with his ruddy mug?

I keep seeing the remarkable colors of the day: beds of crayoned tulips, fat stars of Chinese cherry flowers, slippery dark fruit-tree bark, pink crabapple blossoms. At Sanders, there was a woman in a silver space-cadet jacket and a known Irish writer with manila curls wearing a slim red tie. Each sunny stained-glass window made a kaleidoscope.

Tom, thanks for introducing me to the Grolier Poetry Book Shop on Plympton Street. Some men show younger men the way to cathouses or bars with cheap whiskey, but you chose a gem of a poetry store.

(On September 12, 1977, Robert Lowell died of a heart attack in the back seat of a taxi in New York City. "I thought he was asleep," the taxi driver told a news reporter. The May reading was his last appearance at Harvard University.)

May 1977
"All words with Z in them are suspect," Steve Perrin announced. When he was a kid, he was taunted in the schoolyard: "Perrin is a Huguenot, Perrin is a Huguenot." Just kidding. Back to Z: Bozo, Oz, Cardozo, zed, zenith, syzygy, Yazoo, Zorro, Lazarus, gazebo, garbanzo, Boz Scaggs, ozone, zebu, Zulu. Tom Mofford at times approaches the angelic, his face nearly beatific hovering over a pizza pie. At the same time, Tom is tactile like Doubting Thomas who needed to probe the wounds of Christ.

May 19, 1977
Reading last night at the Parker Memorial Library in Dracut, nine of us with many good new poems. The audience numbered twenty. I read "Smelling Like Childhood," "Boys on Bicycles," "Camille Flammarion," and "Memorial Day Bridges." I introduced the reading with e e cummings' "Advice from a Poet," from the cummings biography by Charles Norman, which I had given to Steve to read. He was recently written up in the Salem, Mass., newspaper—good recognition! He read a fine poem on "Responses." Alice read moving grief poems based on nightmares and her husband's death in London some time ago. Charlie offered four pieces drawn from his antinuke stance and related arrest with Clamshell Alliance protestors at the nuclear plant site in Seabrook, N.H. Cindy read a funny poem about eating out alone. Tom made a flourishing finish after an hour of poetry. Too bad more people could not participate. When they hear it was so good, they'll say, "Sorry we missed it." That's what the unicorns said to Noah as the Ark pulled out of the harbor. We went out for pizza and beer at the Walbrook restaurant down the street.

October 5, 1977
Tom, Steve, Ken, Dave, Eric, Ruth, Cindy, Wayne, Eric, and three new people attended. Eric read his "Snadra Nad Our Snog" poem. I don't know how he got the nutty idea of inverting the "n's" in this piece. But it's funny. Jersey Linder. Eric is from New Jersey. Cindy did a poem for me: "McDonald's & *Marking Fresh Ice,*" referencing my second chapbook. Wayne read "Cromwell Road" with "history mines" and "brandied eyes." I gave Tom a letter about his poetry. 7:30 to 8 p.m. for business; 8 to 9 p.m. for poems.

November 3, 1977
Cindy said her computer-dating poem will be published in a local magazine. Eric read "The Pearl You Spit Is Ancient Fishbone."

January 25, 1978
Alice Davis brought an anthology of Maine poets, *Surf, Sand, Pine,* which has her poem "Pink Trimline Telephone." A review of the book

praises her writing as having "resonance." Alice also reported that she had poems accepted by *North Shore Magazine* and *Dark Horse*. Kathy Aponick had a poem accepted by *Poet Lore* magazine. Steve Perrin landed another poet-in-residence appointment at a North Shore school.

February 23, 1978

Alice shared her poem from a recent issue of *Maine Times* and then read twelve poems about her husband's death in 1968. Wayne read a poem in the voice of a Black soldier in the Civil War, saying it was written in response to Robert Lowell's "For the Union Dead." Florence had a poem evoking California's "golden magnet" and luscious oranges, while Mary read her version, comically fractured, of the legend of Passaconaway, regional Native American leader of the 1600s. Nine people showed up last night.

March 15, 1978

I called Charles Simic to ask about the Master of Fine Arts in Writing Program at the University of New Hampshire in Durham. He said to drive up to see him on March 24, Good Friday.

March 24, 1978

Charles Simic said, "Going through a program like ours won't make you a poet. That's up to you. I may have had a choice when I was eighteen. Now, writing poetry is like breathing. I happen to be teaching here, but I would be writing poems even if I were sweeping streets to make a living." I needed to hear a poet I admire say that.

February 8, 1979

The Eagle-Tribune reported on a reading by the Merrimack Valley Poets, formerly The Poets' Lab, planned for Valentine's Day at the Stevens Memorial Library in North Andover. According to the newspaper:

The group is the nucleus of a poetry revival in the Merrimack Valley, and nearly 50 poets have shared their works in the group setting since 1976. The first major American poet, Anne Bradstreet, lived in North Andover, and John Greenleaf Whittier, famous for *Snow-Bound* and 'The Barefoot Boy,' lived in Haverhill and later in Amesbury. Robert Frost first plowed the literary earth in Lawrence. Lucy Larcom and Jack Kerouac of Lowell are part of that literary tradition. Members of the group include a social worker, a teacher, a bookstore owner, a computer programmer, and a gas station attendant. Their work has been published in books and in local and national magazines. The first edition of their own single-sheet poetry publication called *LOOM* is available.

1979

Alentour Poets

Alentour: One of the Lost "Little Magazines'" (1935-1943).

Invisible Strings

In late 1949, Jack Kerouac wrote to journalist Charles Sampas at his hometown newspaper in Lowell, Massachusetts, to tell him about his first novel, *The Town and the City*, which was due in stores that coming February. Toward the close of the letter, Kerouac asks about friends of his from the early 1940s. Among the pals is Michael Largay:

> So this brings us ... back to the nights when we'd all bump on the Square—Sammy, Ian MacDonald, Mike Largay, Conny Murphy, Eddy Tully, yourself and others like Jim O'Dea and John Koumantzelis and so many others, and chat about what we all felt ... an enriching background for all of us. Strange dark Lowell. ... Where is Michael Largay these days? I hear no more from Ian. The invisible strings got tangled in the night.

When I first read the letter in 1974 in the biography *Visions of Kerouac* by Charles Jarvis, I was struck as much by the familiar remembering of old friends as by the big-idea thinking in the closing—Kerouac compares Lowell to other landmark literary places, such as William Saroyan's Fresno, California. Poet Mike Casey reprinted the letter in the Spring 2002 issue of *The Acre*, the literary magazine he edits and publishes in Andover, ten miles downriver from Lowell. Rereading the letter twenty-eight years later, I knew a lot more, but far from everything, about Largay and his achievement. He was the printer-poet of his generation in Lowell, born into a family of printers in the city's Centralville neighborhood. He died in Southern California in 1991, leaving a modest legacy in New England that has been all but forgotten.

When Kerouac was twenty and shuttling between his family home in Lowell and his various activities out of town, he spent time with Largay and other aspiring intellects in Lowell. In the winter of 1943, reporting to his friend Sebastian Sampas, younger brother of Charles and a soldier at the time, Kerouac wrote, "I saw Michael Largay the other night, we drank beer with Ian, talked, and made an appointment to go see him at his Boston apartment this Thursday with Billy Ryan—we shall feast in a good restaurant, take in a concert, get drunk and discuss all night . . . it should be a memorable evening."

Alentour

Browsing in a used bookshop in Concord, Mass., in the fall of 1989, I noticed a plastic freezer bag in which there were several staple-stitched booklets. Inside were six hand-sized publications with the words *Alentour: A National Magazine of New Poetry* on the faded covers—two issues from 1935, three from 1936, and one from 1937. On the inside cover of one, contributor Arlene Hope had written her name and address, 926 Moody Street, Lowell, Mass., in blue script. The editor was Michael Largay of 3 Hart's Avenue in Lowell. Belle Irene Gillis of 118 West 79th Street in New York City was associate editor. In the lower right corner of the front cover was the price: "Dollar A Year" or "25 Cents A Copy." Gillis designed the magazine and Largay handset the type and did the printing at Alentour House.

The masthead on early issues featured an illustration of a knight bearing a long-handled axe, on guard in front of closed wooden doors that curve to a peak. On the doors are ornamental hinges. The knight's headgear resembles a Saracen's hood, but the face is that of a European. An old etching of a castle atop a rocky hill high above the surrounding territory dominated the cover of the Spring 1935 inaugural issue.

I asked Montreal poet François Pelletier if the word "Alentour" was familiar to him from his readings in French literature. According to *Le Robert Dictionnaire Historique de la Langue Française*, the word originally meant "around a tower." The French "tour" means "une maison en hauteur" or a house that is high or on a hill.

I guess that definition is the closest meaning to the drawing of the castle which is a tower, on the cover of the magazine. 'Alentours' indicates proximity in time and place. The Larousse dictionary gives us 'around' for the definition of 'alentour,' and for 'alentours' the English translation is 'neighborhood.' Regarding the magazine, the name could suggest that the publication is about a well-circumscribed place, like a Little Canada district in New England or like the Beat writers were around ('alentours') North Beach in San Francisco.

I had my hands on a piece of Lowell's cultural history that had been buried by the years. Who knew (or remembered) that young writers had published a poetry quarterly while the city was in the jaws of the Great Depression? There were no copies at the public library, none at the University of Massachusetts Lowell's Center for Lowell History or in the library at Lowell National Historical Park, and none in private collections around town. The lack of mention is odd, given that Lowell's general history had been combed through, sifted, probed, challenged, recompiled, and backfilled by dozens of scholars since the middle 1960s, when people started pushing to make the city a living monument to the American Industrial Revolution.

The Kerouac Connection

My interest in *Alentour* reignited in 1991, when I began cataloguing Kerouac's treasure chest of unpublished, and mostly unseen, papers for his family estate in Lowell. Among the papers was a two-page autobiography written by Kerouac in New York City in late 1943. He was looking for a job as a script synopsizer in the film industry and needed to introduce himself to prospective employers. There are two drafts of the statement; in both drafts he touts his experience as a writer, but in the first version he mentions that he had a poem published in *Alentour*. He deleted the detail in the revised version. He gave no further explanation of the magazine, as if the name should ring his reader's bell. It rang mine.

That reference to *Alentour* became even more important to me after I received a contract from Viking Penguin to edit a collection of Kerouac's early work. Published in 1999, *Atop an Underwood: Early Stories and Other Writings* by Jack Kerouac includes short stories, parts of novels, poems, essays, prose sketches, and plays, all written before Kerouac turned twenty-two years old. I used the second, improved draft of the autobiography to connect the three chronological sections of the book. Although the *Alentour* reference had been excised by Kerouac, I dug deeply to find what I thought might be his first published poem.

In 1997, librarian Renate Olsen of Regis College in Weston, Mass., helped me track down a set of *Alentour* (1935 to 1943), at the Widener Library of Harvard University. There also were issues at Brandeis University, the Library of Congress, Yale University, the University of Pennsylvania, and scattered copies at colleges in Minnesota and Wisconsin—which suggested to me that major libraries had subscribed to the journal while it was live or thought it serious enough to collect afterwards.

I didn't find Kerouac's poem. One explanation could be that the editor had accepted a poem of Kerouac's before the decision was made to cease publication. The editors mention returning manuscripts in the final issue. Since Kerouac was traveling between Lowell and New York City and Merchant Marine voyages in the early 1940s, he may have believed the poem had been published. There is, however, a poem by Jack Greenhill in the Summer 1941 issue. In the summer of 1940, Kerouac had been injured in a car accident while on a road trip with friends in Vermont. Vermont is from the French for "green hill" or "green mountain." It is a stretch, but I could imagine Kerouac using a pen name that was a play on the French. One of his first published pieces about the Beat Generation was signed, "Jean-Louis." The problem is that the poem, "Without Words," is a stilted, formal poem ("He slowly sipped his bit of wine, as she/Drew near, and settled at his feet. Her hair,/In golden length fell softly across his knee;/And from her pretty eyes tears spoke despair."). The writing does not sound like Kerouac, even in those early years, when he was still experimenting with various forms of writing, including some rhyming poetry. In a 1940 note about his writing, he explains why he avoided traditional forms of poetry: "I feel that the words are put backwards. I'd rather have simple prose-poetry, to the point, concise, and more digestible."

Young Prometheans

Alentour was a bridge from Largay's generation to Kerouac's crowd. Ian MacDonald, a regular contributor to *Alentour* by 1940, was counted among Sebastian Sampas's high-minded pals, whom he dubbed the Young Prometheans. It is clear from Kerouac's letters cited earlier that Largay was in the mix, standing out as an older role model. When Kerouac and his literary soulmate Sebastian began to pursue their artistic aspirations as high-school students, they didn't have to look far for examples of others doing the same thing. The presence of Largay and company along with a Lowell-based literary quarterly had to have emboldened them. They could point to a tight-knit group of young writers in the city who were publishing their own work, as well as that of others around the country. On February 2, 1943, in his daily column, Charles Sampas referred to Largay as "Lowell's most authentic poet." The older Sampas likely had copies of *Alentour* in his house from the start, and Sebastian and Jack would have seen the freshly minted poetry.

In their correspondence, Kerouac and Sampas debated the philosophical foundations of their "Prometheanism." Sampas' Promethean notion was bound up with an ideal "Brotherhood of Man" and the hoped-for evolution of a new American with an artful, enlightened soul and eyes filled with love. Here is Kerouac upbraiding his friend for squishy thinking on one aspect of the Promethean vision—the role of the artist:

> ... I want you to get more serious about your poet's station, more diligent, searching, and scholarly—forget the romantic 'outcast' notions and continue observing the phenomena of living, with the patience and scrutiny of a scientist in his laboratory ...

John "Ian" or "Yann" MacDonald, along with Sebastian and Kerouac, had been at Bartlett Junior High School when *Alentour* debuted. He was a charter member of the Young Prometheans. In a sprawling letter to Sebastian in 1943, Kerouac talks about their friend:

> I see within the realms of his truly great mind the wry diamond of Shakespeare's visage, the bejowled heaviness of Beethoven's face, the pale purple vistas of long-ago poetry, long-ago love, trees on the horizon, all the classic meaning of life, pent up in his pale brow like a submissive nightingale . . . .

MacDonald had three poems in the final issue of *Alentour* (1942-43): "To a Young Lady," "Song," and "I Will Not Ask These Things." The poems are romantic flights of language from a young man eager to find the vocabulary equal to the science of his nervous system. His antennae were receiving cosmic transmissions, and he was discovering that he could say things in a poem that did not fit elsewhere in the daily conversation. Here he is in "I Will Not Ask These Things":

> I cannot give my trust to time, I'll buy
>   This 'Now' with every jeweled word I know,
> And sell the formless future for a sigh—
>   If one must pay with sighs who loves you so!

In "A Soldier Contemplates the Fallen Foe," published in 1940, a soldier pleads with his enemy not to die after wounding the adversary severely. He tries to rationalize his action: "I drove the willing blade,/ But steel I never made/Nor hate I bore./I saw the wild blood run,/Thus was my duty done:/ I live today!/But now your hand is chill,/Your eyes reprove me still—/What words to say?"

A National Magazine of New Poetry

Alentour premiered in Spring 1935. On the back cover of volume one, number one, is a full-page ad for "Pollard's, Lowell's Biggest, Busiest, and Best Department Store." The magazine also landed advertisers beyond downtown Lowell—the Autumn 1935 issue had a large advertisement from G. P. Putnam's Sons of 2 West 45th Street in New York City for

Dorothy Quick's second book, *Changing Winds*. Quick is described as a "well-known writer, contributor to numerous publications, and member of important poetry groups." The publisher claims that readers of her first book will appreciate the "spontaneity and charm" of the new poems.

In a practice that would continue through the years, the first issue carried an announcement for awards for the best work in the issue. Winners would receive copies of *I Go A-Walking* by Barbara Young and *From Gold to Green* by Margaret Lathrop Law. For the summer issue, a donor gave a copy of Edna St. Vincent Millay's *Wine From These Grapes* for one prize.

In later issues, prospective contributors were advised to send "experimental forms of poetry" (read free verse) to Gillis in Manhattan and "regular models" or "patterned verse" to Largay in Lowell. *Alentour* was a fair reflection of modern poetry in its time. Examples of spare, visual, imagist verse and haiku appeared alongside poems in closed form. While many of its contributors can be described as "emerging writers" or even less experienced hopefuls, *Alentour* was the springboard for a number of writers whose poems reached larger audiences. The editors were handling requests to reprint *Alentour* poems from editors of anthologies and other publications.

The *Alentour* story has a preamble, as reported by the *Fitchburg Sentinel* (August 3, 1937): "The project began under the name of *Caravel* when Mr. Largay was in the hospital, and it invited others confined within the four walls of a hospital room, so that the magazine might become a ship sailing forth to bring cheer and hope to the confined as well as to others." Largay changed the name when he learned of another literary magazine named *Caravel*.

The Price of Three Lemons

Under the Alentour House imprint, Largay and friends expanded their activity beyond the magazine to produce chapbooks or booklets like George Chapman's *A Song of a Chinese Night*, described as a "light, airy phantasy in the gentle tradition of lyric poetry." This collection was available in the Art in the Mart series for ten cents a copy. Another title in the series was Largay's own *Counterpane*, billed as the first edition of his "hospital poems." Here is Largay's announcement for Art in the Mart:

> The Alentour Associates are comprised of a group of poets who are publishing their own poetry and that of others. They are bringing typographical distinction to poetry that could hardly be achieved by other than a poet.

Within a year, the series had grown to include Philip J. Garrigan's *Nine Poems*, Ralph Lee True's *Among Other Things*, and Mabel Chase Rundlett's *Sylvan Lights and Shadows*, in addition to the Chapman and Largay titles mentioned above. Largay writes:

> Alentour House continues to contribute something new to current poetry in its growing collection of first editions, artistically printed and selling for as little as the price of three lemons. Books like these are usually collectors' items and sold to the few who love good printing, fine materials, and artistry; but belief that song is a close second to what you find in the marketplace has led living poets to leave their eaves and offer these songs in their own span of life.

In 1941, Alentour House released a full-length collection of Largay's poetry, *The Unlistening Street*. Some of his poems had originally appeared in *Bard, Kansas City Journal Post, Lowell Journal, Santa Fe Examiner, The Writer*, and others.

"They Were Intellectuals"

Largay, born in 1911, was "a brilliant student with dark wavy hair," according to retired teacher Mildred Scanlon, who, as an underclassman at Lowell High School, had watched the progress of Largay and his circle. She wrote poetry, too, and mixed with the crowd that gravitated to the school literary magazine, *The Review*. "They were intellectuals, a little different," she said, recalling their effort to organize a writers' workshop. The late Stella Mazur, a classmate of Largay's, remembered him as "popular, smart, good-looking." Class president Largay graduated in 1931 and attended Bard College, where he later solicited poems from students for his new magazine. Mazur last saw him at a high school reunion.

Largay's right-hand man was Philip J. Garrigan, Jr., born in 1914, who served as the first business manager and contributed poems. Tall and thin with close-cropped hair, Garrigan was a classmate and captain in the high school Officers' unit (a kind of pre-R.O.T.C. program). President of the Literary Club, he had poems in *The Review*. He played "Homer, the Wandering Bard" in a 1930 production of *The Iliad*, which also featured Largay as Laertes. "Philip's ego was in full bloom in high school," said Scanlon. He signed her autograph book with this message: "Save this autograph. Someday it may be worth $100,000."

Occasionally, *Alentour* would devote a handful of pages to a featured poet. In Spring 1937, Garrigan was represented by seven poems. Introducing him to readers, Largay wrote:

> It seemed to him, now he came to think of it, very little to have done with twenty-two years: two hundred poems, counting all, half a very dull novel, all a hopeful novelette, some newspaper articles, and the thousands of plans more foolish than all these. It may be, he reasoned, that no one else has done more. But I should have.

One of Garrigan's better pieces is "Northern Mill City," a grim take on the urban scene at his feet: "The full bank and the empty plate/ Confuse them, the cloth not of their weaving,/And why a city built great/Falls in a century, crumbles, only leaving/Weeds in the millyard, a locked gate." The poem concludes with the image of a worker, one of the "simple people," shivering on a bench in the weak winter sun, trying to pull himself together, as the poet forecasts that the next day will be no better. Garrigan also published translations of poems in French by Maurice Vaucaire and Stuart Merrill.

Two other poets from the region earned multipage spreads in the magazine, George S. LaBelle, a Bard College sophomore, and Rose S. Goldman of Lowell, who had attended Boston College. In 1935, Largay prefaced LaBelle's poems with this note: "... he finds time for the craftsmanship of the light shadings and small differences of nuance in poetry, landscape gardening, art, music, and journalism. His background is an early boyhood in New Hampshire, followed by removal to the industrial Merrimack Valley, where he received his education in the cosmopolitan atmosphere of its public schools."

Largay even gives us a description of his friend: "average height, dark hair, hazel eyes, a glowing enthusiasm that sometimes breaks through his reserve, and a love of beauty." LaBelle's contribution includes seven poems grouped as "Poems from the Japanese." Among these imagist poems is "Unbelief":

> the cherry trees
> are blooming again
> on the mountain side.
> if my heart were my eyes,
> I would not believe
> that winter had gone.

Here is Largay's introduction to Goldman's "City Poems" in 1936: "Poetry of the people, city streets, and 'realism' are not often found in good taste and by anybody with anything but bloodshed to offer as a remedy. Too many champions of the oppressed would use them to climb to political prominence. It is with surprise that we see the streets of a large metropolitan city through the hurt eyes of a woman with no propaganda to slant her verses."

In long rhyming lines, she renders an overwhelming cityscape: "The tents of the city have folded, but the demon of speed rides high./Speed is their blood and their heartbeat, pulsating, sullen and cold;/Its rule and lure and its power are tainted like larcenous gold./... I have left behind trees touched by autumn in colors of copper and red,/I have come to the mass maddened city, where the dream and the dreamer have fled."

Featured poets from beyond the region included Jean Paul Talbot of Saskatchewan, Canada, and Arthur Dubois, associate professor of English at Duquesne University and editor of *The Journal of English Literary History*. In 1936, Talbot expressed sympathy for people who do not have "noisy children, a big shabby kitchen with a wood-burning stove, the urge to write, a garden, a white kitten with one blue eye and one brown, a typewriter named Maria whose ribbons must be put in upside down, and two great-great grandfathers who fought under the Iron Duke himself." The same year, *Alentour*'s readers found Dubois' "Grasshopper Lyrics," a selection of "light lyrics, many of them written to be sung to popular music."

"If You Can Be Shocked by Baudelaire, Shame on You."
Alentour's editors made room for book reviews and a Books Received section, features lacking in many of today's literary magazines. The reviewers graded books A to D, sometimes handing out bad marks. There were a few exceptions to the system, such as a 1936 review of Robert Frost's *A Further Range*, which stood on the reviewer's laudatory comments, and in the same year a page-long review of *Flowers of Evil, From the French of Charles Baudelaire*, translated by George Dillon and Edna St. Vincent Millay. The unsigned Baudelaire review begins: "It is not necessary to voice approval or disapproval of the Poe of the Continent; but pass on the merits of the translations done by two gifted American poets. If you can be shocked by Baudelaire, shame on you."

Assessing Frost's latest work, Largay recounts an evening when he challenged a lecturer from Oxford University who made dismissive comments about the New England poet. He writes:

> It is no longer necessary to champion this poet. He has grown on the American people and firmly established his place as one sane and stabilizing influence in the poetic revolution of mumbo jumbo. That he had to go to conservative England to establish himself before we would read him, we had best forget. After all, we still mistreat poets and weep in the cinema.

Among books reviewed were *Stones For My Pocket* by Marion Lee (Dallas: Kaleidograph Press), *Hills of Hope* by Velma Lee Toney (Beebe, Ark.: Underhill Press), and *Without Flame* by George mac Kaye (Fitchburg, Mass.: Aries Press). Reviewer Rena V. Outcalt of

Kansas City, Missouri, is effusive about the poems in *Without Flame*: "George mac Kaye's love sonnets have much of the Chopin appeal and come as the songs of a singer who raises his voice and passes on without announcing himself.... Like Lindsay, mac Kaye is one of the last troubadours."

Alentour also took notice of new anthologies like *The Anthology of Boston College Verse* edited by William C. Kvaraceus (Boston: Manthorne & Burack, Inc.) [Update: Kvaraceus earned a BA at Boston College in 1934 and a PhD at Harvard University. A leader in research on juvenile delinquency, he chaired the Education Department at Boston University. He wrote eleven books and lived to be 101 years old, passing away in 2013.] Also noted was *Chorus for America*, edited by Carlos Bulosan (Los Angeles: Wagon and Star Publishers/Harvey Parker & Craftsmen), an anthology of six poets of the Philippines. About *Chorus for America*, *Alentour* wrote: "This is an interesting and worthy attempt to bring the work ... to the attention of the American that has increased its affection and respect for the people of the islands who have proven that they can fight as well as provide a romantic background. The poetry is, for the most part, poetry of revolt showing a vigorous and independent spirit, maintaining each man's right to absolute freedom."

Alentour's editors were never shy about advocating for poetry even though they had no illusions about the poet's lot. With the coming of David Brook as editor in 1940, the editorial voice of the magazine sharpened. The Winter 1940 issue has two page-long editorials that spell out the *Alentour* agenda. In "Poetry and Pay: The Rewards of Poetry," Brook lays out the flat truth:

> The old picture we have of the poet starving in the attic and writing deathless poetry is as true today as it was in the days of the early bards. However, since the advent of the linotype machine and the flood of printed papers and magazines, we have the rhyme makers and homely philosophers who write for so much a yard and sometimes manage to acquire sleek cars that purr past the humble folk they inspire. Between these writers and the pure poet are many variations. In general, though, nobody who wrote great poetry ever made much money.

PORTRAITS ALONG THE WAY

New England Muse

On the facing right-hand page is an unsigned essay titled "New England Thought," which is more romantic and loftier than Brook's plain potatoes sense. This short composition is a key to understanding how Largay and his circle saw themselves. While the Transcendentalists are long gone from Concord, Mass., the town's river still flows into the Merrimack. The new poets in Lowell imagined tapping the Concord's source by way of the enduring muse. Through poetry, maybe, the worn-out factory city could project a hopeful voice. The anonymous writer imagines the journey of a twig dropped into the river by Emerson.

> Down the serene Concord floated the twig, down the quiet river. It was long in getting to the city and by that time there were piles of dust where many of the mills had been. The people were nervously clasping their idle hands.
>
> It would be good to think that as the twig finally reached the other river with the city of empty mills, the piles of dust, that perhaps a boy playing barefooted by the edge of the river picked up the twig, long from Emerson's hand, and planted it that later it would grow into a tree, bringing life to the ruins. And then because workers were idle and had time to listen, perhaps the birds would come to the tree to sing. Perhaps, again, the muse of poetry, weary from travel would rest a while beneath the tree. It would be good to think this.

When *Alentour* featured Lowell poet Rose S. Goldman's "City Poems," Largay wrote, "She is a spirited member of the modern group not far from Concord [emphasis added]." Like young Kerouac in those years, the *Alentour* poets subscribed to Emerson's vision of the poet in America, as presented in his essay "The Poet":

> Every man should be so much an artist, that he could report in conversation what had befallen him. Yet, in our experience, the rays or appulses have sufficient force to arrive at the senses, but not enough to reach the quick and compel the reproduction of themselves in speech. The poet is the person in whom these

> powers are in balance, the man without impediment, who sees and handles that which others dream of, traverses the whole scale of experience, and is representative of man, in virtue of being the largest power to receive and to impart. ... The poet is the sayer, the namer, and represents beauty. . . .

For a young writer in Lowell, a close reading of the essay might cause a shiver of recognition at the mention of the very city ("In the political processions, Lowell goes in a loom, and Lynn in a shoe, and Salem in a ship."). The passage becomes a kind of mental weld between the Lowell reader's mind and Emerson's old brain. Here he is, or there he was, considering the meaning of Lowell, even briefly, in the towering essay about the poet in society.

Although Kerouac pointed out that his roots were in Brittany, not Concord, he credited Emerson and Thoreau as important early influences. Kerouac's *Atop an Underwood* includes the short composition "The Wound of Living," written in 1943, in which Kerouac elaborates on the subject: "But there is something about the landscape, the weather, the face of New England, where I was born, that has brought out the Transcendentalist in me through the earlier years of my life. For this reason, I call myself of the New England tradition, because my style is New England, my muse aims at simplicity and frankness, and I love pine forests and pure thought."

Poetry in a Time of War

In the Fall 1940 issue, Brook meditates on the darkening prospects of the time:

> It is true that poetry is given little place in time of great national stress; but the lifetime of a personality is not made up of great historical events. Men count their days in terms of simple joys, human dignity, a remembered song. That the fragile artist who is the poet shall have a voice in these troubled times this magazine returns to the poetry field when the little magazines are scattering like leaves in a high wind.

The magazine absorbed the news of the era, and poems written in response to the world war found their way into its pages. Among these poems were Ian MacDonald's "A Soldier Contemplates the Fallen Foe," Celia Keegan's "The Battle," Largay's "A Year of War" and "Air Raid," and Marion Lee's "Reserve Forces." Following are examples:

Paratroops

Death blooms in silhouette against the dark
Like pale moonflowers caressing alien sod;
Some pierced by shafts of flame lie charred and stark,
Some blown to safety by the breath of God.
                    Zita Harris

To a Soldier Husband

You ask me if I miss you. Let me say
Last night I read the paper on the porch
As usual—one green chair I've put away—
The news was maddening—no gains ... The torch
Of coral pink we love was in the west
All spilling along the mountains, and the Ginger
Who pressed so soft against me wished to rest
Right there until you snapped your finger
And poured milk into her saucer. I walked
Awhile to get myself out of my mood—
No use—I met Lucille and Jack—we talked
About you—where you were—It was no good
To pretend longer. But I'm fine, now, Joe.
You asked me if I missed you, so you know.
                    Caroline Eyring Miner

The all-consuming war effort eventually crowded out what time, energy, and resources had kept *Alentour* going in the early 1940s—but not before Brook guided the last four issues into readers' hands. By this time, Largay was designing, as well as hand setting and printing the matured magazine. In the mid-1930s, Raymond Frechette of Beaver

Press in Lowell would set the type before turning it over to Largay's print shop. In 1938, Largay married Rose Cashman, who became the business manager. Associate editor Gillis moved on from New York City. By 1942, it was a Lowell operation start to finish.

In the Spring 1942 issue, a defiant Brook dismissed the notion that a poetry magazine was superfluous in wartime, that valuable paper and metal type should be reserved for the war effort. He wrote, "A poetry magazine is handed from one reader to another; it is something a scholar or a soldier can carry in his pocket. No country is lost because of that." Here is more of his statement:

> The sincere creative expression of fine minds is one of the real liberties we are fighting for. If we become identical to the barbarian, what kind of a victory shall we have? All the poetry magazines of the country could be published for a year on the paper content of one issue of any one of the popular love, sex, movie, or confession magazines.

The Fall 1942 *Alentour* leads with another defense of the magazine by Brook. The Lowell poets must have been feeling terrific pressure to cease operations. The by-product of Brook's editorial, of course, is more beating of the poet's drum, with pounding lines like this: "The poet is the nation's conscience, the country's better self." We can imagine why the *Alentour* faithful had to keep bucking each other up. It is no easy task to produce a quarterly poetry magazine even in relatively safe and prosperous times. Here's Brook on his soapbox:

> In times of peace, when his country is growing soft and complacent, [the poet] sings of arms and men and in times of war he sings of the peace that will come and of what nature it must be. The poet is the nation's conscience, the country's better self. The sharper the truth of what he says, the louder the milling throng would drown him out, and when at last he has been proven right he is again the razor at the throat of thoughtlessness.

It is as the eyes of a beauty-hungry world that the poet is best remembered, however. It is when he comes fresh on the old familiar things and gives them life and meaning again. This is the fruit of the tree.

For the "Little Poets"

Alentour's editors saw themselves as champions of the overlooked and unconnected, in their words, "the little poets." Largay and friends were nothing if not open and generous when they accepted poems. The result was a magazine with a lot of decorative, formal poetry leaning on end rhyme. More often than not, the poems exude a high-art tone that sounds like it comes from the preferred seats in the theater. These are often poems of the young writer who is supersaturated with emotion and big ideas. This is where almost everyone starts. And in the 1930s, these writers were following the prevailing notion of what makes a successful poem.

Importantly, some of the better poems emerged during World War II, when many contributors confronted immediate dangers and found his or her singular voice. Drawn outside the internal struggles that had usually shaped their poems, the writers produced fresher and more urgent works.

One disappointment, especially among the Lowell contributors, is the absence of local reference. There is not much sense that their poetry is rooted in time or place. The war poems stand out. The poems from Lowell contributors aim for the ethereal orbits of the day's textbook poetry. As editors, publishers, printers, organizers, publicists, and distributors, *Alentour*'s leaders are sincere. They act as artists in their community, but for the most part the writing is not distinctive. When the writers engage subject matter in their front yards, the work stands apart, as in Largay's "Inspiration," from his collection *The Unlistening Street*:

> Child, mother and driver of hay rakes,
> Ten-year-old driver of hay rakes,
> Daughter of Canadian raconteurs,
> *Fille de Azarie, le raconteur,*

Singer of songs of voyageurs,
Where are the echoes of your songs,
My sturdy little mother?
The songs you sang to me,
Lilting songs of early springs and racing streams
Roaring at my father, Pierre, who rode the logs,
And small boys who tease their little sisters.
Is it strange I do not see the northern rivers,
The lakes and forests of your songs,
But see only the wistful girl of the hay rake,
And the naïve little mother who comes to the hospital
With word of carnations doing well on the windowsill
And the first few blades of green grass
On the South Common.

"A Beautiful Experiment"

Editor Brook wraps up the story in the Winter 1942-1943 issue. Nine years is a long run for a literary magazine. Author and editor George Plimpton, whose *The Paris Review* is nearing its fiftieth anniversary, says, "Most literary magazines have the life of a butterfly." Poet William Carlos Williams decided that the little literary magazine is one project, a movable production with changing stewards. Commenting on the crucial role played by small publishers such as James Laughlin of New Directions, poet William Corbett writes: "Simple principles. Publish books you believe in and keep them in print so that when the world catches up—Pound figured there was a twenty-year lag—the books will be there."

Michael Largay (editor/typesetter/printer) and Rose Largay (business manager), Belle Irene Gillis (editor/designer), Philip Garrigan (business manager), Rena V. Outcalt (associate editor), Raymond Frechette (printer), and David Brook (editor) took the lead over the years, but the pages needed poets. The little magazine's longevity is a tribute to the stubbornness of the artist, who keeps making art because, as Brook believed, he or she is compelled to do it.

Around the same time that *Alentour* was near the end of its run, newspaperman Charles Sampas was championing poetry for Lowell.

PORTRAITS ALONG THE WAY

At a University of Massachusetts, Lowell, symposium in 1997, Anthony Sampas quoted from one of his uncle's columns in 1943: "Readers keep sending me poems—really lovely poems, and it makes one aware of the need of a poet's corner in this column or somewhere in the *Sun*—I mean a large corner where several of the poems can be published—there are so many really good original ones." Maybe he knew what was in store for *Alentour* and was lobbying for someone to take up the slack

In the final issue, Brook summed up the *Alentour* experience:

> It is with genuine regret that we announce that the pressure of war work makes it necessary for us to suspend publication for the duration. To our many friends we say goodbye for a while and many thanks. Manuscripts and subscriptions will be returned as soon as possible.
>
> *Alentour* leaves at the peak of its career. It was truly a beautiful experiment, one as full of mistakes as the impulsive heart of man. The miracle was that it lived the years that it did, a little magazine run by little people who boldly published the early work of the little poets. It was true faith to have believed that little poets would batten on time's dust and become giants. The dream was dreamed and it lives unafraid, as dreams always do.

Coda

Philip Garrigan served in the Army in World War II and returned to Lowell, where he was known as a church-going man who was active in the charitable Community Chest Association. He and wife, Eugenia, had no children. Physician Richard Sachs, who cared for Garrigan in his later life, said, "He had published some short stories and fancied himself a writer, though I believe he paid the bills working for the state welfare system. I remember seeing among his books one or two American short story anthologies with some of his work." He died in 1985.

Sometime after he shut down the *Alentour* operation, Largay headed for California to make a name in the movies. He remarried and had a son, according to his niece Marjorie Sonia of Peabody, Mass.

Uncle Michael wrote screenplays in Hollywood. He took a job as a professional waiter at the Beverly Hills Hotel to earn a living. We heard stories about the famous people he met, including Frank Sinatra. Michael had a great personality and a strong mind. He and my father, Frederick, a graphic artist and a partner in Alentour House, were ahead of their time. They were hip guys.

2004

Jack Kerouac (1)

For one special game.

On the first Sunday in November the Merrimack Valley is covered in fresh snow, the two inches of white already melting where the sun does its work. I was at the top of Christian Hill this morning watching a flag football game. It's called flag because players wear plastic belts with tear-away strips that must be pulled off to make a "tackle" and stop the play. The guys in their twenties and thirties sported hooded sweatshirts, proper team jerseys, cut-off baseball pants, and all types of cleated shoes. A handful of fans followed the play up and down the field as wind ripped over the rooftops of the Centralville neighborhood and frosted field. Thin snow-like clouds sketched across the pale blue sky.

The hilltop offers a view to the southwest over the river, the university, and farther neighborhoods. There's a large white dome set among wooded hills, one of the structures of the Haystack Observatory ten miles away where scientists monitor sounds from deep reaches of the universe. Huge antennae search heavenward for the one-in-a-billion transmission from a far-off being. The hill, panoramic scene, and football players seemed very Kerouac this morning. He wrote richly of this settlement at the bend in the river.

The clean wind-chilled air cleared my brain as I cheered for an old friend who had invited me to the "free entertainment." Every one of these young men had sampled glory, even if for one special game as with Kerouac in the Thanksgiving Day game of 1938 when 14,000 people in his home stadium cheered when he scored the only touchdown in defeating downriver rival Lawrence High School.

This friend of mine had been a top high school athlete in Dracut, the town that gives the name to the Dracut Tigers football team of the 1930s, when Kerouac lived as a teenager in the Pawtucketville neighborhood that bumps up against the town. My friend went to college in Toronto where he earned All-Canada honors and a tryout with the Miami Dolphins of the National Football League. In practice he hauled in throws from star quarterback Bob Griese, but he didn't make the professional team. Now he was back home diving into the snow to catch the first pass of the day.

These jocks answer the call each season. Almost nothing makes them as happy as to be on the frozen field when everything goes right. Out in the open, repeating a ritual, sharpened by competition, the forever-boys work together and execute—at the same time each of them thinking he is foolish to be running around in the cold at thirty-five years old, risking a broken ankle that would keep him out of work.

How many know they are on Kerouac territory this morning? What would he have written if he had been on the sideline today? He would have heard the voices of girlfriends and wives, seen the shivering buddies swigging beer before noon, and noted the large white numbers on crimson and green shirts. He would have been looking into his own past.

I'm surprised by his enduring and even growing presence among us. Last night, on the Music Television channel (MTV), the weekly countdown came to the number one video in the land: Billy Joel's "We Didn't Start the Fire" from his *Storm Front* album. There is a telegraphed history lesson in the rhymes, including "Pasternak, Kerouac," cultural codewords, the Kerouac code signifying a message of joy and pain for the most part still misunderstood in the larger society. He's part of the social transmission, his signals beaming from Lowell to the wide world, where they can be picked up without satellite dishes, his words as receivable as a well-thrown football.

1989

Gary Snyder

"I can't forget anything I've ever read."

Rain-whipped night outside nondescript auditorium, school hall plain to hold wild ideas, maybe. Slowly building crowd reaches about one hundred—students, Cantabrigians, academic scruffs, a few small kids, casual country-style dressers shaking off the wet.

Someone tells me Snyder asked to make an appearance, saying, "He used to be a hanger-on here years ago," but I can't figure the logic of that since he's from the west This fall, he's teaching just south at Trinity College in Hartford, Connecticut. The Grolier poetry chapel has a book table in back. Microphone test next, and then a video disc player is brought in.

Huge man in plaid shirt overfills a front seat. Two croissant-eating youngsters with blonde mom reading a college paper take seats to my right. Young woman behind me describes a film about the Berlin Wall. Many Snyderish men with beards, ponytails, work clothes. Another woman reads Ovid. Someone with a stack of books for Snyder to sign. Veteran professors in the young-trending audience. Raincoats bejeweled with drops. A host of earth-colored sweaters. Cups of yogurt and steamy coffee. Umbrellas and ponchos shaken. Two black wooden chairs at a fold-up table on stage. Tech director in his booth drinks from a quart of orange juice.

This event celebrates the publication of an essay collection, *The Practice of the Wild*, and reissue of *Riprap and Cold Mountain Poems* by North Point Press of San Francisco, those flinty poems that made such a difference long ago.

Snyder starts reading "Mid-August at Sourdough Mountain Lookout," ends "Looking down for miles/Through high still air." Then he tells on himself: "There's something not true in this poem: 'I cannot remember things I once read'—I could remember Chinese poems. Maybe the truth is I can't forget anything I've ever read."

Then comes "Piute Creek" with "All the junk that goes with being human"— "I was working for the National Park Service at the time."

He next picks up the essays, ten years of work. "How do we resolve the dichotomy of civilization and the wild?"— "What we call wild is very orderly." He reads calmly with witty intonations. The audience laughs and chuckles, they are so happy to be in the room with him. "We have made a lot of this place, but the fishing is no good anymore," a car dealer in California told him.

On stage Snyder is a small-framed man with graying brown hair and a short gray beard wearing a blue cotton shirt open at the neck under a charcoal-gray sport coat. He says, "Very bold people from the '60s are still in play. Everybody's heart was in the right place."

To the guaranteed-to-be-asked question about Jack Kerouac, he replies: "Part of his problem was alcohol . . . He looked to the past but was not necessarily reactionary. He was charming in his way."

And on being the model for Japhy Ryder, he reminds us: *The Dharma Bums* is a novel. "I like *The Subterraneans* better than *The Dharma Bums*, and *Doctor Sax* is my favorite Kerouac novel." Snyder recalls climbing the Matterhorn again—"Range after range of mountains/Year after year/I am still in love."

"Why do you write?" he's asked.

"It helps me organize my own thoughts. It's a way to participate in your community. I never thought of writing as a solitary activity. I always considered it a dialogue."

To another questioner, he responds, "You have to be a working-class person to read a lot."

He talks about community work, political work, cultural work. He says his plan for the next seven years is to finish many writing projects.

"Everyone is busy. Why? They're trying to keep up with things." And near the close says lightheartedly, "My daily life is like everyone else's."

On November 10, 1990, Gary Snyder read his poems and talked about writing and other subjects at Boylston Hall, Harvard University, in

Cambridge, Mass. It was the second time I had heard Snyder read, the first being at Phillips Academy in Andover some years before. He has been a key figure for me since the 1970s when I became serious about writing. His books Riprap and Cold Mountain Poems *and* Turtle Island *influenced my work. His essays are equally important to me. Of special interest is Snyder's stance in relation to communities with which he connects, whether neighbors, sympathetic readers, or environmental activists. His advice about putting a stake down and getting involved in the community of your choice reinforced my instinctive feeling that local engagement is essential.*

1990

Maya Angelou

"All knowledge is spendable currency."

Wearing a long black coat, Dr. Maya Angelou waved both hands to the audience of one thousand community college students who were primed for something extraordinary. She then handed her coat to a helper the way a boxer gives his glossy robe to the cornerman.

For the next ninety minutes, she sang, preached, acted, and danced her way through a fast-paced program as October sunlight filtered through soaring stained-glass windows in a former Protestant church across the street from Lowell City Hall.

"I have not come for nothing!" she declared, ordering the students to take out pen and paper to write the names of authors she was about to reveal. Georgia Douglas Johnson, Paul Laurence Dunbar, and Mari Evans were a few of the African American writers whose poems she recited.

Remembering her grandmother's wisdom, Maya Angelou said, "Poetry puts starch in your backbone."

She described her love of reading and vast appetite for great works, from Shakespeare to Countee Cullen. "All knowledge is spendable currency—read, read, read!" Hers is a message of liberation from the small, mean life that threatens to debase us.

"Everyone in this hall has been paid for by ancestors of every color. Your assignment is to prepare yourselves to pay for those who will come after."

The author shared bold, musical poems of her own about love and the nature of women, as well as a hilarious piece about a "smoking carnivore" who cannot abide the natural food crowd. She advises writers in the audience to "tell the truth, but not necessarily all the facts."

A professor at Wake Forest University, Dr. Angelou is the author of the memoir *I Know Why the Caged Bird Sings* and other works of prose and poetry. Selected as the "common book" of the year at Middlesex Community College, her memoir was read by students across disciplines. Television viewers will remember Maya Angelou in her role as the mother of Kunte Kinte in the acclaimed television miniseries *Roots*.

Editor and writer Donald Hall insists that poetry is not dead, even though he says some critics are trying to murder it. In a recent essay, Hall states: "More people read poetry now in the United States than ever did before."

And their spines are better for it.

1989

PAUL MARION

Charles Simic

"Writing poetry is like breathing."

1.
Under the House and Garden aisle sign, in front of the carved "Barnes & Noble, Booksellers Since 1873," Charles Simic—poet, professor, Guggenheim-, Pulitzer-, MacArthur-winner—gives us his words, all plain and outrageous, some kind of donuts hiding exotic fillings.

Like poetry itself, the writer stands amid business as usual—cash-computer-printer zinging, kids howling one aisle over, front door feeding and discharging customers. His thin, cool voice insists that it should be heard. In the back row, a long way from Oberlin College, Jesse holds her copy of his *Selected Poems*, the favorite pages folded. Polite, but no fool, Charles wraps up early, and takes a seat as the fan-line forms.

At Fenway Park tonight, banjo hitters with million-dollar contracts perform for 35,000 followers sweating with pennant fever. Here in Nashua, N.H., in the Red Sox's sphere of influence, thirty souls attend the church of poetry. And Jesse waits to have her say.

On Good Friday, 1978, I had my chance to tell him what his work meant to me. Considering graduate school, I asked Charles about the creative writing program he taught in at the University of New Hampshire (UNH). "A program like ours won't make you a poet."

When we got to the gritty, he said, "I may have had a choice when I was eighteen. Now, writing poetry is like breathing. I happen to be teaching here, but I would be writing poems even if I were sweeping streets to make a living." Made a note of that.

I had found his poems in *The New Republic* in 1976. "Butcher Shop," "My Shoes," "Watch Repair," "Breasts," "History Books," and others read like I don't know what. Right off, I asked the manager of Prince's Bookstore in downtown Lowell to order *Dismantling the Silence* and

Return to a Place Lit by a Glass of Milk. In the magazine essay, Robert B. Shaw writes, "His determined concentration on the most common things makes reality strange and, even when terrifying, strangely inviting."

2004

2.
"A poem is a secret shared by people who have never met one another."
    —Charles Simic

He wasn't Charlie to me. I didn't know him well enough. To friends and colleagues, he was Charlie. I met him a few times, once in his office and years later when I introduced him to a small audience at a bookstore in Lowell. The manager asked me to say a few words. Since finding him in the 1970s, I had attended a couple of his readings in the area. I bought each new book that was released. I have his signature in two books and on the postcard from 1978 with a typed note telling me when I could meet him at UNH.

He drove himself in the early dark to read from a new book. I was impressed by his commitment to share his poems and by the modest vibe of it all. He had no idea who would show up. There was no pre-reading dinner with university faculty and no after-party with drinks at a local pub. When he was finished signing books and talking to stragglers, he put on his coat and walked to his car. Just like that. I felt stupid after, thinking I should have invited him out for coffee at the Greek restaurant, if not for a drink, with a couple of writers.

A year before I met him at UNH, I had sent him a fan letter with a small watercolor portrait I had made. The 3"x 5" notebook page-painting was one in a series of impressionistic portraits, almost cartoons: William Carlos Williams, Emily Dickinson, Langston Hughes, Robert Frost.

In my copy of *Dismantling the Silence* (1971), on the inside back cover, are lines from a poem I'd written about him: "Against a wall of books, his cub look,/like a good A student/who's second string on the fencing team,/didn't fit a writer of poems/as empty and full as scissor holes,/ . . . I'd pictured a dark-browed, angular man,/with the build of a witch,/a burrower, wild-eyed,/ dragging a bag of earthy tales." He didn't look like that at all, though.

It was bold of me to send the small portrait and I later wondered what Charles thought of the gesture. I had never done anything like that. The image, round face with wire-rimmed glasses like John Lennon's, was based on a photo in a collection of poems by emerging writers. It was my first sight of him. His early books from the publisher Braziller in New York City did not have an author photograph. Maybe that's the way he wanted it.

In the mid-1980s, I collaborated with Sharon Shaloo of the then-University of Lowell on presenting a writers' series that included Charles. In 2023, when the news came down about Charles' passing, Sharon posted on Facebook about the series: "Charles Simic was a featured reader one night at the national park visitor center. He packed the auditorium and stunned us all. These losses are mounting up. It's hard to lose all these voices."

Not long after Charles passed away, poet David Rivard, a colleague of his at UNH, wrote about the new Charles Simic Poetry Prize that had been established.

> Talking with Charlie about poetry [was] an adventure and delight.... What Charlie was looking for in poetry was the intensity of one's presence on this earth—it's what he understood the lyric was looking for too. Something like what Thelonious Monk meant when he said that a genius is a person who is 'most like himself.'

Rivard ends his reflection about his friend with this from Charles' book *The World Doesn't End*:

> I was already dozing off in the shade, dreaming that the rustling trees were my many selves explaining themselves all at the same time so that I could not make out a single word. My life was a beautiful mystery on the verge of understanding, always on the verge! Think of it!

2024

Annie Proulx

"Can't we try again?"

I stood next to Annie Proulx for a group photograph at a Franco-American writers gathering in New Hampshire in 1991. At the time a rising author with a novel and a story collection, she would become a cultural celebrity two years later with her second novel, *The Shipping News*, which earned the Pulitzer Prize for Fiction, the U.S. National Book Award, and the *Irish Times* International Fiction Prize.

Her willingness to drive over from Vermont to join other Franco writers with little or no reputation proved she cared about her Canadian roots. She wanted to connect with us.

Proulx writes about her identity, half French Canadian, in her book *Bird Cloud: A Memoir* (2011), describing "rootless people who have no national identity" and quoting Jack Kerouac about the "horrible homelessness of all French Canadians abroad in America."

With her new novel, *Barkskins*, Proulx turns that attitude around with an epic tale that fills in centuries of blanks and provides a rough-as-bark narrative of the industrious French making a place for themselves on the North American continent.

All this at the expense of the seemingly limitless forests and furred animals of the Northeast and later timber spreads overseas.

I was astonished by the sentences in *The Shipping News*, language that is extravagant, muscular, and often shimmering like a freshly caught fish, which also holds true for this book.

Touted as her masterwork, the new story follows René Sel and Charles Duquet from their scrappy start in 1690s New France (*Kanata* to the native peoples) through their respective descendant lines into the 2000s.

Ambitious European settlers, unlike the longtime tribal occupants, First Nations people, believed the vast dense boreal forest of eastern Canada and New England had been waiting for someone to dominate Nature and turn the splendid trees into money.

In this entertaining and instructive book, Proulx winds the clock back on the cause of today's climate change and has enough pages to bring us full circle to the contemporary Sels doing reforestation from Nova Scotia to Sumatra.

Through the decades, the Duquets morph into the Dukes as their rapacious business empire expands. There is enough bad karma in their genealogical cart to warrant the end Proulx scripts for them.

The Sels, who married early into the local Mi'kmaq culture, fare less well materially but rely on the woods and forest wisdom on their journey.

Superb in her rendering of places, Proulx moves the reader from Quebec and Boston to Amsterdam, China, and New Zealand, taking us through wilderness, preindustrial cities, and oceans.

In 1985, scientists reported a hole in Earth's ozone layer due to the tonnage of chemicals, chlorofluorocarbons, sprayed by humans into the air. Somebody lamented, "We broke the sky." The ozone layer shields us from ultraviolet radiation that wreaks havoc with the ecosystem.

That hole appears to be closing, according to atmospheric experts.

Proulx's driven and at times stumbling characters help us see how breaking the forest to spur progress is ruinous.

In the end, the scientist Sapatisia Sel cries out, "Can't we try again?"

Book review, *Barkskins* by Annie Proulx, 2016

Benjamin Myers

"Place usually comes first."

PM:
In our first installation of "On Coffee" in *The Bean Magazine*, singer and writer Henry Rollins, an enormously accomplished guy, told us he nurses a single cup of coffee each day and favors the taste more than the kick. Do you have a favorite beverage, tea, coffee, or something else, and is there a daily ritual?

B. Myers:
Having met Rollins, I can confirm he is not a man who needs a great deal of caffeine, however being English, I'm both a coffee *and* a tea man. I drink a cup of strong black cafetière coffee in the morning, walk the dog, then have another cup when I start writing. In the afternoon I drink strong black tea, then decaf Earl Grey tea before bed. The landscape where I live in Yorkshire is predominantly wild, wet, and windy moorlands, so I have actually invented my own drink, a sort of Yorkshire Espresso that I call the *Yespresso* ©: it's twice-brewed tea with the bag left in a flask for an hour or two, then drunk black and sugarless in short shots. Each bitter dose is a stringent hit. It's ultra-tea.

PM:
Would a Myers' reader ever catch sight of you with a notebook or laptop in the local coffee bar or café? Do you have a preferred situation for writing, outside somewhere or in the house or office?

B. Myers:
I'm too paranoid my laptop will get stolen, but I do write in cafés with pen and paper. My recent nonfiction book, *Under the Rock*, was conceived and partially written out in the wilderness in some pretty raw conditions. There's still a certain romance to the image of a writer idling away the hours in cafés, though in reality it's a hard grind.

PM:
Your latest novel, *The Gallows Pole*, was described as a "roaring furnace" by judges of the Walter Scott Prize for historical fiction—a story of "social upheavals which have a sharp contemporary echo." The book is due from Third Man Books (TMB) in the U.S. this winter, a project of musician and entrepreneur Jack White. It will be the first novel from TMB. Why did you sign up with them?

B. Myers:
"Why wouldn't I?" is probably the short answer. I'd say the spirit of Third Man Books is entirely in keeping with my own outlook on art and culture: they have a strong DIY punk ethic, coupled with a keen eye for aesthetics and do things for the sheer love of it. They're the best record label in the U.S., so what an honour to be the first novelist on their literary imprint. It's unprecedented.

PM:
Your novel can be seen as a brutal tale wrapped in a counterfeiters' crime story embedded in eighteenth-century history, all enclosed in a landscape masterpiece. If we framed this creation, what would be the ideal exhibition space?

B. Myers:
Either in a dank, moss-covered tumbledown cottage full of sheep bones and dread, or hanging from the wall of The Guggenheim Museum as it's so far removed from the time and place of the novel's setting that the clash between rural gothic poverty and modern urbane sophistication would be interesting to observe.

PM:
You responded to the Brexit vote with "An Elegy for England." It seems the Cragg Vale Coiners from *The Gallows Pole* would have turned Leave or Remain? on its head. They want to Remain on local ground and hold off outsiders while favoring Leave when it comes to the government and power-loom purveyors. Do you see a news hook there?

B. Myers:
Brexit has dominated the British news media for two years and the discourse has become nasty. It has been ideologically driven by chinless middle managers, so I would prefer to see *The Gallows Pole* as an escape from this slow suicide. As a writer, part of me is excited that Britain is on the cusp of something truly catastrophic and I'm quite tempted to fill my cellar with good Italian coffee and French wine. Obviously, I voted to Remain in the European Union as it has been responsible for unbroken peace since 1945.

PM:
From the opening words of the novel the language is near palpable, reminding me of sentences by Annie Proulx and Jack Kerouac and the verbal clots of Seamus Heaney. How much of this comes in the initial outpouring and how much is shaped as you seek texture and sound?

B. Myers:
Once the voice and tone of the book were found, it came. A lot of my initial research concerned slang words and dialect that was true to time and place—the north of England, circa 1770—but there's a lot of rewriting involved too.

PM:
You earned the Roger Deakin Award for excellence in writing about nature. Readers say they've been transported by the descriptions of places in *The Gallows Pole*. Do you think of place as a kind of character in this and other stories?

B. Myers:
Oh, definitely. Place usually comes first. For example, I decided that I wanted my next novel to be set in a tiny former smuggling village on the coast, so then I wrote the story around the idea of this cove, the cliffs, the sea, the farmlands around it.

PM:
You write in different forms. The late American author Meridel Le Sueur said, "To make a distinction between prose and poetry is bourgeois whimsy." How does that strike you?

B. Myers:
I think they feed one another. The prose writer who doesn't read poetry is limiting his or her potential.

PM:
Our media colleagues at *The New York Times* like to ask an author what she or he has on the nightstand. Can you tell us three books and three musical recordings that are in play for you?

B. Myers:
Books: *Don't Skip Out on Me* by Willy Vlautin, *Christie Malry's Own Double-Entry* by B. S. Johnson, and *West* by Carys Davies. Albums: *Peasant* by Richard Dawson, *Rock for Light* by Bad Brains, and *The Complete Noel Coward* by Noel Coward.

PM:
The Beatles famously refused to visit the U.S. until the group had a song at number one on the music charts. Will you go easier on us and tour with *The Gallows Pole* as it makes its way up the bestseller list?

B. Myers:
As with The Beatles I'd just like to be asked, "How did you find America?" To which I will reply, "Turn left at Greenland."

Interview for *The Bean Magazine*, 2019

Jack Kerouac (2)

Introduction to *Atop an Underwood: Early Stories and Other Writings* by Jack Kerouac.

When Jack Kerouac burst onto the American scene in 1957 with his Roman-candle book *On the Road*, he had been a writer for more than twenty years. He later defined what it means to be a born writer: "When the question is therefore asked, 'Are writers made or born?' one should first ask, 'Do you mean writers with talent or writers with originality?' Because anybody can write, but not everybody invents new forms of writing." The clarification was rooted in his understanding of the word "genius" as meaning "to beget." Along with creating more than twenty books, Kerouac knew he had invented a new way of writing—fusing local talk, blown jazz, a scribe's eye, relentless self-examination, the grammar of dreams, memory glee, and gloominess about our short lives.

For someone who felt he was born to write, Kerouac spent his youth "busy being born." And so, this is Jack Kerouac's book about becoming a writer—and an artist. Unlike *Some of the Dharma*, *Book of Blues*, and other books of his published since he died in 1969, Kerouac had not prepared the manuscript of *Atop an Underwood: Early Stories and Other Writings*. He did, however, leave an enormous cache of writings in carefully organized files, the source of this book and others to come. His papers are an extraordinary record of an artist's development.

Atop an Underwood: Early Stories and Other Writings takes its title from a book of stories Kerouac imagined publishing in 1941. Readers of Kerouac's novel *Vanity of Duluoz: An Adventurous Education, 1935-1946*, will recognize the title because he brings it into his story about Jack Duluoz growing up in America. After working all day in a gas station in Hartford, Connecticut, Duluoz would head back to his digs: "I was happy in my room at night writing 'Atop an Underwood,' stories in the Saroyan-Hemingway-Wolfe style as best as I could figure it at age nineteen." Kerouac's readers have long wondered about the real stories written in Hartford in the fall of 1941. Do they exist?

Kerouac's proposed Introduction for "Atop an Underwood" describes the book as a sixty-story collection. One handwritten table of contents for "Atop" includes twenty-five story titles, and another list has six. From the same period, Kerouac left two other lists: "Stories for Blame It on the Heart" numbers forty-two titles, some of which overlap the original "Atop" contents, and "Stories" has forty-eight titles, repeating a few of those on the "Atop" list. An inspection of the author's papers showed that only fifteen of the stories exist; the surviving ones of that period would have made a short collection.

In an essay entitled *"Au Revoir à l'Art,"* written in November 1944, Kerouac assessed his writing output since 1939: "Poems, stories, essays, aphorisms, journals, and nine unfinished novels. That is the record—600,000 words, all in the service of art—in five years." Interviewed by Barry Gifford and Lawrence Lee for *Jack's Book: An Oral Biography of Jack Kerouac*, writer William Burroughs recalled meeting Kerouac in mid-1944: "Jack was quite young at the time. He'd done an awful lot of writing. He'd written about a million words, he said." About 80,000 of those words are published here for the first time.

This book includes the Hartford stories and then some, looking backwards to Kerouac's earliest efforts and past the Hartford period to work he was doing through his twenty-first year—just before he encountered the writer-friends with whom he would make history. The writings include stories, excerpts from novels, poems, essays, sketches, plays, and other work from 1936 through 1943. The contents vary more than the other published collections of Kerouac writings: *Lonesome Traveler* and *Good Blonde & Others*.

It is startling to see how early Kerouac began writing about America, adventurous travel, spiritual questing, work, family, friends, and sports, to name a few subjects that would occupy him. From the start, Kerouac's writings usually centered on his experience. He wrote a novel when he was eleven—a lost manuscript referred to by Kerouac in *Visions of Cody* as "Mike Explores the Merrimack."

Biographer Tom Clark comments on the early "Merrimack" novel: "The same basic story of a tantalizing power that removes one from humdrum existence and takes one on a remarkable voyage can be found underlying almost everything Kerouac wrote for the next eighteen years, up to and including the best known of all these fantasies of life, *On the Road*." An impressive work that survived is the football novella he wrote at sixteen, which opens with a wayward college athlete walking along a railroad track in the American heartland.

As self-deprecating as he was about some of his early writing (dismissing, for example, the stories written in the fall of 1941) Kerouac was proud enough to say the work was "a great little beginning effort." From the résumé-like autobiography that kicks off *Lonesome Traveler* to his memory-laden author's note in the anthology *The New American Poetry*, he recorded his first steps as a writer.

In 1943, Kerouac identified his major artistic project: "Long concentration on all the fundamental influences of your life will net a chronological series of events that will be open to use as a novel—for a novel should have a sort of developing continuity, if nothing else. [. . .] Your life and every other life is stuff for great novels, providing the treatment is good." By 1951, he had refined the concept: "'On the Road' is the first, as the French-Canadian novel will be the second in a series of connected novels revolving around a central plan that will eventually be my life work, a structure of types of people and destinies belonging to this generation and referable to one another in one immense circle of acquaintances."

Jack Kerouac became a serious writer in Lowell, Mass. In a notebook kept when he was barely twelve, he lists writing as one of his talents, along with cartooning and billiards, and reading as his hobby. Whether handling inky type in his father's print shop or soaking up stories told by his mother and aunt on long walks, he was hooked on words. On those walks he heard his family's French-Canadian language, a malleable form of talk with creative blends, rapid musical sounds, and lively inventions. In his 1941 story "The Father of My Father," Kerouac describes it as "one of the most languagey languages in the world. It is unwritten; it is the language of the tongue, and not of the pen. It grew from the lives of the French people come to America. It is a terrific, a huge language."

Kerouac's friends describe him as an imaginative and restless kid, though quiet and mild-mannered, too. He was a standout athlete on local fields and a talker on night porches. Kid Kerouac saw adventure everywhere. He was brave enough to scale Lowell's iron bridges. Jack would entertain his friends with stories, mimic radio characters, and improvise roles. He was as proud of his chess victories as he was of his sports heroics. Kerouac was a keen observer and an intent listener.

By his early teenage years, Kerouac was writing and designing at-home sports newspapers. His reading expanded from French versions of the Catholic Catechism and the Bible, *Rebecca of Sunnybrook Farm*, and serial magazines like *The Shadow* to, by the time he was seventeen, Jack London's adventure novels. He moved on to Walt Whitman's poems, the writings of Henry David Thoreau, and stories by Ernest Hemingway, William Saroyan, and another 1930s luminary—Albert Halper of Chicago and New York City.

A prolific author of the Hemingway-Thomas Wolfe generation, Halper produced a dozen books about people of his day—city people, ethnic people, working people. This book reveals for the first time the crucial impact of Halper's potent writing on Kerouac. In particular, Halper's story of a young writer who wants to write "a big raw slangy piece of work" and who feels "a locomotive in [his] chest" resonated deeply with Kerouac.

In a poem written when he was eighteen, Kerouac described how he would "nibble at some sweet Saroyan" for dessert when he fed his head with books. He and his friends were also impressed by the dramatic products of the polymath Orson Welles. Young Kerouac once listed Wolfe, James Joyce, and Welles as the "Greatest Modern Poets." His writing voice gained definition when he absorbed the sounds, rhythms, and visions of Wolfe, Joyce, Herman Melville, and Fyodor Dostoevsky. He praised Wolfe and Joyce for their "deeply religious feeling for beauty" expressed in artful writings that surpassed the makings of a poet.

Together with a poetic prose, the hyper-local detail, urban texture, self-focus, and "cosmic regionalism" (in the words of scholar Harry

Levin) of Joyce excited young Kerouac. A 1942 novel set in Lowell (titled *The Vanity of Duluoz*) had the markings of Joyce's *Stephen Hero*, an early version of *A Portrait of the Artist as a Young Man*. Shakespeare, Homer, and Tolstoy ranked high on Kerouac's lengthy reading list. He made notes to "delve into Chinese and Hindu thought," along with Celtic and Breton folklore. In his early twenties, he veered toward Arthur Rimbaud, William Blake, and Goethe, going so far as to burn some pages of his writing to prove his artistic fire. He broke through to his own style in his late twenties, with a spontaneous prose form that flowed from jazz method, new ideas about word-sketching, and creative interplay with friends like Neal Cassady, Allen Ginsberg, and Burroughs.

Kerouac found creative people and the arts in Lowell, even as the Great Depression brought economic woe to the city—about forty percent of Lowellians had accepted government assistance by the mid-1930s. His father had introduced him to the performance world with stories about entertainers on downtown stages. Jack attended meetings of the Scribblers' Club at Bartlett Junior High School. He and his friends were great movie fans, and Lowell had the Crown Theatre, the Royal, and others. His gang danced to big band music at the Rex and Commodore ballrooms. In 1940, he and others formed a dramatic group, the Variety Players, and produced a radio play. Friends like Bill Chandler, Bill Ryan, and John "Ian" MacDonald wrote, drew cartoons, and listened to Beethoven. In *Lonesome Traveler*, Kerouac writes, "Decided to become a writer at age seventeen under influence of Sebastian Sampas, local young poet who later died on Anzio beach head."

Sebastian's older brother Charles, a journalist with the *Lowell Sun*, stoked the ambitions of Jack, Sebastian, and others. The elder Sampas was also mindful of Lowell's literary heritage. Nineteenth-century Lowell, the model textile-mill city, had a cultural buzz for a long moment. Charles Dickens wrote about Lowell in his *American Notes for General Circulation*; Emerson delivered twenty lectures in the city; and Thoreau chronicled the region in *A Week on the Concord and Merrimack Rivers*. Kerouac's own Franco-Americans had distinguished themselves as journalists, publishers, and music composers.

Kerouac was friendly with Michael Largay and other writers associated with *Alentour: A National Magazine of Poetry*, a modern-poetry journal published in Lowell from 1935 to 1943. In the unsigned 1940 essay "New England Thought" from *Alentour*, a writer describes the Concord River sliding past nineteenth-century homes of poets and philosophers in Concord, carrying "a twig Emerson may have once broken from a branch" toward the Merrimack River in Lowell. But the once-humming mills are closed when the twig at last drifts into sight:

> Perhaps a boy playing barefooted by the edge of the river picked up the twig, long from Emerson's hand, and planted it that later it would grow into a tree, bringing life to the ruins. And then because workers were idle and had time to listen, perhaps the birds would come to the tree to sing.

Kerouac heard the song in the trees. He read Emerson's essay "The Poet" and Thoreau's *Walden*, and later imagined living in a hut like Thoreau, high atop Christian Hill overlooking Lowell. Analyzing himself in 1941, Kerouac explained why he was a poet: "He is a man, so he does the most man-like thing and writes for his fellow men."

Kerouac recoiled from what he viewed as spirit-killing mill work in his hometown, but he did not flee Lowell in 1939; he built on what he had accomplished there and stepped forward to pursue artistic and material success. Though he was awarded a scholarship to play football at Columbia University, Kerouac was required to spend a year preparing for the rigors of the Ivy League. Accordingly, he attended the Horace Mann School, a private school in New York City. While there in November 1939, Kerouac wrote to fellow Lowell High School football hero Ray Riddick, who had graduated ahead of him and starred at Fordham University. Kerouac asked about free rides with Lowell truckers making the run from New York: "As I'm going to Columbia next year, and then for four more years, it would be convenient for me to start knowing my Lowell brethren truck drivers." He planned to keep town and city linked.

At Horace Mann, Kerouac combined his interests in sports and writing, and then moved to Columbia, where the American romance of Thomas Wolfe defeated football dreams. He had sought New York as the nation's cultural nucleus. Athletic recruiters from Boston College and Duke University could not compete with Manhattan's theater, jazz, and publishers. He mixed with the sharp, upper-class students at Horace Mann, joined the drama club, and dug the city's music scene. With his friend Seymour Wyse, he heard jazz greats at the Savoy Ballroom and Apollo Theatre. In prep school and college he composed themes on Dante, Virgil, Milton, and other giants. At Columbia, he shared his writings with Eugene Sheffer, professor of French, and studied Shakespeare with Professor Mark Van Doren.

Atop an Underwood: Early Stories and Other Writings is arranged chronologically to chart Kerouac's artistic development. The time window closes in late 1943. Kerouac's girlfriend and soon-to-be wife, Edith Parker, introduced him to Columbia University student Lucien Carr in 1944, which led to meetings with Ginsberg, Burroughs, and others in an alternative, avant-garde crowd on the fringe of the Columbia campus. Kerouac, Ginsberg, and Burroughs would become the leading writers of the Beat Generation, a label Kerouac applied when asked in 1948 by his friend and fellow writer John Clellon Holmes to describe their contemporaries. He was referring to a generation of young people with no illusions about their identity and place in the world; these men and women expressed "a weariness with all the forms, all the conventions of the world . . . ."

Later, he associated "beat" and "beatific," emphasizing the spiritual values he honored. *Atop an Underwood* is a roots document for the Beat Generation, whose beginning Kerouac sees in the family house parties and gleeful neighborhood life of the 1920s and '30s. Kerouac's first published use of the word "beat" appears to be in a passage near the end of his first novel, *The Town and the City* (1950), in which he describes Liz Martin, the "hip-chick" and part-time New York nightclub singer, "wandering 'beat' around the city in search of some other job or benefactor or 'loot' or 'gold.'"

This book should help answer how and why Kerouac became an artist. His ideas about love, work, and suffering can be traced back to his apprentice work. The early writings help us understand a North American author who was a cultural free trader with Canada and Mexico long before a continental vision was called up on political screens in the United States. His roots in the industrial, multiethnic milieu of early twentieth-century society connect him to millions of Americans. Taking his life as legend, he asserted his standing as a representative person of his time and revealed the passion, struggles, and dignity of one life. As improbable a candidate as he may have been, Kerouac achieved his goal of becoming an American author.

1999

Patti Smith

"The trouble with dreaming is that we eventually wake up."

Back from the dentist in the city where I used to live, I checked my mailbox in Amesbury, Mass., and found Patti Smith's new book that I had ordered from amazon.com, that big river of products seemingly in the sky overhead. *Year of the Monkey* from Knopf publishers is a far flight from her start in poetry with *Seventh Heaven* from Telegraph Books, a small skinny book that I looked at fifty times when I was a part-time clerk at the big yellow bookstore in Chelmsford, Mass., one town away from where I had grown up. I was out of college a couple of years and had met the owner, Eric Linder, as a customer, and we would chat at the counter, which grew into a friendship, he from New Jersey like Patti. He bought the store after seeing a newspaper notice, eager to try something new after advertising work for Macy's.

    Patti, a public-college student in New Jersey because that's what her family could afford, was a fellow student of a writer-friend of mine, Nancye, a longtime arts-and-entertainment reporter for the *Lowell Sun* who now freelances theater reviews from her house on the Maine coast. In college, she and Patti often exchanged hellos in the student publications office where Patti volunteered for the literary magazine and Nancye edited the yearbook. They didn't engage, which Nancye regrets, now that we know what happened. Patti tells interviewers she wasn't outgoing at that age. She wanted to be a writer, but Nancye didn't save any of the early work if she even had copies.

    The monkey in Patti's book makes me think of the Monkey Bridge in Heidelberg, which has a life-sized bronze animal on a wall near the bridge entrance. Custom has it that a person who rubs the monkey's knee will enjoy good luck. If you rub both knees you are destined to return to the city on the Neckar River that felt like Germany to me, having only been in Germany a few days. Heidelberg has a friendly tone, maybe set by the touristy castle high above the historic business district, or maybe it's the beer. The city is a short bus ride from the Rhine River for travelers like my wife, Rosemary, and me, who spent a day there last August, late in the month, when many of the locals were on holiday in Switzerland, Italy, or France. One souvenir shop outside the castle had a large Ben & Jerry's ice cream poster covering half the front door—Vermont goes to Germany. A popular downtown site is the antique student jail once used to lock up drunks who managed over the years to turn the stone holding cells into a geode of cartoons executed with surprising proficiency. Did the warden hand out brushes and paint pots to the wasted scholars?

The monkey story reminds me of the picaresque scenes of Mark Twain in action or that he reports observing in his book *A Tramp Abroad*, something like autofiction if you were to write it today—This is what I did but not really, not exactly, because I can't show you a movie of my every moment, each of the supersonic thoughts in my brain. Germans have a word, *künstlerroman*, for a book about a writer coming into his or her own as an artist, but that's not what Twain was doing. He spent the summer of 1878 with his family in Heidelberg, Zurich, and Florence, and fashioned his experiences as a long walk, the "tramp" being the excursion, not a reference to himself as a hobo. The tour guides in Heidelberg like to tell Americans that Twain may have chosen "Huckleberry" for a character name after learning that the city was built on what is called Huckleberry Hill for its robust blueberry-like bushes.

Twain hiked with a make-believe friend, twinning fact and fiction, dreams and reality, not unlike Patti Smith's method in the new travel book that takes her from San Francisco to Kentucky to other places, in her case usually solo, unusual for a celebrity but she seems to get away with it, all the while slightly destabilized by a friend's dire medical condition and the decline of playwright Sam Shepard, one time her boyfriend and now an always-friend. From the first friend's bedside in S.F., she heads south to Los Angeles and San Diego, wandering, I could say sauntering in the old sense of the word, a saunterer being a

PORTRAITS ALONG THE WAY

searcher on the road to the Holy Land, "*sainte terre.*" Think about Patti's road, St. Francis (a favorite of her Beat favorites), St. James (Diego), City of Angels (L.A.), St. Ann (Ana), the sainted cross (Santa Cruz), down along the loaded Mission Trail on the coast of the Golden State, not mentioning San Juan Capistrano where Rosemary and I toured the restored mission last winter, taking a photo of the Royal Road (El Camino Real), six hundred miles north and south from San Diego to Sonoma. Patti takes photos all the time when she's on the move. Some of the images are reproduced in her book.

On her improvised journey, Patti meets brain-tunnel types who talk about Roberto Bolaño's powerful novel *2666* and mason jar-canning entrepreneurs. An ethereal Japanese cook materializes and makes soup for Patti's scratchy throat. Like Twain, she's in the moment as well as around and above the moment, instinctively composing the moment for the later story. I don't know how many of these scenes along the road are straight from her notes or jump shots of mind that come later—remembered fragments, some of the passages voiced like clipped Sunset Strip crime *noir* while other segments are outtakes from her brain-movie, Alice from Wonderland and peppy Pinocchio in key roles coming back from girlhood.

Patti's is a dream book but not another *Book of Dreams* like Jack Kerouac's (1960), published by City Lights in San Francisco, the place again looping around, his strange volume with eight years of transcribed fantasmic overnight features in Jack's noggin, the cinematic shorts in his own private moviehouse all *auteur*-like and highly plastic in their reality like the reports from Patti's dreamscape that enter her book. Patti's last words in *Year of the Monkey*: "The trouble with dreaming is that we eventually wake up."

When she came to Kerouac's hometown in 1995 to celebrate Jack-in-heaven, Patti read poems and sang with musician-friends, including doing "Dancing Barefoot" in bare feet on a Persian rug covering the makeshift stage at Smith Baker Center, an upcycled Congregational Church across from Lowell City Hall, the same stage that Allen Ginsberg and colleagues (Corso, Ferlinghetti, Michael McClure accompanied by Doors keyboardist Ray Manzarek) had performed on in late

June 1988 for one thousand people the night before the dedication of the *Kerouac Commemorative* sculptural tribute at French and Bridge streets. (Lowell Franco-American operatic bard Gerry Brunelle and I read that night also but we were like Jimi Hendrix at Woodstock the morning after, not much crowd left when we got up after the stars, squashed cups in the aisles, jackets abandoned on seats.)

The Smith Baker Center, named for nineteenth-century Reverend Smith Baker, is caving in but could be preserved and made to look like a smaller version of Ryman Auditorium in Nashville, the Grand Ole Opry country-music temple. Kerouac wrote about the one-time church's red bricks or "bloodred jags" in his love-and-loss youthful romance *Maggie Cassidy*, another town-and-city story by the master of two-sides. McClure would later tell *California Magazine* that the group reading was the most important poetry reading of the year in America. Manzarek read Mr. K's words sandblasted into polished red-brown granite at the *Commemorative* and declared the whole thing "subversive." He and McClure agreed that shimmering paragraphs and poems are not cut into stone for the ages, a treatment allowed only for politicians and generals, maybe a minister here and there. Thousands of words in granite pillars for as long as they can resist the acid rain.

My friend Nancye had a family event the night of the big reading at the Smith Baker Center, so could not attend, but her pal at the paper Dave Perry, music genius, carried Nancye's college yearbook to the show for Patti to sign, which she did, remembering their student times. I think Patti knew that Nancye had been dancing more than once on the *American Bandstand* TV show in Philly with host Dick Clark. The loop closed for a time-machine second.

A week after Patti's new book arrived, I ordered online an expensive, sun-bleached thumbed copy of *Seventh Heaven* from a bookdealer in Chicago because I just had to have the book after all the years. I don't like the poems nearly as much as I enjoy Patti's memoirs, *Just Kids* and *M Train*, with their smooth revelations and sure sentences, but that's not a fair test to apply to someone who was really just a kid at the time. I have a line in my notes that may be a quote from Nancye or Dave Perry or a comment of mine about the *Monkey* book. Could be from a dream:

"Patti lets you feel like you're a sparrow on her shoulder, seeing and hearing as she moves, even as she sleeps."

Book Review, *Year of the Monkey* by Patti Smith, 2019

PAUL MARION

Stephen King

"It's about getting up, getting well, and getting over. Getting happy, OK?"

In the same year that Lowell celebrated Charles Dickens's famous visit to the city in 1842, UMass Lowell hosted the author who is arguably the Dickens of our time when it comes to readership and popular interest—that would be Stephen King, the guy who grew up in the gritty dooryards of northeast Maine with an outsized passion for reading, writing, rock 'n' roll, and the Red Sox. He brought his one-man literary power station to the Tsongas Center at UMass Lowell last night. "This is my first stadium show," he shouted to the capacity crowd of 4,000 people.

There was a lot of yelling, arm waving, and fooling on stage as he bantered, reflected, and preached. He was both pitcher and catcher to his friend and fellow author Andre Dubus III—and the face of the school's English Department, which gained $100,000 for scholarships on this night. Five thousand dollars came from a raffle of the two armchairs that the guys used on stage and which the featured guest signed boldly in front of everyone at the end of the show.

When I was growing up as a writer, I read about the mass audience for poetry in the Soviet Union. Favored poets would fill sports arenas for their readings. In Lowell, I've seen a 1,000 people show up for a group reading by Allen Ginsberg, Lawrence Ferlinghetti, and fellow Beat writers. Maya Angelou read to 1,000 in the Smith Baker Center for Middlesex Community College. The Lowell Memorial Auditorium drew 2,000 for author David Sedaris last year, and a similar sized audience for radio show host and author Garrison Keillor. I've heard that Robert Frost and T. S. Eliot in their prime filled large performance halls. I've never seen anything like the scene last night. King joked at one point that it felt like a Lynyrd Skynyrd concert. He'd mention a book title like *The Shining* or *The Tommyknockers*, as if name-dropping "Free Bird," and cheers and applause would erupt. Both he and Andre plugged into the electric author-love.

The program came in three sections: Stephen and Andre talking shop, King reading a new story about death and regret, and audience questions. Everything worked as if this was the tenth and not the first time the University had tried something like this. About twenty lucky people got a chance to ask a question, including people who had traveled from Chicago and Pennsylvania—and an eleven-year-old girl who charmed everyone when she said out loud, as if pinching herself, "I'm speaking to Stephen King," before posing her question. To the woman who asked about Red Sox management decisions, Stephen said re-signing David Ortiz was an act of good faith that Red Sox Nation needed.

Stephen said you have to get a buzz off what you are doing as a writer in order to stick with the solitary work. He told touching, gossipy, funny, inspiring, and profane stories about his journey from a rookie writer, whose devoted wife fished the typescript of first novel *Carrie* out of the trash, (he got $2,500 for an advance payment on the hardcover publication . . . and then $200,000 for his share of the paperback publishing rights), to the rarified air of cultural royalty. He honored a request from Bruce Springsteen to meet for dinner in Greenwich Village. "Yes, I'd like that," he told his Rock Bottom Remainders-bandmate and music critic Dave Marsh who had carried the request from The Boss.

Somebody is going to enshrine this Lowell visit by Stephen King in a book the way Dickens wrote about his own visit to the city in the travel book *American Notes for General Circulation*. I hope Andre writes an essay about it. We will have Dave Perry's account from the University magazine. Andre closed out the first part of the program by reading a passage from Stephen's book about writing in which the author describes regaining his strength and capacity to create after being run over by a car many years ago.

Here's his closing thought:

> Writing isn't about making money, getting famous, getting dates, getting laid, or making friends. In the end, it's about

enriching the lives of those who will read your work, and enriching your own life, as well. It's about getting up, getting well, and getting over. Getting happy, okay? Getting happy.

2012

Jack Kerouac & Bob Dylan

Carrying a Torch for *Ti Jean.*

We were talking about Bob Dylan being awarded the Nobel Prize for Literature last week and ole Jack Kerouac having received nothing in his life by way of prizes, and so my friend Sean and I went to the famous gravesite in Edson Cemetery and presented to dead Jack a gold trophy-top from my grandfather-in-law's jewelry-store leftovers in my cellar in recognition of Jack's contribution to world literature, an athlete-figure in a cape and holding a torch, maybe some kind of Prometheus, after all, for the man who stole fire from his book-writing heroes to light the literary underbrush in America in the mid-twentieth century, including a blaze that warmed the heart of young Robert Zimmerman from the Iron Range in upper Minnesota—

young Bob, Joan Baez's "unwashed phenomenon" and Anne Waldman's "ear-poet" who drilled into Kerouac's sound hive, the same Bob who was excited to read Kerouac's "breathless, dynamic bop poetry phrases" even after he set aside his once-bible *On the Road* and gave a nod to Jack in his towering "Desolation Row," the through-story Bob who is living his solo legacy in his seventies on the Endless Tour that has run from the White House to Las Vegas and quite a few truck stops in between, an Endless Tour that recapitulates Henry David Thoreau and his brother John rowing on the Concord and Merrimack Rivers, early road-man Walt Whitman investigating the states of America, Woody Guthrie hopping freight cars, and Jack in a 1940s front bench seat, passenger side, memorizing the prairie pavement and coastal turns—

and then the middle-time Bob who sat on the sunny ground (where my friend stood today) while Allen Ginsberg said poems from *Mexico City*

Blues back in November 1975 when they barnstormed the city with the Rolling Thunder Revue, the tour bus loaded with Joan, Roger, Scarlet, Ramblin' Jack, T-Bone, and crew, "pilgrims landing on Kerouac's grave" is how *Rolling Stone* framed it, and then Bob at Edson Cemetery after a night of old hits and fresh tunes like "Hard Rain" and "Romance in Durango," a show with a lot of "Road" soul, white-cheeked Dylan in plumed cowboy hat and yellow flared pants, a night when the crowd-joy rose to the roof of the university's darkened basketball gym as the bonded sound of Baez and Dylan opened the second half with the wise query: "How many roads must a man walk down . . . ?"—the whole setup like a scenic vista, modern cultural treasures on view, some kind of national park of the soul, sparkling just for our small assembly—

an enduring event I was lucky enough to witness with my girlfriend, Marie, just down the street from my apartment in Pawtucketville, that neighborhood of tenements and broad boulevards across the river from center-Lowell and just this side of the Dracut wild woods, the neighborhood where young Jean/John/Jack patrolled the streets and invented his Doctor Sax atop the sandbank in earshot of the bashing foamy Merrimack, another young guy from a small American place who wanted to go big with what filled him, all this in mind in the autumn heat amid dry leaves red and also gold like the shiny trophy that we notched into the earth right by the simple flat granite marker that bears John L. Kerouac's name and dates, a name that was not spoken from high podiums for his benefit, a name that was not pulled from a sealed envelope at any New York or Swedish ceremony, a name that only rose in the chorus of his readers then and rises again today, a name and a presence that was strong when we stopped by to say, "Take this for what you gave us"—

and when we turned to go more readers from two parked cars were heading Jack's way—and the cemetery staffers will deny it but swear off the record that whenever Dylan plays in Lowell he sneaks in to visit Jack and again close the loop, tying Willy Purple of *Tarantula* to "girlsinger" Lee Anne Burns from *Old Angel Midnight*. Maybe some month on an extended intermission, the Laureate will don his masked welding helmet and produce with his flaming torch a grand gate of keys and strings to mark the path to the maple-shaded sweet spot at Seventh and Lincoln.

2016

PAUL MARION

Henry David Thoreau

"... instead of engineering for all America, he was the captain of a huckleberry party."
—Ralph Waldo Emerson on Henry David Thoreau

The same week that Rosemary and I visited Walden Pond for the water and sights, *London Review of Books* marked Henry's two-hundredth birthday by looking at twenty new books about him and a national museum exhibition. Near the welcome center on state reservation land stands a replica of the writer's handmade cabin that he built in the woods. The original location calls the pilgrim from Concord or Tokyo who pauses for quiet minutes and may toss a tribute stone on the pile that is there.

Under a hazy sky we placed canvas chairs on the narrow pebbly beach and set out towels and our books. Single swimmers made elegant lines in the middle of the pond. Kayakers in yellow vests traced the shore.

Every few minutes another huckleberry-party captain led a small group of people up one of the trails into the surrounding tall pines, firs, and the oak trees whose helmeted acorns distribute themselves on hard-packed paths. This month, walkers see painted signs on stakes that add up to a kids' alphabet of all things Thoreau, like "B" for the honey-makers that fill a niche in a system once overseen by the town's "self-appointed inspector of snowstorms." Lightning strikes and pickerel conventions were no doubt also among his supervisory tasks. There was so much to see and do and account for.

2017

Louise Glück

Poets are writing a single poem throughout their lives.

With the news that Louise Glück had been awarded the Nobel Prize for Literature, Jack Mitchell, conductor of the Lowell Live Feed chat-page orchestra on Facebook, asked me to write something for people who may not know this writer. Jack said he always roots for the home team and was pumped about the global announcement. Although born in New York City, today her home address is in Massachusetts. I dashed off a long paragraph with basics, but there's more to say.

Which American poet is a household name, a living poet that is? Robert Frost died in 1963. Famous Seamus Heaney, a Nobelist, taught for many years in Cambridge, Mass., at Harvard University, but he's Irish. The inaugural poets of Presidents Bill Clinton and Barack Obama have drained from the headlines—the exception being the late Maya Angelou. Billy Collins is familiar from radio appearances and sells a lot of books. But now we have a *bona fide* Massachusetts person getting this grand prize, same one that Bob Dylan earned a couple of years ago. The selection committee praised her poems whose "austere beauty makes individual existence universal."

The writer with ties to Massachusetts who most recently won the Nobel Prize was poet Derek Walcott. He taught at Boston University for twenty years. Born on the island of St. Lucia and a longtime resident of the West Indies nation, Walcott won the award in 1992 for what the selection committee described as "a poetic oeuvre of great luminosity, sustained by a historical vision, the outcome of a multicultural commitment." St. Lucia claims him in a mighty way—a very large portrait of the poet greets visitors arriving at George Charles Airport just north of Castries.

People new to Louise Glück may pause over her name, the two-dot umlaut over the second "u" like a speed bump slowing down the uninitiated. How do you say that? It's Glück like "Glick."

I studied with her for a term in the Master of Fine Arts Program in Writing at the University of California, Irvine, in the mid-1980s. Beyond her award-winning writing, she has been an inspiring teacher to a legion of writers. At Irvine I tested myself in a professional setting and came away encouraged to keep going after being in workshops with her and poets Garrett Hongo (*The Mirror Diary: Selected Essays*, 2017; *Coral Road*, 2011) and James McMichael (*Four Good Things*, 1980).

Many recent media reports mention Louise Glück's passion for teaching. It's not a one-way deal for her. She speaks about what she's gained from the years of working with emerging writers. She has judged manuscript contests, served on prize committees, and nurtured writers who have made a serious mark in the culture. Her latest collection of prose, *American Originality: Essays on Poetry* (2017), includes a group of essays introducing books by young poets. Few established authors would use pages in a book of theirs to give this visibility to writers coming up.

I asked three of my former workshop mates to send their reactions to the prize news. Shawn Levy of Oregon is a film critic and author of many books including his latest: *The Castle on Sunset: Life, Death, Love, Art, and Scandal at Hollywood's Chateau Marmont* (2019). He mentions Louise Glück's energy, joy, and generosity. "She was tiny but spry and could alternate between intense focus and absolutely crackling interest, engagement, participation."

The sound of a composition and its architecture are integral to a well-made poem, one that can bring a reader back time and again. One of her teaching methods is to require students to memorize a poem and recite it—to put the poem in the air and into everyone's ears. One of the poems I learned by heart was "Blackberry Eating" by Galway Kinnell ("... the ripest berries/ fall almost unbidden to my tongue,/as words sometimes do, certain peculiar words/like *strengths* and *squinched,* many-lettered, one-syllabled lumps ...") Shawn brought John Berryman to the table with one of *The Dream Songs*. Juan Delgado (see more below) offered Langston Hughes' "Little Lyric of Great Importance": "I wish the rent/

Was heaven sent," and got busted for brevity. He gave us another poem the next week.

Louise lived outside of Irvine and spent full days on campus when her classes were on. "Always open and available, she kept lengthy office hours," Shawn says, which the writers in the program appreciated immensely. "You wouldn't necessarily know it from her poems, but she loved to laugh and chat and even—at a daytime potluck lunch party at someone's house in Los Angeles—dance, about which we all gossiped astonishedly later."

Another one of our mates, Dana White, a journalist and historian in New York, writes about the poet's arrival in Irvine: "She was small and nervous. The students were in awe. By this time, she had published three books of poems. Perhaps she saw in me the same tendency to place every word just so, the short lines, the near obsession with line breaks and oblique meanings and sexually charged imagery. As a teacher she was never cruel or sarcastic in her criticism, but encouraging of everyone, regardless of style."

Dana remembers a time when Louise asked for help covering a class: "She said she needed a volunteer to teach her undergraduate workshop because she had another commitment. Only two of us raised our hands. She asked us for a few poems and then chose me, saying something like she felt more of a kinship with my work. I went home and cried."

Juan Delgado lives in Southern California, where he taught for many years at California State University, San Bernardino. A poet with several books to his name (*Vital Signs*, 2013) and an innovative visual artist, Juan recalls Louise saying that poets are writing a single poem throughout their lives. "She advised us to collect fragments, passages, and lines as a way to find insightful ways to construct poems."

Sometimes the small particulars of memory are most revealing or at least most intriguing. Juan says, "One day in the workshop she went around the room asking us to name two things that we loved. When it was her turn, she said she loved American soap operas and Neil Young. We didn't ask her which soap operas she watched."

Louise attended a literature seminar on James Joyce's *Ulysses* taught by poet James McMichael. She would just show up. "A couple of times she sat next to me," Juan says. "After one long discussion about narrative, she leaned towards me and whispered, 'Jamesy, what a nut.'"

In 1985, a year after my time at Irvine, I heard Louise Glück read her poems at a public library near Boston. The work was from a forthcoming book, *The Triumph of Achilles*. Her voice is infused with the music of her language, which doesn't sound like a song but rather the music of natural conversation, a clear and strong tone. She breathed into her words, and her whole body seemed to be contained in the poetry. She looked very much the same as in California with a tan and thick hair, a bit wild. She hugged and kissed friends in the room at the start, and we spoke for a minute about my time in her workshop. It was good to see her again.

This Nobel Prize puts her in legendary company of poets from our region, especially the women writers, from the first notable poet in America, Anne Bradstreet of North Andover, Mass., to Phillis Wheatley of Boston, first African-American poet in the nation; from Emily Dickinson, the incomparable, to the underappreciated Lucy Larcom, poet, memoirist, and abolitionist; and then later, Amy Lowell, Edna St. Vincent Millay, Elizabeth Bishop, Sylvia Plath, Anne Sexton, Marge Piercy, Adrienne Rich, and Mary Oliver.

It's worth noting that several major poets of the modern era, white men in Massachusetts and New England, whom we think of as top tier are not Nobel laureates: Robert Frost, Wallace Stevens, and Robert Lowell. T. S. Eliot, who was awarded the Nobel in 1948, touches Harvard University and Cape Ann on the north shore of Massachusetts, but he's from St. Louis, Missouri, and moved to England. Frost won the Pulitzer Prize for poetry four times.

Louise Glück writes beautifully about the natural world and goes deep into the interior, where it can be dark, as she makes sense of the human condition. The poems are often informed by classical myths and religious sources. She bridges the time gap, writing about contemporary life in the context of ages-old experience.

My friend John Suiter in Chicago tells a story about pitching a big-time literary agent in New York City for a book he proposed to write about Gary Snyder and other poets. The agent said, "I don't know Snyder." John pointed out that Snyder had won the Pulitzer Prize some years before. The agent asked John, "Do you know who won the Pulitzer for poetry this year?" John didn't have the name at his fingertips. "Louise Glück," the agent replied, adding, "These people are a dime a dozen." Well, the Nobel Prize for Literature is not a dime a dozen.

Louise Glück has been a poet's poet with a substantial readership, and now, I hope, she will break through the pop culture noise to gain an even larger audience. She told *The New York Times* that she'd prefer not to become as popular as Henry Wadsworth Longfellow in the nineteenth century, concerned for what that might mean about the depth of her art.

It's not "easy" poetry even if it looks that way on first encounter, but if people give her writing a try, they can find something of lasting value, a fresh insight or memorable observation, a sliver of light in the night, or as Robert Frost writes, "a momentary stay against confusion."

2020

PAUL MARION

Merrimack Valley Authors

North of Boston.

The Whittier Bridge connecting Amesbury and Newburyport. Kerouac Park in downtown Lowell. The Robert Frost Fountain on Lawrence's Campagnone Common. Across the Merrimack River Valley, people walk, bike, and drive by places and structures named for writers whose books are part of the American story. My focus in this essay is the lower valley of the river, roughly the water's route from the New Hampshire border to Newburyport, Mass., with a bit of splashing into the bioregion that includes the Transcendental Concord of Thoreau-Emerson-Alcott and the seacoast of New Hampshire and Maine.

Many of us know the Mt. Rushmore-scale authors from our region who have gone from literary notables to being historical figures. Former North Andover Poet Laureate Karen Kline promotes the region as the Valley of the Poets. There is a case to be made that our river valley is extraordinary if not unique among national locations with significant author clusters.

Anne Bradstreet (1612-1672) was the first American woman to publish her poems and the first American poet overall, leading off definitive classroom anthologies. Anne Dudley Bradstreet and her husband Simon arrived in Massachusetts in 1630 and settled in Andover Parish sixteen years later, religious pioneers in the colony that was dominated by Puritans of the Christian faith. Highly educated for an English woman of her time, the devoted spouse and mother of eight children wrote about her inner life, home relations, and spirituality. Her poems were taken by her brother-in-law to London and published in 1650 as *The Tenth Muse Lately Sprung Up in America* by *A Gentlewoman from These Parts*. While her gravesite is not known, she is remembered by a cemetery marker in North Andover where she lived.

A chicken farmer in Derry, N.H., before people knew his poems, Robert Frost (1874-1963) wrote articles for farming magazines and taught school like his mother did. A graduate of Lawrence High School (co-valedictorian with his future wife Elinor White), Frost also touched down briefly in Methuen, Amesbury, and Salem Depot, N.H. He had to take his family to England (1912) and publish two books to get serious attention for his poems. When he returned to America three years later, he had a name in the book world. Through the middle of the twentieth century, Frost personified "poet" in the United States, winning four Pulitzer Prizes and reciting the inaugural poem for President John F. Kennedy in 1961. He remains in the top tier of identifiable poets if someone is given a cultural literacy quiz. Speaking to students some years ago, I asked them to name a living American poet. "Robert Frost," someone shouted. But he had died twenty-five years before.

John Greenleaf Whittier (1807-1892) has the highest local visibility, with two historic houses (Haverhill birthplace, Amesbury residence), an attractive blue bridge over the Merrimack, a large mural portrait in downtown Amesbury, and a few buildings named for him. While not in vogue today, Whittier was a rock star in his day. His long nostalgic and popular book-length poem *Snow-Bound: A Winter Idyl*, about a family weathering a blizzard, earned him at least $10,000 in royalties, which would be about $160,000 in 2019. A staunch abolitionist, he served in the Massachusetts legislature and edited the antislavery *Middlesex Standard* newspaper in Lowell. Whittier, California, settled by Quakers like himself, is named for him.

In 1957, Jack Kerouac, who never really left Lowell in his head, became a one-name celebrity like Elvis after he published the novel *On the Road*, a highway tale about two guys searching for the meaning of life in a society with atom bombs. Kerouac labeled the Beat Generation, whose ideas about liberation, love, spirituality, and the pursuit of happiness flowered in the 1960s when a lot of middle-class kids dropped out of their routines and turned the conventional definition of success on its head. He said he wrote his poetry in paragraphs, but he finished many poems in forms he originated to counter the sonnets and villanelles of old. His tics, pops, flashes, and blues are defined in a sprawling meditation on Buddhism, *Some of the Dharma*.

In the next orbit in, lesser known but highly accomplished, is Lucy Larcom (1824-1893). She moved from Beverly to Lowell where her mother ran a boarding house while young Lucy tended machines in a textile factory with the other "mill girls." Larcom wrote poems and later a memoir, *A New England Girlhood*, that is an early classic of the genre. She was active with *Lowell Offering* magazine writers Harriet Curtis and Harriet H. Robinson, members of a literary circle in the 1840s. Larcom ventured west to teach in Illinois before returning home where she taught at Wheaton Seminary and edited publications. She was an ally of Whittier's in the abolition movement. Her poem "Weaving" expresses solidarity with enslaved Black women harvesting cotton for shipment to Lowell's profitable textile manufacturers. The unholy link between "the Lords of the Lash and Lords of the Loom" held fast until the Civil War ruptured the business partnerships.

Henry David Thoreau (1817-1862) turned north at Lowell in his 1839 boat trip with his brother John, chronicled in *A Week on the Concord and Merrimack Rivers*, stroking upriver past Nashua to Concord, N.H. In the lower valley, as a child he lived briefly in Chelmsford before his famed residency in Concord. He is known to have given one lecture in Lowell—to Emerson's twenty in the heyday of the lyceum circuit.

Introduced to Harriet Beecher Stowe (1811-1896), President Abraham Lincoln reportedly said, "So you are the little woman who wrote the book that started this great war." After having published the enormously consequential *Uncle Tom's Cabin; or Life Among the Lowly* in 1852, Stowe moved to Andover the same year with her minister husband, Reverend Calvin Stowe of the Andover Theological Seminary. Only the Bible sold more copies in the nineteenth century than her novel, which greatly advanced the abolitionist cause.

The mid-twentieth century was John P. Marquand's time in the literary sun. With roots in Newburyport's robust seafaring era, Marquand (1893-1960) graduated from Newburyport High School at a time when his extended family had fallen in status. After Harvard College, where he wrote for the *Lampoon*, and a stint doing magazine articles, he won the Pulitzer Prize for *The Late George Apley* in 1938, a novel and sly memoir that makes sophisticated fun of Boston's upper class. In *Imagining Boston: A Literary Landscape* (1990), Shaun O'Connell writes that much of Marquand's fiction "articulates the quintessential Boston myth of loss" and exposes the city's provincialism. His Mr. Moto espionage stories, the basis of films starring Peter Lorre, gained him a wide readership. Marquand published more than twenty novels and four short-story collections. He's buried in Newburyport.

Two of the most admired American prose writers since World War II called this region home.

Pennsylvania-born John Updike (1932-2009) came to our state via Harvard College in 1950. He lived in Ipswich and Georgetown, bordering the river valley, spending most of his adult life in northeast Massachusetts. Awarded the Pulitzer Prize for Fiction twice (*Rabbit is Rich* and *Rabbit at Rest*), he was prolific in his output of fiction, poetry, essays, and art criticism. Critic James Atlas writes that Updike, "translated his life into a masterful chronicle of middle-class anxiety and infidelity . . . ." It's notable that Updike mocked Kerouac's *On the Road* as naïve in a piece called "On the Sidewalk" for *The New Yorker* at the height of the Beat author's newsmaking.

Andre Dubus II of Haverhill was young, sixty-two, when he passed away in 1999 after years of health challenges. His reputation grew among readers as publisher David Godine of Boston issued one collection of stories after another, the work drawing accolades from reviewers, including Updike. Dubus's fortitude paid off as the "writers' writer" crested the literary hill into "readers' writer" elevation and then to an even higher level with wide attention. His stories are being reissued in handsome volumes by Godine with introductions by Ann Beattie, Richard Russo, and Tobias Wolff.

In 1986, I wrote to Dubus to invite him to Lowell for a writers' series. He accepted gladly and read on April Fools' Day in the national park auditorium, paired with Peggy Rambach who read her own gritty local stories. My journal tells me he read his story "Townies" from the book *Finding a Girl in America*, and to this day my wife Rosemary recalls the deep empathy in his reading of "The Fat Girl." We adjourned to an Irish pub where we talked about trains, Raymond Carver, a triple-murder in

Hollywood, and of course the Red Sox, with him reciting his preferred lineup for Opening Day. That night I wrote: "He's on the verge of breaking through to a huge audience, but for now he's not out of reach and still among us."

I have my worn yellow paperback of *Separate Flights* (1975) with blurbs on the back cover saying Dubus is the nation's "most underrated writer" (*Atlantic*) and comparing him to Chekhov (*Los Angeles Times*). How satisfying it is to see this author's work flying gracefully through the wide blue sky of book-land today.

Not many areas compare favorably to our region's depth and breadth of authorship and literary influence when we look around America. Cultural meccas of big cities make their statements: New York, Boston, San Francisco, New Orleans, Chicago. But among "blue highway" places, our Merrimack Valley holds a high rank. John Updike describes this place as "the New World's first real industrial belt," but its collective literary power has yet to be framed for appreciation as effectively as the Industrial Revolution mills noted in every U.S. History textbook. Again, in *Imagining Boston*, Shaun O'Connell writes:

> Good country people lost their old place in the pastoral order, then found their new, less certain place in urban industry. The literary record presents the story, from many compelling angles, of this dream: found, lost, and remembered. The mighty Merrimack, by route of the sluggish Concord River, links Boston, like a blood line, to the landscape, fact and image, north of Boston.

We can use a telescope and microscope to understand what is going on today, which is as vital as in past times. There's a bundle of writers connected to the river valley, some of whom like writers Jane Brox in Maine and Elinor Lipman in New York City are "away" like Robert Frost going from Lawrence to Vermont, and some who've stayed like poet Michael Casey of Lowell and now Andover, who has been as steady in place as valley resident John Greenleaf Whittier.

One Sunday this past February, Brox and Lipman, who grew up

in Dracut and Lowell, respectively, were featured authors in *The New York Times Book Review*, the gold standard for book notices. The *Times* said Brox "writes beautifully" in *Silence: A Social History of One of the Least Understood Elements of Our Lives*, while *Good Riddance*, Lipman's "caper novel" was described as capable of inducing "a very specific kind of modern joy." Both authors were A-list presenters at the Newburyport Literary Festival in late April, drawing enthusiastic fans, many of whom left smiling, signed books in hand. Brox and Lipman return to the area when their latest books appear, tending to familiar community bonds.

So here we have a couple of major-league writers who are easily integrated into what has become the premier literary event in the region, the annual festival in Newburyport, a platform for dozens of writers. This is infrastructure as much as the Whittier Bridge over the Merrimack and Lucy Larcom Park in Lowell were built to benefit public life. The organizers work year-round to bring readers and writers together for a weekend at the mouth of the river.

One of the marquee authors in the program this year was Andre Dubus III, a neighbor in Newbury. He gladly participates in local events, this year doing two sessions in Newburyport, one about his latest novel, *Gone So Long*, in which he "probes the limits of recovery and addiction," and a second being a discussion with author Peter Orner about the legacy of his father, who "instructs the heart" with his stories, writes the *Atlantic*.

The poet Gary Snyder, a friend of Jack Kerouac's, remarked that his two favorite invitations to read his work came from the Library of Congress and his hometown fire station down the hill from his house in the California high country. It's a special reward to have one's work read by people who an author sees in the local supermarket. The Jabberwocky Bookshop in Newburyport, another piece of the literary infrastructure, displays a list of its customers' most popular books to date. Andre Dubus III's *House of Sand and Fog* and *Townie: A Memoir* make the top twenty.

A longtime member of the UMass Lowell English Department, Dubus III played a pivotal role in bringing Oprah Winfrey to the Paul Tsongas arena last fall for a conversation before more than 6,000 people, a benefit event expected to yield $1.5 million for scholarships until

Oprah announced spontaneously that she would match that to reach $3 million. Andre's past networking led to popular appearances by Stephen King and Meryl Streep. On his night, Stephen King said, "This is my first stadium show!"

Jay Atkinson of Methuen scored in a big way with his rugby culture-based thriller *Caveman Politics* (1997) and has barely taken a breath since, publishing six more books of fiction and nonfiction. *Men's Health* magazine calls him "The bard of New England toughness," and he wears the label like a badge. For his award-winning *Massacre on the Merrimack: Hannah Duston's Captivity and Revenge in Colonial America* (2015), Jay retraced Duston's escape route on the river in harsh conditions. He's made a practice of testing himself in extreme conditions for magazine articles in which he finds the story in roads less traveled. He teaches writing at Boston University and as always has a new book in the pipeline.

On another level but as meaningful, the literary grassroots are nutrient rich. One evening last spring, thirty people jammed the Teen Lounge downstairs in the Amesbury library for the monthly reading hosted by the Amesbury Poet Laureate Stephen Wagner. Writer and visual artist Ann McCrea of Newburyport read poems in various forms, from a pantoum and haiku to ekphrastic pieces composed in response to artworks. After the poems, more than a dozen questions kept the session going. Near the front, award-winning poet Rhina Espaillat of Newburyport nodded her encouragement for a poet stepping out in public.

Espaillat, author of several collections of poetry, including *And After All* (2018), has been instrumental in the creation of a robust core audience for poetry in the lower river valley. The Powow River Poets group, which she cofounded in 1992, is a force with its workshops and literary events. Espaillat has won the T. S. Eliot and Howard Nemerov prizes as well as the Richard Wilbur Award.

Up and down the valley, similar scenes play out. The Grey Court Poets of Methuen hang poems on the railing of a city bridge. The Chelmsford and Dracut libraries host authors. North Andover's Poet Laureate Mark Bohrer uses Facebook for publicity. The Whittier Birthplace in Haverhill and Whittier House Museum in Amesbury keep John Greenleaf's foliage fresh. At Merrimack College, the Writers' House feeds student interest in books. Faculty and students there are trying to locate the North Andover grave of poet Anne Bradstreet.

There's a Cambodian-American Literary Arts group in Lowell. Middlesex Community College has a conference showcasing Latino poets and others in translation. Jerry Bisantz's Image Theatre sponsors Femnoire for women playwrights. Merrimack Repertory Theatre turned forty years old this year. Lawrence honors Robert Frost with the monthly "hoot" reading at Cafe Azteca. Friends of the Frost Foundation were saddened to learn of the death of Foundation director Jessica Nesbitt Sanchez last April.

Raymond Mungo didn't hear about Robert Frost going to Lawrence High School when he grew up at 58 Bowdoin Street after World War II. His grandparents from Scotland and Ireland met on the boat to America in the early twentieth century. His mother was one of twenty children, his dad one of fourteen. He may have one cousin left in Lawrence.

"I could read and write by age four-and-a-half, self-taught from my older sister's first-grade books. At age eight, I stunned the South Lawrence Public Library by needing an adult card because I had exhausted the children's library."

Mungo published fifteen books between 1970 and 1996 and wrote for scores of magazines. He made his own way to serious writing, encouraged to read by nuns at St. Patrick's School and to write by elderly, chain-smoking Brother Rudolph, an English teacher at St. John's Prep in Danvers, which Ray got to via a scholarship paid for by the Ladies' Solidarity of St. Pat's.

Mungo never met an author until college where he began to read the region's greats like Frost, but especially Jack Kerouac, "a sainted uncle of sorts" to him. "I was justly proud of them and inspired."

He came into his own as an anti-war activist and counterculture inventor in the late 1960s at Boston University, a cofounder of Liberation News Service, an alternative to the mainstream media. With the publication of his just-in-time memoirs, *Famous Long Ago* and *Total Loss Farm*, the campus radical became a national figure. Anticipating by decades the popularity of memoirs, Mungo's books are classics of the genre and remain in print some fifty years later.

He would publish fiction, a guide to getting published, and even an offbeat baseball book before switching career paths. Recognizing that the freelance writing life would not be enough as he got older, at age fifty he trained for social work and counseling and helped people with AIDS and mental health challenges.

At his California home, he's pleased to hear about the literary vitality of the region. His experience illustrates what it takes to write and to reach readers. The Raymond Mungo Papers in the archives of the University of Massachusetts, Amherst, are available for research and enjoyment. UMass calls him "one of the most evocative writers of the 1960s counterculture." In this year of remembering the Woodstock music festival and the moon landing, Mungo's voice remains fresh.

The active legacy-tending, community building, and productivity of writers combine to make the Merrimack Valley a literary hot spot and point of pride.

2019

Rosemary & Joseph

"Simply Beautiful"
  —St. Lucia's slogan

"Hate to tell you, but I could live like this," says Rosemary, my wife of seven years, as the local paper noted this fall in a cultural gossip column. "I could do this." She puts down her book, smiles the wine-smile, and bites a cookie.

I can't see them from the balcony, but they're down on the sunny curved beach, the best two-thirds of my homemade family pie chart—Rosemary, Joseph, bronze ants in line.

Joe says we have to stay in the shallow part of the pool where the sides are painted white. He says, "No diving allowed, Dad, because your head will go kaboom." He shivers down the steps, afloat on orange wings. When I chase him underwater, he struggles to keep his chin up and dog paddles like every starter. "Swim like Scooby," I tell him. Joe craves both pool and sea, the lukewarm water worlds away from icy waves we jump at the end of Boston Avenue at Hampton Beach up north.

Bread line on the railing. Ruby-throated blackbird snits at a lesser bird pecking at our gift. Another flier parks behind. They claim huge portions relative to their body size, then bounce back to near branches to feast on the golden toast, pinned by wire feet.

Joe says, "Dinosaur bones," when he steps on crumbled coral about ten feet out into the water and picks up a blanched joint for later play. The new toy hunters with plastic German jeep will stow the bones.

Dots of pyrite in hills above the bay. One droning plane angles to the airport. Deck lamps on a liner slicing north. Clouds and stars and the moon wedge. Far house lights pulse, pulse in the air's cool breath.

The lime bars at the minimart, so good. Just so you know, I ate one every day.

Joe's happy at night with his video cartoons, many of them going back to his parents' childhoods—*Peanuts, Looney Tunes, Merrie Melodies, The Flintstones, Batman, Scooby-Doo*—the animated America archives, Declaration of Entertainment.

Three staff guys in the jitney when it grinds to a stop outside Villa 8. The one with a two-way radio says to Joe, "Don't forget your seatbelt," and my Joseph laughs, knowing nobody is strapped in. "Tell me why there are no seatbelts, Joseph," another guy says. "Watch this, he will have the answer." And Joe thinks and thinks and starts and stops and at last says, "Because we have to keep getting out."

Six months of salads to get thin, Rosemary says, looking sweet in a royal blue two-piece—model mother, the vision, the look, perfect-perfect Mum says the son.

A skinny cat weaves between tables at Jammers. The lunch crowd lets it be, but my son, although curious, shoos the *"chat,"* as the little French boy calls it, asking his *Papa, "Est-ce que je peu caresse le chat?"*

Joe saw three dinosaur birds yesterday. Birds the size of lounge chairs, legs like golf clubs. The storm grounded them. Surf sprays tables full of empty brunch plates. The spastic red hazard flag snaps on its beach pole.

Rasta-man near the table tennis table offers Joe his steel drum, size of an Irish hand-drum, and two mallets. This happens during a rain break, all of us ducking under an overhang, and Joe bings out a tune.

How the sea gives up its color to the setting sun, the dazzling highway to sundown, white, no, brighter, more than white, a metal glow on the bay's skin.

2000, Labrelotte Bay, St. Lucia, Caribbean Sea

Frank P. Putnam

Our back pages.

There's nothing like a snowstorm to get you into the cellar, attic, and back closets during a housebound morning. My family lives in the South Common Historic District in Lowell, close to the state courthouse and train station. Built for managers of the Appleton Mill Company in 1860, the house has been in my wife Rosemary's family since the 1930s.

Occupants in the first seventy or so years left a few things. One curiosity is a shelf of books from the 1800s, titles from personal libraries that were passed down as the house changed hands. That's my guess, unless the last occupant collected the mixed bag of books. Rosemary says the books have always been in the house. I'm interested in Lowell's cultural history and intellectual history. The books people read are a window into the mind of a community. The titles are anecdotal evidence of people's interests and the conversations of the times. Poking through the books again this morning, I was struck by some coincidental dates, which spurred me to write about them.

There's a handsome, three-inch-thick copy of *Byron's Complete Works, Illustrated* (Phillips, Sampson and Company: Boston, 1854) signed: "Mrs. Sarah E. M. Goodrich, January 1st, 1855." [I'm writing this on New Year's Eve, 2008.] This volume contains "unabridged, line for line, word for word, the complete works of Lord Byron" in 1,071 gilt-edged pages, including "his suppressed poems and a sketch of his life." We have a two-volume set of *The Ingoldsby Legends; or, Mirth and Marvels* by Thomas Ingoldsby, Esq. (The Rev. Richard Harris Barham), published by W. J. Widdleton of New York in 1866. These are illustrated stories in verse about French musketeers, knights and ladies, *The Merchant of Venice,* smugglers and buccaneers, jackdaws, witches, milkmaids and nurses, and ghosts. What caught my eye today is the inscription on the title page: "F. P. Putnam, Lowell, Dec. 31, 1867"—signed 141 years ago to this day. Sometimes history jumps into your hand.

This is the same Mr. Putnam who inscribed another book "Frank P. Putnam, Christmas 1872, from Eliza." Frank received as a gift *Rambles of an Archaeologist Among Old Books and in Old Places* by Frederick William Fairholt, F.S.A., published by Virtue and Co. of London in 1871. A book written in French that seems to go with this one is *L'Age du Bronze: Instruments, Armes, et Ornaments par* John Evans D. C. L., L. L. D., published by *Librarie Germer Bailliere et cie.* of Paris in 1882. There's also *The Monumental History of Egypt as Recorded on the Ruins of Her Temples, Palaces, and Tombs* by William Osburn, R. S. L. (London: Trübner and Co., 1854). In the style of the time, several of these volumes have marbled or feather-design end papers in green, blue, red, and gold.

Mr. P. had other interests also, because his name shows up in an unusual book, *The Hasheesh Eater: Being Passages from the Life of a Pythagorean*. In the vein of tales from the East, this mysterious author recounts the secret to the "Eastern narrative" and mind. His subject is "Cannabis indica," the resin of which is hasheesh. He writes: "From time immemorial it has been known among all the nations of the East as possessing a powerful stimulant and narcotic properties . . . ." Harper & Brothers of New York published the book in 1857. The explorer proceeds with his narrative through stages of curiosity, ecstasy, pain, and torture to, finally, "abandonment of the indulgence." Sounds a little like a nineteenth-century version of the 1936 film classic *Reefer Madness*. Forget what you may have heard about Jack Kerouac. Is Putnam the missing link in "Beat" attitude in Lowell? In an appendix, J.W. Palmer, M.D., citing medical journal articles and experiments in India, makes a case for medical use of the herb, all of which is timely given the new law in Massachusetts regarding use of the substance.

Putnam appears in real time in the *History of Lowell and Its People* by Frederick W. Coburn, Volume III (Lewis Historical Publishing Company: New York, 1920). There's a full-page photo of him in business attire with a white handlebar mustache and a cigar in his hand. Here's his profile:

Frank P. Putnam was born in Lowell, Massachusetts, November 15, 1848, and has ever resided in his native city and added to her mercantile greatness. He attended the public schools of the city, but at the age of fifteen years left high school to go into his father's store, business life greatly attracting him from boyhood. This was in 1863, or 1864, the clothing store of Addison Putnam [the oldest of Lowell's men's clothing and furnishing stores] then being located at the corner of Market and Central streets. He rapidly absorbed the principles upon which the business was conducted . . . and upon arriving at legal age [became his father's] partner, the firm trading as Putnam & Son. He later became president . . .

In the not always peaceful arts of trade he has won eminence, and in his native city of Lowell is well-known and highly esteemed as merchant and citizen. There are few men, who, if fortune had been kind to them in a financial way but would develop some special interest which often amounts to a passion, sometimes a hobby. Mr. Putnam is not an exception, his passion being the cultivation of flowers, carnations, and single chrysanthemums being his specialty. Many are the prizes and first premiums which adorn his home, where four large greenhouses are stocked with the specimens and varieties which most appeal to the owner's tastes.

Mr. Putnam married, in Lowell, November 1, 1898, [at the age of 50], Sarah Barry. The family residence is at North Tewksbury, where the greenhouses are Mr. Putnam's especial pleasure, and a generous hospitality is extended.

2008

Jim Casselton

Rings of Saturn.

Standing on the oval track, Jim Casselton and I studied the three-quarter moon in the soft blue sky, the dents and ridges making a mottled milky surface that was papery in its translucence, as if the rock of a moon held its place as neatly as a shape cut out of a blank sheet.

Way beyond, after seven years of transit over vast miles, the latest celebrity spacecraft, *Cassini-Huygens,* was perambulating Saturn, having deked its way between swirling ice chunks and universal gravel—sending back photographs of Saturnine moons like a tourist. But instead of a loud shirt and plaid shorts, a familiar flag logo adorns the underside, shielded as much as possible from the elements on the extreme ride.

Jim said, "That moon seems especially large. And there's something odd about the light."

A muscular man who stands five feet, eight inches, Jim wore a Patriots sweatshirt, the one from the second Super Bowl win. When he saw me, he pointed to his blue cap and then to my Oakland A's cap, and said, "Tonight," meaning the A's would be playing the Red Sox at Fenway.

Jim lives in "the housing" near the Common, a residential complex named for a local priest who became a bishop. He's usually finished with his workout before I arrive. Underfoot were dozens of spent red and blue casings of firecrackers from last Sunday's Fourth of July celebration. About the holiday, he said:

> I had my window open and heard the party until all hours. It's not as tough as it used to be out there. Summer carnivals were stopped after a guy got stabbed years ago. You have to keep your eyes open.

Before I retired from the sheriff's office, a bunch of us would run in South Lowell on weekends. When I came to Lowell from Florida in 1959, that area was run down. It still has some inner-city problems but look at the grapevines and fruit trees. People are keeping up appearances.

Did you know Mr. Homer, the fisherman? He'd come around with his truck to the section where a lot of the Black families lived and put out tubs of fish on ice, all kinds. He'd say to my mother, 'Go ahead, Mrs. Casselton, take a couple more. There are plenty of fish in the ocean.'

2004

PAUL MARION

Luther C. Ladd & Addison O. Whitney

"We shall have trouble today."

Luther Ladd was seventeen. Seventeen years old when he was killed by a "see-sesh" mob, on his way to shield President Abraham Lincoln from secessionist soldiers within reach of the nation's capital. Luther Ladd was seventeen. A boy from Alexandria, New Hampshire, the Granite State. He had followed his three sisters to Lowell in their search for jobs, classic Yankee mill girls. He found a position in the Lowell Machine Shop, a high-tech lab of its time, making manufacturing equipment and locomotive engines.

Luther joined the City Guards. He was ready to go when the fire bell called citizen-soldiers to the armory in the Market House Building on Market Street. It was April 17—the country was headed for the worst. Southern states were in revolt. In South Carolina, the American Fort Sumpter had been blasted by rebel artillery. He had drilled three times a week. The special bell meant "war." Luther Crawford Ladd was seventeen years old.

Addison Otis Whitney from Waldo, Maine, was twenty-two. Both were in Company D of the 6th Massachusetts Militia. Whitney had been in Lowell two years, working in the Number 3 spinning room of the Middlesex Corporation, one of the thousands of New England migrants who came to the city for paid work.

Ladd, Whitney, Sumner Henry Needham of Lawrence, and Charles A. Taylor of Boston, died on the street in Baltimore, Mary-Land. A rebel mob killed the men from Massachusetts. The first soldiers of the Union Army to die in "the great rebellion," as Governor John Andrew called it in 1865 at the dedication of the Lowell Monument.

Gray Concord-granite monument. Twenty-seven-and-a-half-feet high. Same look as the Washington Monument, the shape of Cleopatra's Needle, 3,000 years before. The obelisk for eternal remembrance. In June 1865, the Monument anchored Merrimack Square and gave it a new name: Monument Square. Later, a castle-like City Hall added an epic backdrop.

Luther Ladd was seventeen. What did he think? What made him a patriot? He was born three days before Christmas in 1843 and was named for a local minister. His biographer tells us he admired Alexander the Great and our nation's Founders. "He delighted in farming and nature," wrote a fellow New Hampshire citizen. He was not tall. We know him by his deeds. He volunteered. He trained. He answered the call.

He was killed on April 19, 1861, while passing through Baltimore with his comrades. They wanted to defend Washington, D.C., from secessionist troops of the emerging Confederate States of America. He showed up to fight in a civil war. He was seventeen. He was a boy. He was an only son. His mother died when he was seven years old.

Did he admire President Lincoln or was he moved by Governor Andrew's antislavery speeches? Historians report that he praised the U.S. flag with his last words. We have his likeness, an ambrotype made before he boarded the train for Washington. He wore a "tall bearskin hat and a long frock coat with black braid." He carried a Springfield rifle. One of his sisters kept the original image that appeared in his biography, which sold for twenty-five cents in 1862.

At the Monument's dedication, the Governor called Luther and Addison "martyrs" and described them as "two young artisans" from the city whose motto is "Art Is the Handmaid of Human Good." More than 4,000 people attended the public tribute. On the day they had left Boston for Washington, one of their fellow soldiers said, "We shall have trouble today, and I shall not get out of it alive."

2011

PAUL MARION

Daniel R. Turner

Hero square.

Iron chops the sky up and down this coast, from Camp Pendleton to the Marine Corps Air Station El Toro. Maybe it's the palm trees or because I'm picturing the surf sliding into Vietnam on the other hem of the Pacific Ocean, but I can't help thinking the helicopters are from the war, the ones that carried wounded kids out of fire zones long enough ago that Hollywood movies about the war seem old.

I didn't have to go but can't get rid of it in my head. My military draft number was low, the riskiest, in 1972 when the call-ups were suspended. I don't know what I would have done if I'd been ordered to report for duty. At twelve years old, I brought home brochures about the Green Berets from the town library. My father had been in the army. Two years later, 1968, I had turned on the war. I'm haunted by my near miss. I still read Mike Casey's *Obscenities* and Michael Herr's *Dispatches*, drawn to the mayhem.

I wonder if young Daniel Turner from my home back east spent time in California before his flight to Vietnam. Six years older than me, he was a sergeant in the Air Force when he died in Gia Dinh province in 1969, a "ground casualty," per military records. A quiet guy who lived up the hill from my house, his name now tops a steel post set in a grassy crossroads where I caught my high school bus. It's a hero square: Turner Square.

When I visited the bright black Wall in hot and steamy white-stone Washington, D.C., and felt the incisions in its mirror-face, I searched for Sergeant Turner's name among the names that hold up all the signs at all the intersections. His dates are 31 Jan 48, 17 Aug 69. Daniel R. Turner. He's on Panel 19 West, Row 57. Just like the neighborhood sign.

1984, Capistrano Beach, California

Eddie Franzoni

Screwed.

Waiting at the Lowell train station to pick up a friend one afternoon, I overhead two cab drivers talking—one cabbie had the best story, probably one of a hundred from his days and nights on the streets.

> I had one guy, picked him up at Shaughnessy Terrace, wanted to go to Papa Gino's in Burlington—said he had to see a guy—so I take him, and when we get there, he says, 'The guy inside'll cash my check'—
>
> Oh, beautiful, I say, and I follow him in—he says, 'What're you doing?'—I say, I'm making sure you pay me—he says, 'I'll be right out'—he comes out, says, 'He won't cash it'—Now the guy owes me thirty-four bucks—course I figure he just made his drug sale and now wants back to Lowell—so he says,
>
> 'Take me back to my mother's in Lowell—she'll pay you'—Okay, back to Lowell—another thirty-four bucks—now he owes me sixty-eight bucks—get to his mother's house, and it's total chaos—she comes out, yelling, 'No money, no money'—kids are screaming—she's hollering at the guy—he says,
>
> 'Take me to my friend's house in the Highlands—he owes me money'—So we go—now he's up to owing me about seventy-five—he gets out near Cupples Square and says, 'It's right here'—I stop and watch, and he starts to run—Vroom!—I pull out and chase him in the cab—he legs it across a parking lot, and I stop and jump out—I had called the cops on the radio—I caught him and beat the piss out of him—the cops said they

couldn't do much because he owed me less than a hundred-fifty bucks—I heard in New Hampshire you can get a guy pinched if he screws you out of five bucks.

2009

Hamid Ismailov & Juan Ferrer

The beast underneath.

I wake up early every day, but today I got up even earlier to check on our young cat that came home from the vet yesterday after being spayed. We were told to watch her closely for several days to be sure she recovered as expected. I was awake, listening to New Hampshire Public Radio's overnight broadcast of the BBC *World Service*, when I heard the rattle of shopping-cart wheels on the sidewalk through the window. It was barely first light, but a middle-aged couple was making the rounds on trash pickup day. They fished in the recycle bin for cans and bottles to redeem.

A tall, thin, older jogger passed them on his way toward the courthouse. He was alone, but there are guys the same age as him who run this route in a group, probably jumping off from the Family "Y" on Thorndike Street. The clock read 4:32. Big cities like New York and Boston come to mind when you think about cities that don't sleep, but Lowell has its own 24/7 tempo—ask any police officer about the night rhythm. This time of year, the birds keep time in the trees. Their music rises with the light.

On the BBC, the news as usual was angled toward war, money, and politics. The Republic of Congo is marking its fiftieth year of independence from Belgium. Chaos and brutality have dominated the nation for five decades. At one point, ten African nations were fighting with or against political factions in Congo in what was called "Africa's World War."

I also heard a report about Hamid Ismailov, an Uzbek novelist and poet from Kyrgyzstan now living in London. He's a writer-in-residence for the BBC who blogs about the turmoil in his homeland, where the Kyrgyz are fighting people with roots in Uzbekistan who live in Kyrgyzstan. Listening to him, I was reminded of my friend Steve talking about the Irish Civil War and the more recent indiscriminate bombings when he was studying at Trinity College in Dublin. The Kyrgyz-Uzbek writer was asked if he was losing faith in human nature, given all the violence.

About the interethnic strife in his nation, he said, "I felt as if my hands were cutting my legs." He had written on his blog, "Are the crows that do not peck out each other's eyes more human than us?" and "Is civilization as thin as the shirt we wear, covering a beast underneath?" He said the stories of human kindness coming out of the war zone make him feel hopeful.

You don't have to cross an ocean to encounter violence. Last week, a nineteen-year-old man from downriver in Lawrence was shot and killed in the Back Central neighborhood, a short walk from where my family lives. Juan Ferrer's death was a page one story in the newspaper.

Two days after the shooting, yellow police tape lay on the pavement in the alley outside the building where he had been visiting friends who hosted a cookout. A black kettle-top grill stood in the alley and dark curtains blew in an open window above.

Born in Puerto Rico, Juan grew up in Lowell and then in his teens moved to Lawrence with his mother. The father of a two-month-old daughter, he worked in a Haverhill factory cleaning machines. He didn't have enemies, his girlfriend and family told reporters. "He was just a good dad," they said.

I asked a neighbor who knew him what happened. The man said, "There was an argument, and somebody had a gun." That statement fits the old Irish situation, Afghanistan today, fifty years in Congo, Kyrgystan, and on and on.

A colleague of mine has been writing about the origins of human beings and most recently, "What makes humans unique?" One of the traits is the capacity for abstract thought. We can imagine peace and tranquility, but there's a behavioral glitch that manifests itself in individuals and social groups that prevents some people from rejecting violence as a way to solve a problem. We tell children, "Use your words and don't hit each other."

2010

PORTRAITS ALONG THE WAY

Doug DeNatale

Listening to a memory worker.

On a sticky spring morning, I'm in Carrboro, North Carolina, to see how Dr. Douglas DeNatale is doing on his book about Lowell's culture. A down-to-earth scholar who is curious about everything, he's in a blue short-sleeved shirt and khaki shorts, offering me icy lemonade. Doug directed the Lowell Folklife Project, an ambitious survey of the community sponsored by the American Folklife Center at the Library of Congress. I was his bureaucratic partner as cultural affairs director of the Lowell Historic Preservation Commission, an agency of the U.S. Department of the Interior that was helping the National Park Service in Lowell. We became friends.

From June 1987 to May 1988, Lowell's way of life was under a microscope. Folklore fieldworkers, most of them PhDs, fanned out across the city—recording songs, making photographs, taping interviews, and collecting stories. Their efforts paralleled a project undertaken after Congress established Lowell National Historical Park in 1978. Buildings in the historic district were rated for their significance and condition in a multivolume report called the *Inventory of Cultural Resources*. Those researchers focused on the built environment only. The folklife project is a record of Lowell's people during the course of a year.

Doug is sifting through the digital and hard-copy data in his redbrick bungalow in a suburban neighborhood outside of Chapel Hill. The heat is up to ninety degrees at 10:00 a.m. On the porch a hummingbird sucks red syrup from a tube. Artifacts cover walls and shelves of the living room: a dulcimer, a small mud-green ceramic catfish, Hmong story cloths. One wall has two black-and-white photographs from Lowell: a picture of a Portuguese woman singing at the Four Seasons Restaurant on the edge of downtown and a group portrait of young skateboarders in the Acre neighborhood.

The survey team collected a truckload of information. The book will explore subjects as various as daily tenement life in the remnants of the French neighborhood of Little Canada and the informal names for favorite swimming spots along the Merrimack River. Doug has considered the meaning of ethnic flag-raising ceremonies at City Hall and listened to anecdotes repeated by Park Rangers who meet retired mill workers on canal boat tours. Readers will find a Greek recipe for baked lamb, transcriptions of Puerto Rican song lyrics, and harrowing accounts of journeys out of Southeast Asia told by Cambodian refugees.

Here's Doug:

> I've lived a divided existence. When I was in graduate school in Pennsylvania, I wrote about Southern mill villages; and now here I am in North Carolina writing about Lowell. When you get away from a place, and look back, you begin to see some of the patterns more clearly.
>
> I'm struck by the waves of immigration and each group rediscovering Lowell and finding ways to integrate into the city. Many of the patterns repeat. One of the most important aspects of Lowell is the relationship between religion and culture. People are deeply rooted in their religion; this has shaped the city's culture in some very important ways. Although there was a common language of faith among many of the early peoples in Lowell, their ethnicity became even more important as each group defined its identity and community—its particular form of Christianity or Catholicism. Of course, there are other, smaller religious sects in the city, too, some of them with a long history, like the Jewish community.
>
> It's clear that there's a high level of historical consciousness in the community. Lowell is in the memory business, and that's a wise decision. When you wipe the slate clean, you have nothing to start with. People read each other's experiences in the city by what they understand their own history to be. Their understanding of their grandparents comes down to them, and

they apply it to their view of others in the city. That is not the best basis for understanding new immigrants. You are as far away from your great-grandparents' experiences as you are from the experiences of new people to the city.

This book is not saying what Lowell should be, but, among a lot of other information, it reflects what people are thinking about where the city should go. Lowell has plenty of lessons for any city that has experienced industrialization and immigration. At the same time, Lowell is atypical because of the recent revitalization, a process not easy to duplicate.

The best book about Lowell will have to be written by somebody from Lowell. It would be impossible for me to define Lowell. I hope people will find something that they had forgotten or see something they don't know about. I'm pulling together diverse strands into a unified response. I'm sure some people will say, 'Well, that's good, he knew about that in our community, but he didn't know anything about this, and it's the most important thing here!'

1989, Carrboro, North Carolina

PAUL MARION

Douen "Duey" Kol

"History is story. It means nothing else as a noun. Herodotus was the first to use the word . . . and he used it as a verb: to find out for oneself. Then you tell."
—Charles Olson, *The Special View of History* (1970)

Duey Kol came to Lowell for the first time in 1999 to see the Southeast Asian Water Festival on the north bank of the Merrimack River above Pawtucket Falls. This wide, relatively straight section of the river has been called one of the best stretches for rowing in the country. For years, the community has hosted competitions like the Textile River Regatta. Every August, the Southeast Asian Water Festival draws tens of thousands of people to the riverside for music, dancing, food, people watching, and the Khmer long-boat races similar to those held on the Mekong River.

Kol was born in a refugee camp in Thailand while her parents waited for an opportunity to move to a safe new home. Their next stop was another camp in the Philippines, and then in 1984 on to Chelsea, Mass., which, like Lowell, had become a place where Cambodian families were resettling in increasing numbers. Her family was sponsored for resettlement in the United States by Boston Catholic Charities. She was three-and-a-half years old when she arrived with her parents and younger brother and sister. For the first six months the family lived on welfare payments and shared a three-bedroom apartment with two other Cambodian families.

As a youth she learned traditional Khmer dance and performed with the Reaching Out for Chelsea Adolescents Dance Troupe. Her mother had been a dancer before the Khmer Rouge overran Cambodia. Artists were targets during the genocide. Kol later met members of the acclaimed Angkor Dance Troupe of Lowell. She remembers her high-school teacher Sylvia Schernbaum urging her and fellow students to "Think big, dream big." She did just that, winning acceptance to Simmons College in Boston. After graduation she worked for a time as an insurance agent in Waltham, Mass., concentrating on the immigrant and refugee communities in Lowell and Lynn, Mass.

In 2004, she was recruited by George Chigas of the Angkor Dance Troupe in Lowell to help manage the organization. With a Theodore Edson Parker Foundation grant, Chigas and Samkhann Khoeun of the Cambodian Expressions Project of Middlesex Community College brought her on board as a shared program manager. When the national park in Lowell advertised a special events position, Kol applied and was selected. She worked on the Lowell Folk Festival, Lowell Summer Music Series, and other events. A rising star, Kol was recruited in 2012 to work in the office of the Assistant Director of the National Park Service in Washington, D.C., which oversees interpretive and education policies. She already had been helping with the agency's nationwide Diversity and Inclusion Project.

> Those of us who are bicultural have to create a separate idea that is not one or the other—we have to manage a blended identity. It's important to develop year-round relationships with the people whose cultural traditions we promote on special days. We have to get beyond celebration. We of the Park staff must be able to exist in a condition like the state of 'therapeutic irritation' that comes with holding a new and different pose in yoga. We should be able to hold ourselves in that place that is uncomfortable and to be okay with that. At the same time, visitors should be comfortable asking difficult, complicated questions on tours, in museums, and at public activities.

Kol advocates multitrack storytelling.

> We have to ask ourselves, 'How do you decide what to present? Which stories do you choose to tell?' We need the best storytellers, more people who have lived the stories. With a topic like immigration, we can be relevant in what we talk about.

And what happens to people not interested in displaying their culture in a public demonstration?

It's our responsibility to explore and probe, to record more stories in Lowell because this is where we have been asked to preserve part of America's history and relate it to people. ... There's an online TED talk (Technology, Entertainment, Design) by Nigerian novelist Chimamanda Adichie in which she cautions listeners about 'the danger of a single story' and how this can lead to a fundamental lack of understanding of another person or place. She says, 'The single story creates stereotypes, and the problem with stereotypes is not that they are untrue, but that they are incomplete. They make one story become the only story.'

2014

Helga Becker

A single potato.

On the Rhine River trip are two French guys in their late fifties, one of them an eye doctor, the other an architect, on their honeymoon, both previously married—one with a son and two daughters. They come from the same New England town full of French Canadians, and their parents were members at the local golf club.

They talked about a ninety-three-year-old friend, Helga Becker, whom they know from their condo association in North Carolina where they vacation. She had survived the World War II aerial bombing of Dresden, Germany. In early February 1945, with the Allied forces gaining ground on Hitler's military, 1000 British and American bomber planes dropped tons of explosives on the city, killing as many as 30,000 people. The ensuing conflagration consumed large sections of Dresden.

A direct hit on Helga's house killed twelve family members while she was two streets away looking for food. She fled Dresden at fifteen years old with a single potato in her pocket and in time found help at a U.S. Army camp where she was hired as a translator. There she met an American officer who fell in love with her. The man pursued the beautiful, six feet tall teenager, but she kept her distance, blaming his countrymen for destroying her family.

Helga put the chocolates and oranges from the captain in a desk drawer, untouched. When she learned through German contacts that her father had been out when the bomb hit, she asked the American to find him. He did.

2023

PAUL MARION

Francis "Pinky" Roy

My mother's younger brother Frank, or Pinky, whom I remember as always wearing sunglasses and a golf sweater, usually a dark cardigan over a light shirt, combed his black hair back and wore a fancy ring. He was always good for a memorable monologue.

One Sunday afternoon he pulled his sea-blue Cadillac into our driveway in Dracut and stayed for an hour, talking to my folks non-stop at the kitchen table. He was somewhere between California and Florida and New England in his travels. Behind my bedroom door, lying on the floor listening, I scribbled as fast as possible in my notebook. Here's a sample of what I caught:

>That ashtray's so big you can do laundry in it!
>
>What are you up to now? Still reading those deep books? Make a communist out of yourself yet.
>
>In this country, all the politicians are doing all day is building a big bureaucracy. Liberals are ruining the country.
>
>People don't give a goddamn—they say, 'Leave me alone. No matter what those guys are doing up there in Washington, what the hell, there's nothing I can do.'
>
>They're fed up. You can smell something going on. When it happens, it'll happen so fast it'll blow up.
>
>Everything is bad, nothing is good, it stinks.
>
>People who are one step ahead buy land and put a trailer on it. Taxes are ridiculous.
>
>Lawyers are running us. Lawyers are wrecking the country. It's unreal.
>
>And you, my sister, you need help. I don't know if anyone can help you.
>
>And your husband there, he's a jewel in the rough. What

are you gonna do with an old horse like that—leave him in the stable, put a blanket on him?

Have you heard from that homely girl I used to see, the other one there? She married the crazy rich guy from Texas that she was running with? Well, Holy Jesus!

Hey, remember Ma and her beans when we were all living at home? Ma would bake beans, and the old man would give her a pigeon, a pigeon in the pot—best damn thing I ever ate. I make beans, good beans, with molasses and bacon fat.

Hey, I gotta go. Thank you, yup, bye now.

1976

SIX

Leymah Gbowee

"Peace is justice. Peace requires the provision of our basic human security needs."

When I learned this morning that Leymah Gbowee of Liberia, now Ghana, had been awarded the Nobel Peace Prize in a three-way share with two other women leaders, I felt good for her—and excited because I know this person. The other recipients are Ellen Johnson Sirleaf, the President of Liberia, and Tawakkol Karmen, a journalist and democracy activist in Yemen and the first Arab woman to earn this recognition.

I was fortunate enough to get to know Leymah when she was in Lowell for three weeks last April, serving as the Greeley Scholar for Peace Studies. Each year, UMass Lowell invites an outstanding individual who has advanced the cause of peace and social justice for a multi-week residency on campus.

Leymah organized women to use nonviolent tactics to oppose the tyrannical president Charles Taylor during a long civil war in Liberia. We reached her through Kathy Reticker of our Greeley Committee, whose sister had directed a film about the peace-building work in Liberia, *Pray the Devil Back to Hell*. Kathy is executive director of Acre Family Day Care of Lowell, a key neighborhood resource.

The lesson I took from Leymah is that there are times in your life when you have to put yourself on the line. You have to risk what's important to you when the cause is more important than your own comfort, your reputation, and even possibly your safety. She was determined to do what she could to stop the killing.

She brought together women of Christian and Muslim faiths for public protests, the Liberian Mass Action for Peace. The goal was to stop the violence that was destroying the lives of their children. One tactic echoed a play from 411 BCE. In *Lysistrata* by Aristophanes, women withhold sexual relations from their partners to pressure the men to negotiate a peace treaty. The women also seize the civic treasury.

Leymah believed that Liberian women had more common sense and decency than the angry, hostile, power-hungry men who were endlessly fighting. Her movement, and she would be the first to say it was not all about her, broke the pattern of conflict.

She stayed with us for three weeks, living at the the university's Inn & Conference Center with a young daughter, one of her several children. Her husband joined her at the end of her stay. She spoke in a dozen settings on campus and in the area, including to school groups. She believes it is especially important to reach young people while their minds are open to finding a better way to behave than resorting to violence to solve problems.

A woman from Acre Family Day Care took care of her daughter while Leymah was at events. One day the woman told Leymah about a women's shelter in the city where she volunteered after work. Leymah asked to go there. It was the end of a busy day of meeting people, but she insisted on going to the shelter. As we know, it's what you do when nobody is watching that proves what kind of person you are.

A group of us at the university had lunch with her the day she arrived. We were captivated by her accounts of the struggle in Liberia and the work she was doing at that moment during the political and military crisis in the neighboring country of Côte d'Ivoire (Ivory Coast). She was urging women there to try the approach that had worked in Liberia, but not enough people were cooperative.

Sitting at the long table in the gallery at the Allen House on the South Campus, a view of the Merrimack River through the windows, I remember thinking that this person has come to us from the front lines, from a war zone, where people are jailed or murdered for challenging the authorities. A formidable presence with a ready smile, she projects calmness and self-assurance and is easygoing in her own way. Leaving conflict resolution aside at another lunch, she spoke enthusiastically about NBA basketball. She knows the American teams and rosters better than I do, following the games on satellite broadcasts in Africa.

On a return visit to Lowell in 2014 for a student forum with other peace builders, Leymah told the *Boston Herald*, "Find the thing that keeps you up at night, that thing that gets your adrenaline going. Find what you believe in and go for it. I have no regrets. Everything I've done has been to ensure my children don't have to go through the struggles."

2011, 2014

In May 2024, Leymah Gbowee received a $20 million award from Melinda French Gates as one of twelve global leaders who will make grants to "charitable organizations they consider to be doing urgent, impactful, and innovative work to improve women's health and well-being in the U.S. and around the world." French Gates has pledged $1 billion of additional funding in this effort by 2026. Along with the Gbowee Peace Foundation, recipients of the French Gates' funding include former New Zealand Prime Minister Jacinda Ardern, filmmaker Ava DuVerney, and Olympic athlete and Black maternal health advocate Allyson Felix.

PAUL MARION

Patrick J. Mogan (1)

Taking action.

In the final quarter of the twentieth century, federal and state agencies, City government, community development groups, and private investors spent hundreds of millions of dollars in Lowell to renovate old mills for businesses and apartments, fix streets and improve the water treatment plant, build a baseball stadium and civic arena, lay walkways along the river and canals, and construct houses, schools, and museums. More than 400 historic buildings were restored, creating a distinctive downtown setting of vibrant rose-red structures, cobblestone streets, vintage lampposts, an esplanade and stage along the river, and contemporary sculpture along the canal system.

One lead figure in the story emerged, a man who combined the seriousness of Yul Brynner's magnetic hired gunman in *The Magnificent Seven* with the quirky, metaphysical seer qualities of *Star Wars*' Yoda. Pat Mogan—Dr. Patrick J. Mogan—was not born in the city. There is extensive preamble to Mogan's passion for a restored Lowell. The successes link back to earlier activists, fathers and mothers on redevelopment boards and civic improvement committees. Still, more than forty years on, he remains the consensus choice for main actor, as in "taking action," at the start of Lowell's modern turnaround. Although he operated in concert with a variety of people—teachers, parish activists, planning consultants, City bureaucrats, politicians, neighborhood leaders, local historians—Mogan most clearly and most consistently described what the city could be and expressed a rationale for mobilization. Mogan and his ambitious band reconceived Lowell as a city-scale lifelong learning laboratory. The grassroots effort embodied the rock-ribbed American value of progress through education.

The unlikely guru was an Irish American reading teacher from Norwood, Mass., with light hair and large, black-framed glasses. In his town south of Boston, he had seen the Irish community assimilate in a way that gradually diminished its distinct identity. He read this as an early warning sign of social alienation and the related problems.

With his marriage to Mary Pollard, he was embraced by a prominent Lowell family. Through a willful reshaping of community expectations, he made the place his own the way an author can take hold of a place with language and an artistic vision. *Boston Globe* reporter Ian Forman had cited Mogan's success as a principal at the Reilly Elementary School in the Belvidere neighborhood, including constructive work with the Parent & Teachers Association. The Reilly Elementary School in 1963 was regarded as one of a few dams holding back a potential flood of families into the highly absorbent suburban towns.

Mogan composed the "elevator speech" about Lowell's singular importance. He would recite the speech countless times between 1966 and 1978, and then some. The audience might be ten people in a church basement or a phalanx of congressmen at a Washington, D.C., hearing. He would tell them about merchants from Boston who took a runaway river, a bankrupt canal, pilot technology, and an available labor pool of young rural women and created a template for industrial success. They connected parts picked up along the Merrimack River and fashioned a humming cloth production complex on a scale and of an efficiency never before seen in the United States. Plentiful falling water and a practical mill town combined to forge a hinge of history, the place where America could be seen transforming from a dominant agrarian culture to a society tilted toward factories, wage earners, and teeming cities.

To his parable about the past, Mogan added a balancing future side that suggested how Lowell could reclaim its special place in American history: the city would be reshaped into a museum without walls, a platform for lifelong experiential learning, a living exhibit of the process and consequences of the American Industrial Revolution—a place so compelling visually and expressively that visitors would fill city streets, scholars would come to write books, and chief executive officers would establish businesses in an inspiring, purposeful renaissance city. Mogan gave anyone who showed interest a homework assignment designed to push the vision forward an inch.

Mogan was on the reclamation job by 1966. He had connected the prevailing negative community mindset in Lowell with lagging educational achievement and poor self-esteem among schoolchildren. "There appeared to be a complete disassociation between the present and the past," he said. "This was very serious, for scholars have been saying for a long time that people need 'roots' and a positive sense of being as prime ingredients for development." Students in the inner-city neighborhood schools were a year-and-a-half behind the "educational norm" when they reached the eighth grade. Lowell had hired fifty remedial reading teachers, but for many the improvement was stalled.

Young Martin T. Meehan, the future congressman, knew the educational opportunities in Lowell were unequal. He attended a school close to home in a working-class precinct in the southern end of the city. "When we got new books, we had to erase the names in the book—they came from other schools that got the new books. My father said it was wrong." In the sixth grade he took a bus across the river to the Pawtucketville Memorial Elementary School, where he saw for himself what it was like in a neighborhood that got more attention. City planner and development specialist Jim Milinazzo is about the same age as Meehan. As a boy he went to elementary school near home in Belvidere, an upper-tier section. Pat Mogan was his principal at the Reilly. "It was *the* school to go to," he said.

In Mogan's analysis, "No single agency, including the schools, could meet people's needs." He began talking about "a community-type school" that policymakers in the state education office dubbed "The Everywhere School." His answer for repairing the breach between "Who am I?" and "Where do I come from?" was to focus his thinking on the fact that Lowell was a place to be proud of because of the role it played in the formation of America.

With his allies, Mogan sought to bring a national historical park and heritage state park to the city. He always added that the parks themselves were a "means—not ends in themselves—for achieving the stated goals. These means were intended to utilize the physical environment and the cultural environment as two interrelated attributes worthy of being celebrated and shared with people around the United States and the world."

As a coda, he stressed this point: "We believed the cultural or 'people' element was our prime focus." Upon learning that the National Park Service and other decision-makers in Washington, D.C., would be more at ease talking about the value of "the artifacts of the industrial city" as opposed to "the human story," Mogan and company, ever-pragmatic, stopped calling their project a "cultural park" and accepted the standard "historical park" category used by the U.S. Department of the Interior. Mogan was the first to admit that the physical development was needed as "props" around which the people's story could be told. He knew the built environment was the strongest evidence of Lowell's unique character as much as he was convinced that the innovative new park's true value would be in enshrining the nation-building contributions made by generations of immigrant workers in Lowell.

Mogan urged Lowellians to flip their value assessment of the city's resources. The conventional wisdom inside and outside of the city limits held that outmoded mill buildings, a working-class labor heritage, and a mostly low-schooled multiethnic population were drags on the community efforts to climb the progress ladder. Mogan said, "No, what you think is bad is really good—the perceived liabilities are actually assets, and the past is the gateway to a better future."

Pat Mogan wanted everyone to be an entrepreneur contributing to the renaissance. He would say, "Never underestimate the capacity that is in the average person to contribute to the common good." He liked to tell stories on himself, chuckling as he recalled this or that episode. One of his favorites went like this: "Years ago, a man standing near the Merrimack Canal said to me, 'Someone could make a good living by running a wire around the edges of the canal, attaching small boats like Boston's Swan Boats, and powering the whole system with a bicycle.' I said, 'You're crazy.' He laughed and said, 'Well, you're crazy, too!'"

Much of the early funding for park planning came to Lowell through federal Great Society programs like the Model Cities Program and innovative state programs for urban revitalization, which Lowell qualified for because it ranked so high on the "misery index," explained Mogan's colleague at the time, Peter Stamas. A local Greek American and Harvard University graduate, Stamas went on to teach mathematics and serve as headmaster of Lowell High School. All the while, he urged along the local revival in various roles, from championing a vision of Lowell as "The Flowering City" (promoting beautification and environmental sustainability) while president of the Human Services Corporation to helping to create the Greater Lowell Community Foundation to boost local philanthropy. Asked by the *Boston Globe* in 2002 about his community work that led to a national park, Stamas said he got involved in the beginning "to help the kids in the Acre neighborhood with education."

Mogan was feted by the National Park Service on the 30th anniversary of Lowell National Historical Park. In one of the last formal photographs made of him, he wears a green Park Service jacket in the front row among dozens of staff members with the Patrick J. Mogan Cultural Center in the background. He died in December 2012.

2014

Patrick J. Mogan (2)

Mogan speaks.

The thinking prevalent in my youth was that to become something better, you had to become something else. My section of the town of Norwood, Mass., was called Dublin, and virtually everyone spoke Gaelic. We were referred to by the public schools as second-language problems. When you have an institution as powerful as the schools referring to your background as a problem, well, whether it was deliberate or a reaction to what the educational institution was saying, my people killed their culture so we could live better.

You won't find much learning, you'll find instruction, in school. There's not a lot of learning in schools. Some people confuse knowing something with understanding something. You'll never understand anything unless you apply it in some circumstance and find out if it's working or not and whether you have to make a further accommodation. That's the only time learning occurs.

Your learning occurs with some kind of dialogue that is not happening in the schools but is happening outside of the schools. The school is a small factor, maybe a twenty percent factor, in learning, and your home, neighbors, and peers combine for an eighty percent factor in learning. I had the concept for years of making that eighty percent factor a school, a school in a different sense, but a learning environment that was going to help people when they got into the twenty percent factor, the school. And I'm still consumed with that idea.

Lowell was not considered a good address in the 1960s. Our industrial city aspect and our ethnic city aspect were looked upon as deficits. There was an alienation being built up between the people and their community.

We created a process that enabled people of various disciplines to come to Lowell and work with the community to think, plan, and develop concepts, which allowed us to express a vision of the future. In our Model Cities program, we knew we were involved in a process that was going to take time to develop.

We used the words of historian William Bundy, who said, 'Every great civilization (I say, every great city) has one thing in common—that's a positive sense of the future infusing the present with a sense of purpose, hope, and expectation.'

(From *Mill Power* by Paul Marion, 2014, quoting from the video documentaries *Roots of an Urban Cultural Park* and *Patrick J. Mogan: Visionary and Realist* by Page One Productions, 1991, 1995.)

1995

Paul E. Tsongas (1)

"How do you discard a city?"

After graduating from college, Paul Tsongas spent two years in the Peace Corps in Ethiopia in the early 1960s. He remembered a *Sports Illustrated* article from that time. In a story about Abebe Bikila, the gold-medal marathon runner of the 1960 Olympics in Rome, the national hero of Ethiopia, the reporter compared the destitute hometown of the champion marathoner to down-and-out places in the United States. Paterson, New Jersey, and Lowell, Mass., were offered as the abject examples. Tsongas never forgot how his hometown had been portrayed. "I remember vividly that the audience of *Sports Illustrated*, in reading that, would think that Addis Ababa was in terrible shape," said Tsongas.

Tsongas had his own version of Lowell Economics 101. Arguing in favor of a pro-business platform for the Democratic Party in 1991-92 when he was running for his party's presidential nomination against the likes of Arkansas Governor Bill Clinton and Senator Bob Kerrey of Nebraska, Tsongas told his story in a plain gray pamphlet titled *A Call to Economic Arms*. The eighty-six-page pamphlet was a campaign phenomenon for its tough-love talk about the American future. The candidate distributed hundreds of thousands to voters starved for substance. Tsongas wrote about growing up in Lowell:

> My childhood was spent experiencing the economic decline of my home city.... My father (a Republican) owned a dry-cleaning shop, and the entire family worked in the business. My father worked 6:30 a.m. to 6:30 p.m., six days a week, fifty-one weeks a year. Sundays were spent doing books and repairing the machinery. By any fair standard, this staggering workload should have resulted in just rewards for him. It didn't.

> No matter how hard he worked, no matter how conscientious he was, the forces of Lowell's economic decline were too much to overcome. The remembrance of those days has left me with an inability to view economic dislocation casually. (*A Call to Economic Arms: Forging a New American Mandate* by Paul Tsongas, 1991)

A 1958 graduate of Lowell High School who went on to Dartmouth College and then Yale University Law School, Tsongas talked about a "psychological numbness," the feeling "that somehow there's not a lot going on and you are sinking into the mud. You don't want to be part of that, particularly if you are eighteen years of age." The atmosphere suppressed the local ambition to do well in the city. Tsongas said that too many residents, especially the decision-makers, felt it was acceptable to say, "Lowell may be a dump, but it's our dump, and we control it."

Like many of his contemporaries, he decided that the way up was to "go on to the greater world and do what he could." Ten years later there was still a lot of that in the air. David Marion is a professor of political science at Hampden-Sydney College in Virginia. In the mid-1960s he attended St. Joseph's High School for Boys on upper Merrimack Street in *St. Jean Baptiste* parish. He recalled the afternoon when one of the Marist Brothers who taught there walked into his class and said, "Somebody should just drop a bomb on this place and start over." A couple of blocks away in what had been Little Canada it looked like the bombs had already exploded. Not everyone shared that view, not everyone sped out of town; even Paul Tsongas came back in the mid-1960s and got elected to the Lowell City Council.

Reflecting on what Lowell had been through, forty-year-old Senator Tsongas wrote:

> Under the free enterprise system, useless items are discarded in favor of more productive ones. How do you discard a city? Very simply—by allowing it to decay. Who makes the decision? Everyone. . . . Watching a city decline is like watching a fire dying out. The critical mass necessary for continued dynamism is no longer present: even while there is still both heat and

light, the eventual outcome is obvious. (*The Road From Here: Liberalism and Realities in the 1980s* by Paul Tsongas, 1981)

Tsongas would jokingly refer to himself as a "pinko" when the talk came around to social issues, but he was as hardheaded as his Republican father the dry cleaner when the topic was the importance of business and partnerships. He had seen his father struggle in economic quicksand. As proud as he was of the historical park bill, he was convinced that Lowell needed a vigorous business sector and a pro-business climate citywide to survive long-term. Tsongas is the one who said to his fellow Democrats, "You can't be pro-jobs and antibusiness."

Tsongas teamed up with then-City Manager B. Joseph Tully, a gruff but effective political boss-type who favored a cardigan sweater over a shirt and tie at the office—an unlikely dance partner for him. A former state senator, Tully was City Manager from 1979 to 1987. They devised mechanisms to foster collaboration between government and business sector leaders. Veterans of the Lowell renaissance swap stories about Tsongas and Tully using their considerable powers of persuasion in two-on-one meetings with downtown landlords whose buildings were detracting from the overall progress, either in appearance or down-market activity. Sometimes the agenda items were agreed to on the merits, but there are tales like the one involving a Public Works Department crew showing up unannounced on the street in front of a landlord's ranch house in an upscale neighborhood; the workers proceeded to excavate in search of a broken water pipe, shutting down service to the house. Message received. Tsongas liked that the Manager could get results on the city side. Tully, however, came to grief in 1988 when he broke the law concerning a property transaction.

Making notes one night on a napkin in a riverfront restaurant appointed like King Arthur's Court, Tsongas and Tully had outlined a strategy for cooperation among leaders in the public and private sectors. Out of this meeting in 1979 came the second of two related organizations: the Lowell Plan Inc., a roundtable of business, government, and community leaders that Tsongas described as "a chamber of commerce that actually works." The first organization was a quasi-public banking entity called the Lowell Development & Financial Corporation (LDFC), founded in 1975, through which local banks pooled funds to make low-rate loans for local projects. With these innovative tools, leaders forged a collaborative approach to city development and aligned the private interests behind both business ventures and other initiatives that contributed to the public good, for example, a master plan for city development and an assessment of the public schools.

2014

Paul E. Tsongas (2)

"When the legislation passed, he was just ecstatic, absolutely ecstatic."

While the Lowell National Historical Park proponents were often condescended to by officials in Washington, D.C., whose reflex response was that the Lowell project was just another cut of pork for a clever Congressman, U.S. Representative Paul Tsongas was adamant that the people whom he had to persuade must see the larger concept. He also resisted attempts to minimize the scope of the project. Fred Faust, who was on the congressman's staff, recalled a discussion with National Park Service (NPS) Director Bill Whalen, who pushed for an easy-to-manage operation with ten buildings owned by the federal government.

> Paul said, 'No, you know, you're missing it. This is the living part. This is the story. There's a story that has to do with this. There are elements of the story that are all over the downtown. They're in the buildings, they're in the people.' There were times when he could have got things through, but he was holding out for what was important.
>
> We had great people who were working on the ground. I mean we were talking to Pat Mogan every day, and he was lobbying people. I remember working with Bob Malavich in the City planning office. He was the technical point man. And it would be, Bob, you know, we need a better picture of this or a line drawing of that.
>
> We got the Congressional subcommittee to come to Lowell. We were pulling our hair out because that day it was forty degrees outside. Today, it's easy, you're on the canal. Well, I had to call Mel Lezberg [from the Locks and Canals Co.]. I said, 'Mel, next Monday bring your boat up from Lexington [Mass.]

because we're going on a canal ride.' Mel said, 'I have to cut the fence open,' and I said, 'Cut the fence open.' And they were cooperative. (Fred Faust interview with Mehmed Ali, 2003)

Former Lowell National Historical Park historian Gray Fitzsimons described the Lowell Historic Canal District Commission's work in an unpublished paper:

> [The Commission's work] was the result of combined efforts of a Boston-Cambridge group of consultants; the Lowell Team; and a subcommittee of Commission members representing the state, the U.S. Department of Transportation, and the National Park Service. Employing language and concepts used in earlier studies for a national park in Lowell, the report called for the creation of a 'cultural park,' though this was later changed to 'historical park' at the behest of the NPS. The Commission stated: 'The creation of a Lowell National Cultural Park by Congress ... is the appropriate action for the federal government to take in order to preserve Lowell's historical and cultural resources and to interpret the city's special role in the American Industrial Revolution.' (George Ohar and Gray Fitzsimons, unpublished paper, 'Lowell National Historical Park Administrative History,' 2004)

Making the canal system the centerpiece of the plan, the Commission dodged the consistent skepticism within the NPS about the critical mass of historical structures in Lowell. The proposed park would have a "broad preservation zone and a smaller intensive use zone," which would be downtown-centric and the purview of the NPS. The preservation zone would be overseen by "a new management entity," which became the Lowell Historic Preservation Commission (LHPC), charged with directing preservation and regeneration, both economically and culturally. The projected cost over the first ten years would be $40 million for development, not counting the annual operating budgets of the new park unit and allied LHPC.

> The Historic Canal District Commission recommended the most ambitious alternative of six sent to the Congress. The Concentrated/Large option would include several attractions that were expected to draw as many as 750,000 visitors annually, on a scale comparable to 'major attractions in New England.' The Summary Evaluation of this alternative indicated that 'this scale of park should be sufficient to encourage substantial private investment such as that proposed for the Lowell [Market Mills] and Boott Mills centers. Park activities encircling downtown should improve the economic climate and provide a strong impetus for private restoration. Although this scheme would be among the more expensive to develop, its return to the city and to the federal government per dollar spent is likely to be the greatest.' (George Ohar and Gray Fitzsimons, 2004)

The march to a park took another large step forward in April 1977, when Congressman Tsongas put forward a bill to establish Lowell National Historical Park. Democrat Jimmy Carter was now President, having defeated President Gerald R. Ford, who had ascended to the presidency upon Richard M. Nixon's resignation the previous summer—and then pardoned Nixon to "end the long national nightmare." At the same time that Tsongas had introduced legislation for the Lowell Park, the Advisory Board on National Parks, Historic Sites, Buildings, and Monuments of the Interior Department rejected the advice of the Canal District Commission to make Lowell part of the national park system. The board members, appointive products of the two previous Republican administrations, preferred traditional parks and wild open spaces to the new urban ventures for which U. S. Secretary of the Interior Walter Hickel had argued. In the fall, the board met again, this time with a number of Carter appointees, and decided that the Lowell canal system was nationally significant.

Richard Arenberg was a premed student at Boston University in the late 1960s when he decided that politics was his true passion. After some grassroots work in Boston, he signed on with Tsongas' first campaign for Congress in 1974 and stayed with him through his Senate years.

PAUL MARION

In 1975, Tsongas cast a crucial ballot in a contest for Democratic Majority Leader of the House of Representatives. In a five-way contest, Tsongas sided with California Represetative Phil Burton, who eventually lost to Representative Jim Wright of Texas—and Tsongas had let Burton know how his "secret ballot" had been cast. Burton was a high-ranking member of the Interior Committee in the House, who became chairman of the subcommittee on national parks. In Arenberg's telling: "Burton held hearings on the park and moved it right through. The day that we were apprehensive about the mark-up, Burton came in and called the subcommittee to order, and said, 'We're going to report the Lowell park bill today.' Bang, bang, bang, hit the gavel, and out it went to the full committee."

Arenberg stresses that it is important to understand what an achievement the Lowell park bill was for a second-term member of Congress. He said it was a tribute to his boss's "single-mindedness" about Lowell. That Massachusetts had a powerful Congressional delegation in the 1970s was a huge plus, but the accomplishment was nonetheless extraordinary.

The House Interior Committee had a decidedly "western tilt" because of its oversight of vast tracts of public lands from the Mississippi River westward. Tsongas had proven himself to his colleagues from Wyoming, Alaska, Arizona, and elsewhere through diligent work on issues like hard rock mining. He had also gained respect for his leadership in preserving the environment in Alaska, legislation that he later steered through the U.S. Senate as the Alaska Lands Act of 1980 and which President Jimmy Carter described at the time as "the most important conservation legislation of the century."

The National Parks Conservation Association goes further than Carter in describing the Alaska National Interest Lands Conservation Act (ANILCA):

> Often called the most significant land conservation measure in the history of our nation, the statute protected over 100 million acres of federal lands in Alaska, doubling the size of the country's national park and refuge system and tripling the

amount of land designated as wilderness. ANILCA expanded the national park system in Alaska by over forty-three million acres, creating ten new national parks and increasing the acreage of three existing units. (National Parks Conservation Association)

The day after his Valentine's Day birthday in 1978, Tsongas refiled his park bill with some changes, including a more robust role for what was now called the Lowell Historic Preservation Commission (LHPC). The NPS staffers pushed back on the stronger LHPC, and Tsongas agreed to a ten-year limit for the innovative agency. There were a few more legislative hoops to get through. Speaker of the U.S. House of Representatives Tip O'Neill of Massachusetts interceded before the final House vote. The first vote had failed to garner a three-quarters vote under suspension of the rules, a legislative means to fast-track passage. Now needing a simple majority to assure the bill's passage, O'Neill's staff volunteered to help—an insurance policy for a then-concerned Tsongas. They recommended that Tsongas prepare a letter restating the case for the members who had voted nay.

Legislative aide Faust worked the language for hours. What began as a carefully crafted, single-spaced one-page argument in favor of the bill was eventually revised by an O'Neill lieutenant to a one-sentence letter signed by the Speaker: "Paul Tsongas and I would appreciate it if you would vote for the Lowell National Historical Park legislation." House passage came on April 11, 326 in favor and seventy-six opposed, and the Senate approved the bill on May 18. President Jimmy Carter signed Public Law 95-290 on June 5, 1978. It had been six years since Congressman F. Bradford Morse, representing the Lowell-area district, brought the matter to the floor of the House of Representatives; the community-bred idea dated from 1967.

Recalling her husband's efforts on the park bill, now-Congresswoman Niki Tsongas said:

> The work never stopped. He pursued anybody who could make a difference in getting the legislation through. It never

stopped.... When the legislation passed, he was just ecstatic, absolutely ecstatic.... And now, the park has done so much for old cities everywhere because people look at old buildings and instead of seeing things you want to tear down, they see things you want to save. You recognize their intrinsic beauty. And quite apart from the history of the Industrial Revolution, in terms of immigrant culture it has generated a lot more respect for what people contributed to the making of this country. (Niki Tsongas interview with Mehmed. Ali, 2003)

Sister Lillian Lamoureux of Lowell's Model Cities Program and Human Services Corporation reflected on the process in 1991: "I am convinced that if we had not gone to all those meetings, if we had not written all those grants, then none of this would have happened."

What began as a mission by teachers and local organizers to make life better for those in Lowell being left behind in the churn of callous economic and political markets had morphed into a city-wide renewal strategy. A community had reconciled its past with its future. No longer did history, the long-ago local story, emit a bad odor. What was heterogeneous now radiated positive value. Patrick Mogan always believed the perceived liabilities could be turned into assets. Paul Tsongas said it was immoral to kick the whole city into the ditch because it was broken. He did not use the term "generational responsibility" until he ran for president, but that is what he meant in the 1970s. Led by the Congress of the United States, the National Park Service took Lowell on board and now brags about it.

2014

Harry Callahan

Harry at the Lowell Conference.

He told us twice that he had dropped out of high school, but Harry spoke as well as any old politician at a hotel banquet. He asked why the United States and South Africa are the only modern countries without national health care.

He called President Ronald Reagan "a turkey," and described a White House full of smoky mirrors. Union leader Harry Callahan said the First Lady's idea of cruel and unusual punishment is being dragged to a Sears department store and forced to pick a dress off the rack.

Harry isn't sure that Labor should be a political party but won't rule it out. "We're like rats," he said, "and when cornered, we'll fight—fight dirty if needed."

Harry went to the Soviet Union. He said they have hearts and put pants on the same way we do. "Why shouldn't I go to learn something? The Pepsi and Caterpillar executives go twice a month."

He wonders why Americans don't know their own history. He said most people want to be in unions but aren't, and that anyone can see that union workers make more money each week.

Harry said, "The democracy has problems. There's no democracy at work—never has been. American businessmen want authoritarian systems at work."

He said he might be the first guy to put a bullet between the eyes of a capitalist if the fight goes to the street. He tells that to businessmen, he said, and they listen quietly, confident that it will never happen.

1986

PAUL MARION

Dith Pran & Sophin Chea

"Don't watch the lips, watch the hands of those who profess to make a better world."
—a survivor

The Governor's aide says the ceremony marks the first time a Cambodian flag had been raised at a City Hall in the United States. The year is 1985 in Lowell. After the political speeches, a recording of the American national anthem plays, then a red-and-blue flag with a white image of Angkor Wat in the center inches its way up the pole. The Khmer anthem blares for the hundreds gathered on the plaza named for President John F. Kennedy.

Volunteers made food for everyone. I taste beef soaked in ginger sauce, which is served on cooked but cold noodles, and sample the fried chicken, spicy coleslaw, mashed beans formed into a small roll, and a dessert of coconut-topped clear gelatin. A thin, older woman offers me a New Year's treat: a sweet rice cake wrapped in banana leaf.

Young dancers in gold, green, and blue costumes perform, accompanied by musicians playing a drum and string instruments. In the middle of the plaza, people had built a "Food Mountain"—a mound of loose rice on a table and piles of other food items for the poor and the Buddhist monks. Families carried their New Year's food to the celebration in decorative silver canisters with handles. The tall, round containers have five interlocking compartments that stack up.

Two monks and a Cambodian priest chant blessings at a low altar topped with incense, a Buddha figure, and cut flowers. Earlier, people had lit incense and offered prayers. They knelt on colored straw mats around the altar.

Children play a piñata game—five clay bowls wrapped in bright tissue hung from branches of one of the locust trees on the plaza. Blindfolded kids swing wildly with a baseball bat. The crowd cheers when anyone makes contact, showering coins and candy on the pavement.

The evening celebration moves to a former church across the street from the City Hall complex. There's a large community event space on the first floor. When I arrive with my friends Joan and Jim a raffle is in progress. A rock band cranks out Santana's "Black Magic Woman." Dancers in their dressy best don't change a step when the sounds shift from Asian music to rock 'n' roll.

Joan and I spend a long time talking to Sophin, a seventeen-year-old high school student. He and his mother had been in a refugee camp in Thailand for five years before finding a sponsor to bring them to America four years ago. His father was killed in Vietnam in 1971 while fighting with the Americans against the Viet Cong.

Sophin grew up in Phnom Penh. He says the film *The Killing Fields* is true and told us he had cried as he watched. His twenty-five-year-old brother is in Cambodia, a lieutenant in the Khmer Free Army, which is fighting the Khmer Rouge for control of the country. At the same time, both Khmer armies are battling to drive the Vietnamese Army out of Cambodia.

Sophin had seen a film about the abuse and murder of Jewish people by Nazis in Germany during World War II. It was the same in his country he says. A person can be killed simply for carrying a camera. His uncle had been tied up by soldiers and taken away without explanation.

"I want to return to help my people. I want to help the Cambodian refugees in Thailand. I have to do something. I have to say something about this."

A few months later, Dith Pran, *The New York Times* photographer who survived the Khmer Rouge genocide and whose story is told in *The Killing Fields* film, spoke in the red-brick courtyard of Market Mills in downtown Lowell. He urged his countrymen to speak out. Monks wrapped in rust-colored robes listened to his story:

> Don't keep this in your heart. Talk about it.
> I ate crickets, rats, and leaves. I wished I could have had a lizard every day.

I saw the Khmer Rouge were not from the same planet. They are monsters, crazy. They forced people to work fourteen hours a day.

They killed babies. They killed old people. They killed intellectuals and their families. Millions were killed. They killed their enemy. They killed children, their future enemy. They killed honest people.

I lied. I said I was a taxi driver. Every day we were scared. The world did not help us.

The movie *The Killing Fields* is mild. If it were too real, people would not watch. The killing is not over. It goes on around the clock around the world.

1985

John Ogonowski

Severe clear sky.

On a rise on the south bank just below the rocky grill of the riverbed, students at his alma mater carved into stone his name and those of six others from the school family to remember John, the compassionate guy from the Polish side of Lowell, whose family later migrated to Dracut, a green town across the river—

and he grew up to be a pilot and a farmer, who shared his land with Asian refugees who had resettled in the city and who wanted to grow vegetables as they did in Cambodia, Vietnam, and Laos, a region from which John had flown home soldiers hurt in the battles—

John, the preservationist, who saved open space in his town, called *Augumtoocooke*, a place in the woods, by native people who had been on the ground in the vast riverside forest for thousands of years—

John, who on September 11, 2001, lifted his passengers into a "severe clear" sky, nothing but blue on the route west—

John, who guided American Airlines Flight 11 out of Boston's Logan Airport, where so many of us have flown away with faith in the promise of technology, scientific management, and civilized behavior—

John, who carried his travelers into boundless air on a day when he had as usual driven in early from Marsh Hill to captain his plane across country, that day like any other in the late summer, not officially fall even though school was in session—

that day like no other by the end of the morning, by the end of the paper rain and ash-cloud, by the end of the twisted steel and burnt ground, by the end of John's life—

on that day from which we have not fully recovered the bounce that always made people elsewhere believe Americans can figure out a problem and invent the next dazzle—

a day that moved John's neighbors and even strangers to drive slowly up the winding hill road that leads to his farm, where they heaped flowers, handmade signs, candles, and sympathy cards in front of the wide white gate leading to the farm, piled high the colorful cut flowers, placed in silence—

and past the white gate up the driveway a giant crane held an American flag that looked as big as the flag that covers the left field wall at Fenway Park on Opening Day—

and past the crane and flag was the farmhouse of John's family, his wife and daughters, who needed him to come back so he would sit next to them at the table in the house one more time.

2017

PORTRAITS ALONG THE WAY

Meetinghouse Hill Figures

Cut from American cloth.

In the middle of the nineteenth century, workers in the red-brick mills of Lowell each year produced enough cotton cloth to wrap the world. More importantly, the city known for manufacturing textiles produced the stuff of America itself: ideas and merchandise, entrepreneurs and generals, politicians and artists, religious leaders and labor champions, sports heroes and movie stars, inventors and criminals, and a multitude of citizens from the immigrants, refugees, and migrants who crowded its streets.

To understand America, a good place to start is where you are. In my case, it is Meetinghouse Hill, the rise on the far side of the South Common opposite my house. With my wife and son, I live at 44 Highland Street in Lowell. In 1830, my great-great grandfather Marion trekked from Canada to find work in this burgeoning northeast Massachusetts mill city, and I was born in a neighborhood across the river nine years after my father returned from World War II. Like my father's people, my mother's ancestors traveled the Normandy-Quebec-Lowell route. My wife Rosemary is Irish on both sides, with Lowell roots winding back to the 1870s. Our son is named for the original Marion in Lowell, a carpenter, and Rosemary's grandfather, a longtime jeweler in the city—all Josephs.

Built in the 1860s, my family's house was once owned by the Appleton Manufacturing Company, which was formed in 1828, five years after the first mill began producing cloth in Lowell. The Appleton's managers who lived in the house through the late nineteenth century could see the tops of their factories from the second-floor windows. Our house was bought in 1940 by Rosemary grandparents, Joseph Foley and his wife, Gertrude O'Neill Foley. Joe Foley's mother scrubbed floors and washed dishes in the mansion at 42–44 Highland Street not long after she emigrated from Ireland. Imagine the satisfaction and sense of class revenge in Joe's heart as he signed the purchase papers.

On special occasions, when we sit for dinner in our elaborately detailed front room, I picture a scene in *Doctor Zhivago*, the one in which the poet-physician returns to Moscow from his forced service with fighters in the hinterlands only to see that the Bolsheviks have confiscated his family's house. When he looks up at the scruffy crowd hanging over the upstairs banister and asks what is going on, one of the comrades tells him the arrangement is "more just." In the moment all he can do is agree. "Yes, more just."

From my bedroom window, I look across the Common to the redbrick Eliot Presbyterian Church atop Meetinghouse Hill. In 1930, the Massachusetts Bay Colony Tercentenary Commission installed a bronze plaque near the church, marking the location of Reverend John Eliot's log cabin chapel in 1648. Adventurer Simon Willard, who had clashed with local peoples since arriving in the colony, built the cabin to use as a frontier court—it was the first structure built by Anglo settlers in the place that became Lowell.

A graduate of Jesus College of Cambridge, Eliot started out as a school assistant in Chelmsford, England. After converting to Puritanism, he fled to Massachusetts in 1631 to avoid persecution. Eliot was the first Christian preacher to journey from Boston to the village of Wamesit, named for its tribe, at the confluence of the Merrimack and Concord rivers. Beginning with a first trip to the northwest woods in 1647, Eliot often traveled with Major General Daniel Gookin, Superintendent of Indians in the colony, who "saved Eliot's neck more than once," writes Reverend David Malone, former pastor of the Eliot Church.

In 1653, colonial officials designated the broad wedge of land bounded by the Concord and Merrimack for the Pennacook peoples— to be their property. Everything around them had already been signed away by Passaconaway, leader of the local tribes who has come down to us through European accounts as a shaman who could set water aflame, generate a live snake by rubbing its shed skin in his hands, and make trees vibrate. Passaconaway deeded to the English a vast tract of land between present-day Newburyport, Mass., and the lower Merrimack River. Fifteen years later, he committed his people to the governance of the Bay Colony. His strategy of accommodation hardly satisfied the settlers' appetite for land and control. By 1660, English settlers had moved deep into the interior, and all evidence suggested more of them were coming. Passaconaway gathered his people for a farewell address—the substance of which was reported by an English observer with partial understanding of Algonkian. "I am going the way of all the earth," the sachem began.

> I am ready to die and not likely to see you met together anymore. . . . Take heed how you quarrel with the English. Hearken to the last words of your father and your friend. The white men are the sons of the morning. The Great Spirit is their father. . . . Never make war with them. Sure as you light the fires, the breath of heaven will turn the flame upon you and destroy you . . . .

According to legend, Passaconaway withdrew to the northern mountains and some years later was swept into the sky in a huge maple sleigh drawn by flying gray wolves.

The area to the right of my house steps down to the western bank of the Concord and until recent times was called Wamesit Hill, though the only Native American in sight now is the one positioned at the center of the state emblem that appears on the Tercentenary plaque on Meetinghouse Hill and on the flag of the Commonwealth of Massachusetts displayed outside the Superior Court House nearby and at the Gallagher Transportation Center a block away.

In the early winter of 1943, twenty-year-old Jack Kerouac had a night job parking cars at the Hotel Garage on Middlesex Street, on the back slope of Meetinghouse Hill. He was in sight of a handsome brownstone train depot, since demolished, a short way down the tracks from Gallagher terminal. Long before he composed his signature "October in the Railroad Earth," he sketched the local scene during down time in the garage office, itself now gone:

> One night, returning from work in the casual, squalid atmosphere of railroad yards, warehouses, switch towers, idle boxcars, and one lonely little lunch cart across the tracks, as I was approaching the rail crossing near the old depot that we have in my home town, I had to lean against a sagging fence (black with soot-years) for fully ten minutes while a mighty locomotive went by freighting ninety-six cars: coal cars, oil tanks, wooden boxcars, all types of commercial rolling stock. While I loafed there with a cigarette, watching each car rumble past and checking the cargoes, a thought came to me with swift and lucid impact, with the same jolt of common sense and disbelief in the scantiness of my own intelligence that I had felt when first I understood the working of a mathematic equation. 'Why,' I asked myself, 'does not this rich cargo, these cars, that terrific locomotive belong to me? . . . and to my fellow men? . . . Why are they not, like my trousers, my property? Who covets these great things so that myself and my fellow men are not heir to their full use?' Then I asked myself, 'Are we not all men living alone on a single earth?' ('The Mystery' [1943] by Jack Kerouac in *Atop an Underwood: Early Stories and Other Writings*)

The morning freight train slides behind the long red flank of a former patent medicine lab and continues past the terminal while passengers wait for the 9:07 a.m. run to Boston. Copper flashing gleams on the adjacent roof of gray granite Keith Academy, once the turreted city jail and since renovated into upscale apartments. The boxcars are blocks of American place. Apalachicola, Port St. Joe Route, Soo Line, Maine Central, Rio Grande, Milwaukee, Santa Fe, Illinois Terminal, Penn Central, Southern Pacific, Bangor and Aroostook, Atlantic and Western, Boston and Maine—national freight, movable goods, raw material, made things—the weight that spreads cross country. Everything seems to come through Lowell. Burlington Northern, Springfield Terminal, Canadian Pacific.

What happened to the Canadian Sausage Company of Lowell? The red-and-white trucks scooted around the city, delivering fresh meats to grocers and butchers. Like the freight cars of place, the sausage trucks stood for the French-Canadian presence. If you were French Canadian, you noticed when the truck passed by. You saw that word "Canadian." It was like seeing maple leaf cookie packages in the crackers-and-cookies aisle at the market. And it made you think of grandparents, who served plates of maple leaf cookies and offered Christmastime gift boxes of painfully sweet, grainy, creamy maple candies.

On a siding just north of the station, there's a scrap train—ground-up fenders and stoves and corroded pipes en route to the smelter, the chopped ham of American industry. In the rail yard, freight-car murals in graffiti code, the blocky colored letters like harsh plastic alphabet-magnets on a refrigerator door.

Next to the train station stands the ugly mill building on Thorndike Street that you cannot miss, if you listen to local cable TV commercials from Comfort Furniture. The wavy wooden floors of the four-story complex creak and squeak when customers wind through aisles between the tons of sofas, recliners, dining room sets, lamps of all types, coffee tables, bunk beds with matching desks, and assembly-required home entertainment center shelf units. There is only a hint of the patent medicine production plant that thrived in this factory. Running sideways up the tapered brick chimney is the word "Hood's," for C.I. Hood & Company, one of the city's two massive patent medicine operations of the nineteenth century. Cartons of vegetable pills, tooth powder, olive ointment, and syrups promising cures for everything from rheumatism to syphilis filled the loading dock. When it was built in 1893, the Hood laboratory was the world's largest medicine manufacturing building. Charles Hood's specialty was a bottled syrup called Sarsaparilla, which promised to "cure neuralgia pains."

Lowell's patent medicine firms helped shape the future of not only entrepreneurship, but also mass advertising in this country. Pill-making and bottling plants were combined with on-site printing shops. Hood's main competitor in Lowell was J.C. Ayer & Company, which, at its height around 1900, published promotional literature, especially *American Almanac*, in various languages around the world—fifteen million copies. Master salesman Ayer showered emperors, pashas, and even the Czar of Russia with fancy cartons of his Cherry Pectoral respiratory elixir. The medicine industry picked up some of the business slack when textile manufacturing sagged. One of its lasting effects is that people in this region still ask for a "tonic" when ordering a soft drink. Outside the office, on the second floor of Comfort Furniture, the owners have a display of colorized postcards, a "Sarsaparilla Rainy Day Puzzle," and crinkled photographs from the Hood firm.

For the first seventeen years that I lived on Highland Street, every weekday at 3 p.m. during the school year a dozen or more yellow buses pulled into the semi-oval driveway in front of the Rogers Middle School that faces my house. The school was a microcosm of New Lowell, with Cambodian Americans making up more than half the building's population—the rest were Portuguese-American kids from long-settled families around St. Anthony's parish in the Back Central section and newcomers from Brazil, Cameroon, and Guatemala, along with the third-, fourth-, fifth-, or sixth-generation Lithuanian, Greek, French Canadian, and Irish American youngsters. The descendants of the native peoples and early English colonists are as scarce as heirloom species in the flower boxes under the windows on Elm Street a block away. In the school lobby students with newcomer DNA could read about Edith Nourse Rogers, who still holds the record as the woman who served longest without interruption in the U.S. House of Representatives (1925-1960). The Great Recession of 2008-09 claimed the Rogers as City Hall budget cuts led to its closing—despite the "Rogers School Rocks" protest signs waved by kids and their parents.

In *Cotton Was King: A History of Lowell, Massachusetts* (1976), Mary H. Blewett, longtime professor of history at the University of Massachusetts, Lowell, writes:

> Congresswoman Rogers was a liberal and an internationalist, typical of successful Republicans of the northeast. She voted for most of the key New Deal programs of the Thirties—the Wagner Act which protected union organization, the Social Security Act of 1935, and the minimum wage law of 1938—in line with the needs of her Lowell constituents, if not with the Republican leadership.

A Mainer by birth, Rogers married into a wealthy textile industry family in Lowell, where she had studied in a private girls' school. She succeeded her husband, Congressman John Rogers, when he died in office. "Mrs. Rogers" became the veterans' best friend, her experience with the military having begun with agencies serving the wounded in France during World War I. In 1939, moved by reports of abuse of German Jews, especially the brutality of *Kristallnacht* (the sanctioned night attack on Jews in their homes, shops, and synagogues), she and U. S. Senator Robert F. Wagner of New York filed a refugee aid bill that would have allowed 20,000 German refugee children into the United States. President Franklin D. Roosevelt withheld his support, and despite lobbying by children's advocates across America, the bill was defeated at the committee level. Mrs. Rogers backed laws creating a Women's Army Auxiliary Corps in 1941 and the G.I. Bill of Rights, the latter providing a range of social, financial, and educational benefits to World War II veterans. She was seventy-nine when she died in 1960, in the midst of a reelection campaign.

Mrs. Rogers was in the middle of a line of Republican U.S. Representatives from the Lowell area who controlled the seat from 1859 to 1974, with the exception of a single two-year term for Democrat John K. Tarbox (1875-1877). It took a man who grew up on Highland Street to break the Republican streak.

Sitting at a desk in his father's dry-cleaning shop on Gorham Street in June 1968, just days after Senator Robert Kennedy was assassinated, twenty-seven-year-old Paul Tsongas wrote a letter to the editor of the *Lowell Sun*:

> I read with dismay your editorial attacking foreign reaction to the tragedy of Robert Kennedy. Your advice for them to 'keep their stupid mouth shut' is not the kind of reasoned awareness for which these times call. No one has much patience with those who allege conspiracy in the murders of President Kennedy, Medgar Evers, Martin Luther King, Robert Kennedy, and whoever should follow them. Certainly, many foreign capitals wish us ill and will resort to misrepresentations. This however should not obscure the fact that the world

beyond our borders, including our closest friends, stands horrified at our shoot-em-up mentality.

I was in a small village in Ethiopia with the Peace Corps when President Kennedy was slain. My grief and agony were shared by the Ethiopians among whom I lived. They shed tears over the senseless death of such a '*Tru Sew*' (good man). They felt that he belonged to the world and the promise of a brotherhood, and his death did indeed diminish us all.

This was at the time when *Time* magazine would arrive with graphic pictures of Bull Connor and his dogs brutalizing Southern blacks. We did what we could to defend America. It became very difficult when four of my Ethiopian students came to the United States and received the stinging backlash of racism. They returned to Ethiopia forever disillusioned with a nation that professes to believe that 'all men are created equal.'

The next year he won a seat on the Lowell City Council and set out on his own "journey of purpose," to quote the title of a book of his speeches and essays.

He and his fellow Democratic members of the "Watergate Class" dominated the 1974 Congressional election and took office the following January with a mandate to reform the government. The son of a Harvard-educated small-businessman, Tsongas was raised in a large white house on the corner of Highland and Thorndike streets. He caught the public service fever from President John F. Kennedy and, ultimately, as a former U.S. Senator challenged Arkansas Governor Bill Clinton one-on-one in the 1992 presidential primaries, winning New Hampshire and eight more state contests before an empty war chest forced him to withdraw. Through his Washington years he had a red-phone connection to Lowell's City Hall and made the city's rebirth his passion. It became an article of faith with him that one must honor the toil of past generations and respect the potential of future generations.

The reclaiming of Lowell came to symbolize that faith. Tsongas embodied the "Don't Quit" character of Lowell that explains in part the community's resurgence. He wrote the legislation that created Lowell

National Historical Park in 1978, adding his hometown to the list that includes the Grand Canyon and Statue of Liberty. The cradle of the American Industrial Revolution would be preserved. The renaissance sparked by the park made Lowell a model of urban regeneration. In the last thirteen years of his life, he was as well known for his high-profile fight against cancer. He died of pneumonia in 1997.

Places change, people enter and exit the stage—we won't see Paul Tsongas jogging through the South Common, we won't see Brother Gilbert who taught at Keith Academy after mentoring the young sportsman George Herman Ruth (the "Babe") in Baltimore or Ruth Meehan who organized U.S.O. shows around the world and drove a candy apple-red coupe out of the driveway at 48 Highland

Some buildings are lost entirely. The Commodore Ballroom, later Mr. C's Rock Palace, once commanded the middle of Thorndike Street. The big bands and blues greats made it the favored nightspot. In the 1960s, major acts like Paul Revere and the Raiders headlined on weekends, and local phenoms like Little John and the Sherwoods opened for the hot artists of the month like The Yardbirds and Neil Diamond. You have to find it in pictures on the web now.

Somewhere in my local travels I heard a story about Jim Morrison of the Doors arriving early for a gig at the Commodore in the fall of 1967 when "Light My Fire" was still torching the competition. He had heard Kerouac was living on Sanders Avenue, about five minutes away by car, so he got a ride over to see the forty-five-year-old author who by all accounts was in serious physical decline. When he got to the house, Mrs. Kerouac refused to let him in. Ragged young visitors materialized on the doorstep all the time. There would be no grand encounter of bare-chested pop poet and booze-bellied Beat Pop. Jack was sleeping.

From my front porch, I can take in the site of Simon Willard's court at Wamesit Village and the present Superior Court of the county, where Daniel Webster argued cases and then stayed for dinner. With St. Peter Church razed, only one of Highland Street's great gray bookends remains, the sturdy Lowell Jail that became a Catholic high school for boys—which, to some graduates, was not a substantial change of use at all. On mornings when I circle the track at the bottom of the Common's green bowl, I scan a roster of names tied to the ridgeline of buildings—Reverend Eliot, politico Charles Gallagher, Hood the Medicine Man, theatre-magnate Keith of the Academy, and Congresswoman Rogers.

These names are entwined in history like the signature grapevines of the neighborhood, hundreds of them planted through the decades by Portuguese immigrants—green signs marking the presence of people who turn open space around their modest homes into miniature farms along the narrow, hilly ways. In season, waiting a minute before starting their cars for the drive to work, my neighbors, gardeners Joe Veiga and Natalie Silva, hear the larks and the locomotive pulling toward Boston.

2012

PAUL MARION

Acknowledgments

In this compilation, certain selections, sometimes in different versions, appeared in newspapers, magazines, journals, anthologies, books, documentary videos, a pamphlet, as blog posts, and as a broadside. Thank you to the editors, producers, and publishers of the following publications and media productions.

Atop an Underwood: Early Stories and Other Writings by Jack Kerouac
The Bean Magazine
Beat Scene (England)
Cut From American Cloth
Dimitri Hadzi at The Brush Art Gallery & Studios
History as It Happens: Citizen Bloggers in Lowell, Mass.
Kerouac on Record: A Literary Soundtrack
Lockdown Letters & Other Poems
Lowell Gallery Broadsides
The Lowell Review
The Lowell Sun
The Massachusetts Review
Merrimack Journal
Merrimack Valley Magazine
Mill Power: The Origin and Impact of Lowell National Historical Park
The Offering
Patrick J. Mogan: Visionary and Realist
PaulMarion.com
Poetry Face-Off (Canada)
Résonance
RichardHowe.com
River Muse: Tales of Lowell & the Merrimack Valley

PORTRAITS ALONG THE WAY

Roots of an Urban Cultural Park
Union River: Poems and Sketches
University of Lowell Magazine
What Is the City?

Index

Acknowledgments, 248
Alentour Poets, 113
Angelou, Maya, 138
Antoinette & Wilfrid, 3
Astronauts of Project Mercury, 29
Baez, Joan, 84
Becker, Helga, 205
Callahan, Harry, 231
Casselton, Jim, 190
Chea, Sophin, 232
Conigliaro, Tony, 45
Davis, Bette, 73
DeNatale, Doug, 199
Depp, Johnny, 82
Doris & Marcel, 15
Dylan, Bob, 79, 98, 165
Eovaldi, Nathan, 57
Ferrer, Juan, 197
Franzoni, Eddie, 195
Gbowee, Leymah, 211
Glück, Louise, 169
Gorky, Arshile, 96
Gumba & The Fly, 48
Guy, Buddy, 91
Hadzi, Dimitri, 86
Ismailov, Hamid & Juan Ferrer, 197
Jones, Dalton, 55
Joel, Billy, 93
Kennedy, John F., 38
Kerouac, Jack, 133, 149, 165
Kerouac, Jack & Bob Dylan, 165
King, Stephen, 162
Kol, Doeun "Duey," 202
Ladd, Luther C. & Addison O. Whitney, 192
Marion, Antoinette Héroux, 3, 6
Marion, Doris Roy, 3, 6, 15
Marion, Joseph, 185
Marion, Marcel, 3, 15, 21
Marion, Paul, 61
Marion, Wilfrid, 3, 6
Meetinghouse Hill Figures, 237
Merrimack Valley Authors, 174
Mogan, Patrick J., 214, 219
Murphy, Katherine O'Donnell & Arshile Gorky, 96
Myers, Benjamin, 145
Noon, Rosemary, 185
Ogonowski, John, 235
The Poets' Lab, 103
Pran, Dith & Chea, Sophin, 232
Proulx, Annie, 143
Putnam, Frank P., 187
Rosemary & Joseph, 185
Roy, Francis "Pinky," 206
Ste. Thérèse de Lisieux, 32
Samsonov, Sergei, 53
Simic, Charles, 111, 140
Smith, Patti, 157
Snyder, Gary, 135
Thoreau, Henry David, 168
Tsongas, Paul E., 221, 225
Turner, Daniel R., 194
Whitney, Addison O., 192

A Note on the Author

Paul Marion (b. 1954) is the author of *Union River: Poems and Sketches* and *Lockdown Letters & Other Poems* and editor of Jack Kerouac's early writing, *Atop an Underwood*. His book *Mill Power* chronicles the modern revival of the historic textile factory city in which he was born, Lowell, Massachusetts.

His work has appeared in *Alaska Quarterly Review, The Café Review, The Massachusetts Review, Wisconsin Review, Yankee Magazine, Cholla Needles, So It Goes*, and *poetsreadingthenews.com*, as well as in anthologies and other literary magazines in the U.S., Canada, Japan, and England. He is featured in *The Grifter, the Poet, and the Runaway Train: Stories from a Yankee Writer's Notebook* by Geoffrey Douglas.

He is a graduate of the University of Massachusetts, Lowell, and studied in the MFA Program in Writing at the University of California, Irvine. His career work involved communications and cultural affairs in state and federal government positions.

In 1978, he founded a small publishing company, Loom Press, which has released more than fifty titles: fiction, nonfiction, poetry, photography, and anthologies.

With his wife, Rosemary Noon, he lives in Amesbury in the Merrimack River Valley of northeastern Massachusetts.